Praise for NO SUCH THING AS A BAD KID...

"*No Such Thing As a Bad Kid* is a well-organized, clearly written book giving practical recipes for helping children. And like the chefs whose love of food inspires great cookbooks, the author shares these recipes from his heart and soul. His obvious love for children shines through on every page. This is a nutritious and delicious book written with loving care to feed and fill all who work with young people."

Bernard Levine, PhD
Clinical psychologist
Former clinical director, Walker Home & School, Inc.

"This book provides a wealth of insight as well as practical suggestions for people involved with challenged, high-risk kids. Teachers, foster parents, counselors, and others will benefit greatly from this rich, experience-based work. I personally learned a tremendous amount from the perceptive approach the author uses. He 'becomes the kid,' offering a unique understanding of these young people."

Mary Allen
Editor, *Treatment Today*

"This book is a *must read* for any teacher or principal who is working with children who demonstrate challenging behaviors. Charlie Appelstein's comprehensive 'no fault' approach helps adults develop a greater understanding of problem behavior while providing concrete, tangible, and effective strategies for helping students maintain greater self-control. The ideas, guiding principles, and strategies that Charlie has given our staff have been immeasurably helpful. Our teachers have gained greater confidence and expertise in handling disruptive student behavior. While we haven't eliminated undesirable behavior, our teachers now have a much better capacity and a set of procedures in place to help students make better choices. This book is invaluable for professional educators."

David Castelline, EdD
Principal, Underwood Elementary School
Newton, Massachusetts

"*No Such Thing As a Bad Kid* is a comprehensive blend of theory, example, and instruction that should be a staple for foster parents, residential centers, classrooms, and clinical offices. Written as though the author were conversing with the reader, it is free of jargon and complicated theory; the concepts are tried-and-true and are presented simply and understandably. The descriptive anecdotes woven throughout these pages will be motivating and rejuvenating to anyone who works with children. Empathy, humor, and sound interventions abound, along with practical insights and strategies. Ultimately, this book offers validation and support to caretakers by normalizing frustrations, mistakes, poor decisions, and burnout, and by providing helpful, hopeful, and refreshing solutions."

Foster-Care Team
ComCare Foster Care Program

"*No Such Thing As a Bad Kid* is sure to be an instant classic. It challenges the reader to recognize that misbehavior is indicative of a child's response to abuse, neglect, environmental stress, low self-esteem, and certain developmental deficits. It also reminds us that potentially disruptive situations can be diffused when careful attention is given to a variety of specific issues. In addition to practical, hands-on, easy-to-read techniques, it offers multiple exercises and charts workers can use for training, supervision, role-plays, and actual application. These tools ensure that the book will augment efforts targeted at helping youngsters become empowered, self-actualizing, productive citizens. Thank you, Mr. Appelstein, for your important contribution to child- and youth-care practitioners, teachers, trainers, parents, and others interested in the well-being of troubled children and youth."

Dennis J. Braziel, MSSA, LSW
Senior Consultant, Child Welfare League of America

No Such Thing As a Bad Kid

Also by Charles D. Appelstein:

The Gus Chronicles: Reflections from an Abused Kid

The Gifford School is a nonprofit special education day school with over thirty years of experience providing quality educational and clinical services to students with moderate to severe academic, behavior, and emotional needs. The Gifford School participates in several partnerships between public and private agencies designed to advance innovative educational and therapeutic practices. As part of its mission to improve the quality of education for all students, Gifford also sponsors professional conferences and offers training and consultation. For information about these programs, please contact the school at 781-899-9500.

No Such Thing As a Bad Kid

Understanding and Responding to
the Challenging Behavior of
Troubled Children and Youth

Charles D. Appelstein, MSW

THE GIFFORD SCHOOL
WESTON, MASSACHUSETTS

Published by: The Gifford School
                177 Boston Post Road
                Weston, MA 02193

Edited by Amanda D. Irwin and Ellen Kleiner
Book design by Richard Harris
Cover design by To The Point

Printed in the United States of America

Publisher's Cataloging-in-Publication Data

Appelstein, Charles D.
    No such thing as a bad kid : understanding and responding
  to the challenging behavior of troubled children and youth /
  Charles D. Appelstein. — 1st ed.
    p. cm.
    Includes bibliographical references and index.
    Preassigned LCCN: 97-74764
    ISBN: 0-9659836-0-9
    1. Problem children—Education. 2. Problem children—
  Behavior modification. 3. Problem children—Counseling of
  4. Self-esteem in children.   I. Title.

LC4801.A77 1998   371.93
                                             QB197-41183

15 14 13

If you're lucky enough, you meet people along the road of life who touch you, inspire you, and make you feel good about humanity. I dedicate this book to four such people:

> To the memory of Reverend Robert and Idolyn Crabtree, both of whom walked this earth with undying compassion and with a sweetness and grace that brought sunshine wherever there was darkness. I hope there's opera up in heaven, Bob.

> To my "little" brother DeWayne, as well as his wonderful family. DeWayne, you're one of the most courageous kids I've ever known, and I couldn't be more proud of you. We're brothers for life, man.

> And with love, to my mother, Tiby Appelstein. You were the one who taught me how to make a kid feel special. Don't ever stop—this kid still likes it!

Acknowledgments

Ever since 1977, when I started working with troubled kids, some truly wonderful teachers and role models have inspired me, making it possible for this book to be written. I offer my personal thanks to Ellen Kenney, whose wisdom, passion, and commitment to children is ensconced in my brain and continues to guide me; Bernard Levine, who opened up new worlds to a "dubious" student; David Villiotti, a great professional who has always stood by me; Neil Pare, who proved that miracles can happen when you don't give up on a kid; Jill Hopkins, the best child-care professional I have ever observed; Dennis Braziel, whose heart and passion for the work continues to inspire me; Rick Small and Floyd Alwon, for believing in my work; as well as the staffs, past and present, of St. Ann's Home and the Nashua Children's Home.

I offer special thanks to those who contributed to the writing of this book: Kevin Kennedy, my ex-professor at Simmons College School of Social Work; my two outstanding editors, Mandy Irwin, who created a strong foundation for this work, and Ellen Kleiner, who used her wizardry with words to build the rest; Barbara Selwyn, who provided a steady commitment to this project; Mike Bassichis, executive director of The Gifford School, as well as the school's board of directors, who had the courage and commitment to offer the technical, emotional, and financial resources needed to make this book a reality; and my fantastic wife, Cheryl, who rendered tireless support throughout the two years of writing.

Finally, I thank every kid I have ever worked with, each one of whom has touched and enriched my life.

Contents

Part III: Responding to Challenging Behavior

List of Figures

Chapter 13

FOREWORD

THIS RARE BOOK DESCRIBES INTERVENTIONS WITH THE PRECISION OF A manual and the wisdom of a spiritual text. If children in treatment were asked to review it, they would cheer and weep. Cheer, out of pleasure that Charles Appelstein knows who they are, what they need, and what they deserve. Weep, because they may have long ago given up hope for being so well-known and cared for.

Charlie has managed to write *No Such Thing As a Bad Kid* in the "voice" of effective treatment—sensitive, direct, humble, alternately firm and tentative, and profoundly compassionate. While reading these pages, I had the impression that I was following the journey of a gifted clinician and teacher from his first bouts with rage, despair, physical and emotional attacks, and profound confusion and sadness to the satisfactions and unassuming competence developed by a more seasoned helper of children with serious emotional troubles. It is the wisdom picked up along the way that makes this book so extraordinary and useful.

Throughout, Charlie is aware that the quality of our work with troubled children depends on mastery of our own feelings, which are never very different from the children's feelings. Rather than set adult "experts" apart from "mentally ill" children, he points out that we need to "stay in control of ourselves" before we can begin to foster more adaptive strategies for self-control in the children. Illustrating this theme, as well as numerous others, are clinical vignettes that demonstrate lessons the author has learned from his interactions with individual children.

At the heart of Charlie's wisdom are several core beliefs: there are no bad kids, only "bad" behaviors; initiating and sustaining a relationship with a child is the only context in which other interventions can succeed; all bad behaviors need to be "decoded" for treatment to proceed; and good treatment involves appropriate "symptom management" and sophisticated resolution of the underlying issues. These tenets put the *why* back in behavioral treatments and the *child* back in "biomedical" diagnostic approaches.

Like Fritz Redl and David Wineman before him, Charlie Appelstein portrays with vivid clinical examples the fundamentals of relating to children. Not only does each vignette in this book model imaginative and effective verbal interventions but several chapters "x-ray" empathic therapeutic verbal exchanges with a focus on the communication dynamics of affect, tone, word choice, and body language. I would recommend that on the first day of work, a childcare worker, teacher, social worker, nurse, psychologist, or foster parent carry the table of fourteen basic verbal techniques (figure 10–1) with them at all times. The strategic verbal interventions (chapter 11) would be invaluable for the second day. The capacity to say the "right thing," or at least avoid saying the "wrong thing," is crucial to the relationship-building side of therapeutic management.

An additional aspect that distinguishes this book from most others in the field is that it is divided into three main sections reflecting the three big jobs inherent in this work: understanding, preventing, and responding to challenging behavior. Charlie makes it clear that *all* child helpers will need to avail themselves of strategies in each phase of therapeutic management. Even if we master the art—and to some extent, the science—of understanding and preventing challenging behaviors, we will need to know, and our children will need us to know, how to effectively respond to challenging behavior, primarily through limit-setting interventions and behavior modification.

I find *No Such Thing As a Bad Kid* both inspiring and pragmatic. What's more, it meets my ultimate criterion for useful information on therapeutic management, for it provides a resounding *yes* to the question "Does this approach bring out the best in the child?" Interestingly, it goes even further by offering an approach that brings out the best in the *child helper.* At the beginning of the book, Charlie relates a story about the nerve-racking antics of a child named Andy who is about to throw important documents out the window of Charlie's moving car. His creative response diverts Andy. By referring to him as a friend, Charlie creates a more positive self-image for Andy than he had of himself. Andy was then "forced" to live up to this new image rather than act in accordance with his previous image as a troublemaker.

In addition to Andy, I, along with every other child helper who reads this book, would like to thank Charlie Appelstein for helping us see ourselves in a more positive light by bringing out the best in our work.

Nancy S. Cotton, PhD
Clinical developmental psychologist
Author of *Lessons from the Lion's Den*

PREFACE

THE GIFFORD SCHOOL STAFF HAS WORKED WITH THOUSANDS OF children, families, teachers, and clinicians over its thirty-three-year history. Whether we work with, live with, or teach youngsters who have behavioral, learning, or emotional problems, we all know how challenging it can be, how our morale can be eroded, how helpless we often feel when nothing seems to work. Conversely, we also know the satisfaction of finally *getting through* and making progress with a child who is burdened with such difficulties.

Troubled kids often struggle with compelling problems that put them at particular disadvantage in the day-to-day encounters of home, school, and community. Whether they face learning difficulties, behavioral or social predicaments, or histories of abuse and neglect, these kids all need a supportive "safety net" composed of caring individuals and skilled professionals. For those of us who, by choice or default, find ourselves part of such a support network, the mandate is clear: we must find new, more helpful ways to work with the vulnerable youngsters in our care. Our goal in publishing *No Such Thing As a Bad Kid* is to provide an invaluable guidebook for doing just that.

Gifford is pleased to have collaborated with Charlie Appelstein on this book. Charlie is a highly respected child-care specialist whose work with troubled children has distinguished him in the field of behavior management. His constructive messages about behavior have hit a responsive note among teachers, parents, and child-care workers alike. Unlike most books about challenging behavior, *No Such Thing* is a hands-on guide that helps us understand how to maintain a balanced perspective, reminding us of both the challenges and the rewards inherent in our relationships with kids who may "push our buttons."

From classrooms and residential centers to foster homes and community centers comes a resounding call for help in dealing with difficult behavior. We at Gifford are committed to helping all children succeed and to improving the emotional and behavioral outcomes for children and teens at risk. *No Such Thing As a Bad Kid* is an inspiring and vital resource for all who share that mission.

Michael J. Bassichis, LICSW
Executive Director
The Gifford School
Weston, Massachusetts

INTRODUCTION

THIS BOOK IS FOR ANYONE WHO WORKS WITH TROUBLED CHILDREN OR youth. Unlike most books about challenging behavior, this one is not academic; it is a hands-on guide designed to help you relate more effectively to children and adolescents who consistently display impaired social functioning due to adverse histories—in short, kids "at risk."

Whether you are a teacher grappling with difficult classroom behaviors, a camp counselor with more heat inside the cabin than out under the noonday sun, a social worker contending with an unruly four year old, the foster parent of a rude and defiant teenager, or an overwhelmed residential child-care worker, you know what challenging behaviors look like. You also know what kinds of feelings they evoke in you. You may even be on the verge of burnout, ready to walk away from the seemingly hopeless task of creating order out of chaos. If so, take heart—your every interaction *does* count. The practical insights and interventions that follow can help you hang in there with renewed vision and a variety of useful skills.

To illustrate these approaches, each chapter contains several anecdotes. In those that draw upon my own experiences, I look pretty good. But please remember that for every positive interaction you read about, there are at least twenty in which I messed up big-time.

Like most people, I do my best learning by analyzing mistakes. And when you make a mistake with a child, you end up hurting inside, so you try to learn from the experience and do better the next time.

Many of the personal anecdotes are from my work in residential care centers. These facilities double as giant "learning laboratories" where one can discover a wealth of helpful interventions that can then be generalized to less troubled populations. Feel free to extrapolate from these stories as you wish.

By the same token, if you come upon sections of this book that are not germane to your situation, move on. Please remember, however, that reading about challenging behaviors is one thing and grappling with them quite another. With at-risk children, there are no quick fixes, no shortcuts. To the contrary, these children require great patience, fortitude, sacrifice, and sustained love. Because they want to believe in us, they continually "test" us to see if we are worthy of their confidence, to make sure our actions support our words. When we stay true to our words, the children connect to us and, through this link, grow stronger.

That is what happened with Al, a man I recently met. After spending a decade as a businessman, Al discovered that the corporate world did not jibe with who he really was. Making a radical change, he took a job at a residential school for troubled kids. Two years into it, he still loved the work and knew he had found his true calling.

Around this time Billy, an angry and resistant twelve year old, entered his program. One Friday afternoon, Billy began acting out, whereupon Al decided to keep him after school to work through the problem. When school let out, Billy refused to speak and continued to act in a rude and belligerent manner.

"Billy, I'm going to keep you here until we talk about what is going on with you," Al calmly asserted.

Billy scowled, laughed mockingly, then shot back: "Go ahead, keep me here. I *live* here, you idiot. *You're* the one who goes home at three o'clock. *I'll* keep *you* here *all night!* "

Al replied: "Billy, I love it here. Working with you guys is the best job in the world. I'm never going to leave. If I need to stay late tonight, that's okay. In fact, I've already called your unit and they'll be sending your dinner down in an hour."

Billy grew silent. Soon afterward he began talking about his day and some of the pressure he was under.

Two years later, Al was ready to leave the program. Used up and feeling as though he had nothing left to offer, he gave notice. On his last day on the job, Billy volunteered to help him move his things to the car. As they made their final trip to the parking lot, Billy suddenly stopped and looked him square in the eye.

"Do you remember that day a few years ago when you kept me after school?" he asked.

"Yes, I think so," Al replied.

"You said you loved this job and would never leave. Why are you leaving?"

Al looked into Billy's eyes and saw heart-wrenching despair. After a few ponderous seconds, he announced, "Put all the stuff back in my office."

That was five years ago, and Al has been there ever since.

This story attests to the power of relationship. It reminds us of the degree to which troubled children want to believe in adults, and of how critical it is to stay the course with them. It is easy to get angry at a kid and act impulsively. It is equally easy to walk away from behaviors that push us away. Yet those behaviors are silent calls for help. When we listen for the messages and stay in control of ourselves, we begin to make a difference.

There is no such thing as a bad kid. Just bad luck . . . and eventually, provided that we persevere, new, more promising circumstances.

PART I

UNDERSTANDING CHALLENGING BEHAVIOR

CHAPTER 1

MISBEHAVIOR: A CODED MESSAGE

I WAS DRIVING ALONG ELM STREET, A HEAVILY TRAVELED ROAD, WITH my twelve-year-old passenger Andy, a resident at a treatment center for troubled youth. Before coming to the center, Andy had been severely abused by his parents. His behavior was described as provocative, rude, wild, and aggressive. He trusted no one.

As the social work intern assigned to Andy, I was taking him out for his fourth therapy session. Our first three sessions had gone well, though he had tested me a bit. Even so, I liked him; he had spunk. With each session, it had become easier to see through his tough facade. I sensed a lonely and hurting boy under there—someone longing to connect but fearful of relationships.

As we passed a busy intersection, Andy began rummaging through my glove compartment. "Not the glove compartment!" I thought to myself. Inside was a stack of bills I had just paid, neatly wrapped in an elastic band and ready to be mailed. I tried to stay calm while he removed the elastic band.

"Hey, Andy," I said with as much composure as I could muster, "why don't you put those back. They're just crummy old bills."

Andy ignored me. He studied the sealed envelopes in his hands, then glanced out the side window. "Not the window!" I thought, as we inched along the busy road.

"What would you do if I threw these out the window?" he asked with a provocative glint in his eyes.

My mind flooded with the consequences I would administer. "Throw those out the window and we won't be driving together for a l-o-n-g time!" I imagined saying to him. A moment later I silently added, "Because you'll be grounded for a month!"

Get control of yourself, a familiar inner voiced chimed in my head. *What you say will make a difference.* I took a reflective step back, analyzed the situation, and changed my tune. "Andy," I explained, "you're my friend and I don't think you would do such a thing."

He stared at me for a while, looked at the letters, then quietly returned them to the glove compartment. I started to breathe again.

We never discussed the incident. As far as I could tell, he forgot about it. Yet I never did, for I could see that beneath Andy's bravado was a kid seeking to connect and needing to test our relationship.

Looking beyond Behavior

Children like Andy, who push our buttons, are usually attempting to relay a message. They are trying to tell us: "Something isn't right. I need help!" But when we've just been verbally assaulted, or asked to picture our bills flying one by one out the car window, anger and frustration surge to the fore, temporarily overriding any inclination we may have had to decode the underlying message.

When our buttons are pushed, the natural tendency is to focus our attention on what the child did and what should be done about it, rather than on *why he did it*. In the glove compartment incident, Andy's threat to toss the bills out the window was symptomatic of a deeper issue—namely, his inability to trust his connections with people. Andy lacked trust in adults and wanted to know if I would turn on him like his parents had.

To grasp the difference between symptoms and core issues, imagine an athlete who has torn the cartilage in his knee and is experiencing pain. A strong painkiller may temporarily ease the situation, but it will not remedy the underlying problem. The pain is a symptom—a message that something is wrong. If the athlete's doctor treats only the symptom, the condition may in fact worsen. Good treatment entails appropriate *symptom management* (pain relief) and sophisticated *problem resolution* (surgery). Both are essential.

Disciplining children without considering the cause of their problematic behavior is like dispensing medication to people without searching for the cause of their symptoms. If a problem is significant, symptom management alone will not be enough. Andy, for one, needed more than behavioral limits; he needed to know he could count on me not to hurt him.

Decoding the Message

To get to the root of troubling behavior, we must decode the underlying message. Linda, an elementary school art teacher, was having a tough time holding the attention of her fourth grade class. Tommy, a defiant student seated at the back of the room, kept disrupting the others. When Linda stopped to think about the boy behind the behavior, she realized that Tommy had trouble drawing as well as the other students, never seemed satisfied with his work, and appeared to have low self-esteem.

To improve his chances of succeeding, Linda decided to let him tackle less complicated projects. At the start of each class, she presented her students with the exercise for the day, inviting Tommy to choose from a number of simpler ones. Over time, he stopped acting out. By the end of the year, he was able to work on the same projects as his classmates, with satisfactory results. The message behind his unruly behavior was: "I can't draw like the other kids, and I'm sick and tired of being the worst at everything. Help me!"

Decoding was also essential with Mary, a young teenager with a traumatic history of mistreatment who was recently placed at a residential treatment center. Socially immature, she was incessantly ridiculed by her public school classmates and would often return to the center in tears. Mary wanted desperately to switch schools and attend a local special education facility with some of the other residents. The staff agreed that the change would make sense.

Weeks later, while the paperwork was still in process, Mary's therapist, Eileen, reported a serious problem: Mary was running away in the middle of their psychotherapy sessions. Eileen suspected that from Mary's perspective, the staff had not acted quickly enough, and that she was turning her back on her therapist in much the same way that the staff was turning its back on *her*. When confronted with this interpretation of events, Mary acknowledged that she was indeed running away because her request to change schools had not been taken seriously. Eileen relayed this message to the administrators, who promptly arranged for Mary's transfer. Assured that her needs were being addressed, she stopped running from her therapy sessions.

In both these instances the adults in charge were able to decode the message behind the misbehavior. As a result, they managed to address the issue troubling each child and arrive at a helpful course of action.

While decoding such messages, please remember that the proclamation "Something isn't right" does not necessarily imply that you are doing something wrong. Neither Tommy's disrespect nor Mary's escapes reflected on the actions of the adults in charge; they were merely the people interested enough in unraveling the triggers for the disruptive actions.

Many of the triggers for problem behavior are biological. Children with Attention Deficit Hyperactivity Disorder (ADHD), learning disabilities, visual or hearing impairments, or other physiological difficulties frequently act out—in part, to call attention to their conditions, which have either gone undiagnosed or received improper treatment.

Temperament, too, can play a role. An active child born to reserved parents, for example, may be destined for conflict. Many children who are temperamentally mismatched with their parents revert to problematic behavior any time they are asked to act in ways that do not mesh with their personalities. The message behind this behavior is: "Treat me as I am, not as who you want me to be."

Interestingly, some acting out that occurs is developmentally appropriate. Perfectly adjusted teens, for example, will do things that drive us crazy—that's adolescence! Understanding normal development and the deviations that occur among troubled youngsters can help you identify the roots of problem behavior. (For insights into developmental factors, see chapter 3).

Whether you are decoding a behavioral message or trying to understand its origins, be sure to *avoid hasty interpretations*. For one thing, children hate pat explanations of their actions. For another, you may be considerably off base. In either case, jumping to conclusions can hinder the growth of your relationships with children.

The person who taught me to beware of quick interpretations was Elroy, a thirteen year old who was referred to the court clinic for counseling. His mother reported that six months before, an older relative named Gene had been tragically killed. He had lived in the boy's home, and the two had developed a strong attachment to each other. Initially, Elroy displayed little response to Gene's death, but he had recently begun to show signs of depression.

Elroy and I met for weekly therapy sessions to help him through his delayed grief reaction. For the first nine months of our twelve-month program, he felt too uncomfortable to open up. Then he let down his guard and began to cry for his lost buddy. The more he grieved, the more his depression lifted.

Only one uncomfortable piece of business remained. From time to time, I would end our session by inviting Elroy, with his mother's permission, to join me for an ice cream cone—my treat. Every time I asked, however, he politely declined. "The kid isn't ready for intimacy," I thought to myself. "I'm a nurturing male figure and being with me reminds him of Gene, so I shouldn't push it. Man, do I have this kid pegged."

In our eleventh month of therapy, after considerable work on his part to open up and deal with Gene's death, I again asked Elroy to join me for a cone. I thought for sure he would agree to celebrate the triumphant culmination of our work together. Again, he politely refused.

"What gives?" I wondered. "I *know* this kid. In the past, his refusal was a message—'I'm not ready to handle the intimacy.' But now he should be ready. Haven't we worked through the grief issue enough?" Perplexed, I began to have self-doubts about Elroy's course of therapy.

During our next to last session, no longer able to stand the suspense, I came right out and asked Elroy why he refused to join me for a cone. I should not have forced the issue, or put my needs before his; I should have had more respect for his boundaries.

"You're dressed a lot better than me," he calmly replied. "I'd be embarrassed going out there with you."

"That's it?" I thought to myself. "Just the statutory shirt and tie?"

The following week, I broke code. I chucked the button-down shirt and tie, and we enjoyed a few scoops of ice cream together.

The moral of this story is: Search till you're sure. This story lesson holds true for more problematic behaviors as well. Any time a challenging kid misbehaves, set your sights on the deeper problem. The more sensitive you are to why the child is acting out, the more effective your response will be. In the end, although good and timely symptom management is essential, long-term success in diminishing troubling behaviors is more likely when the underlying issues are properly addressed.

CHAPTER 2

RESPONDING VERSUS REACTING

IT IS NOT ALWAYS EASY TO LOOK FOR HIDDEN MESSAGES WHEN A CHILD is pushing your buttons. It is far simpler to say, "I don't give a hoot why this kid is provoking me. She needs discipline—now!" We bark out the words, reach for our behavior management tools, and often, in the heat of anger, misuse them. Why? Because we are "wired" for self-protection and, when threatened, may react to provoking situations in vengeful, nonproductive ways.

This is what happened to Frank within hours of leaving a training workshop on behavior management. At the workshop, he had smiled and nodded his head in understanding; but later that night, when his sixteen-year-old foster daughter arrived home two hours after curfew with liquor on her breath and proceeded to vomit on the new living room rug, he screamed at her and grounded her for three months. Anger had taken over. As a result, his newly acquired learning slipped to the back of his consciousness and he forfeited a golden opportunity to ferret out the meaning underlying his foster daughter's rebellious behavior.

Why do many caring adults become so upset with children that they react to them in nonproductive ways? One major reason is that when children in our care misbehave, we are likely to feel inadequate and psychologically attacked. Upon experiencing such an assault to our self-esteem, we are apt to retaliate by yelling, intimidating, and inappropriately disciplining them. The crux of the problem is that when kids act out, we tend to take it personally, because we believe that their behavior is a reflection of who *we* are.

The key to good behavior management is staying cool and *responding* to situations rather than *reacting* to them. Responding requires us to acknowledge the fragility of our self-esteem, then take time to look for the message behind distressing behavior, rather than immediately levy consequences. To do this, we must first learn to manage our *own* behavior.

Self-Management Techniques

More often than not, a teacher whose class is out of control feels incompetent. A residential counselor who cannot help a child improve his behavior feels inadequate. A foster parent whose disruptive child is removed from her home feels like a failure. All these feelings, and more, prompt a reaction rather than a response.

Imagine that you are a foster parent and you receive a call from the school principal informing you that your son Carl, who has been behaving well lately, has been suspended for three days because he was caught writing, "Mrs. Reilly is an asshole" on the school walls. How do you feel—embarrassed and humiliated? Do you wonder how this behavior will reflect on you as a parent? No doubt, your self-esteem has taken a serious hit and your confidence as a foster parent is shaken. You are waiting for little Carl to get home so you can lower the boom. That is the proper thing to do, right? Wrong!

Yes, Carl made a serious mistake and should experience the consequences of his actions. If you overreact when he arrives home, however, you will most likely sabotage your ability to work through the incident. If you listen calmly, on the other hand, you may find that an older student bullied Carl into writing the inscriptions.

How do you avoid overreacting? The best way is to take a moment for reflection by counting to five, ten, or *one hundred,* or by briefly leaving the scene. Then, once you have regained your composure, reflect upon the distressing incident, identify how it has made you feel, and consider how it has affected your self-esteem. Remember, your goal is to *respond* rather than *react*.

For effective self-reflection, try cultivating an observing ego, a voice that will talk to you when your self-esteem has been wounded and your emotions are flaring. If you have an active imagination, this voice can even guide you to other realms of consciousness.

Dialoguing with Your Observing Ego
A conversation with your observing ego can take your self-esteem off the hook and stop you from reacting precipitately. The conversation might go something like this:

YOU: I'm gonna kill that kid! Why is he doing this to me? He's ruining my life! How the hell can he write, "Mrs. Reilly is an asshole" on school walls? Just wait till he gets home—he'll be grounded for six months!

OBSERVING EGO: Now, (your name), it's okay to be mad. You're a human being. But remember, you haven't heard Carl's side of the story.

YOU: What could he possibly say that would excuse such behavior?! I'm furious!

OBSERVING EGO: Why so furious?

YOU: He embarrassed me! He's made me question my parenting skills. Maybe I'm not as good a foster mother as I thought. Other foster parents don't have kids who write graffiti on the walls. This is awful.

OBSERVING EGO: (Your name), what you're experiencing is normal. We all question our abilities when we take a hit to our self-esteem. But remember, it is only a wound and wounds heal. You've suffered a *narcissistic injury,* and in a few hours you won't feel so bad. *Don't make any rash decisions in your present frame of mind.* Be careful about what you initially say to Carl. Listen to his side of the story first; then after you've heard all the facts, decide on an appropriate consequence if he deserves one. Whatever you do, discuss the matter without yelling, threatening, or finger pointing.

Using the "Force"
This technique can help you avoid inappropriate knee-jerk reactions in times of physical or emotional exhaustion when your self-esteem has been injured, support is lacking, and the pull is to act punitively toward the child. Indeed, it has been said that *anyone* who works with challenging kids is apt to become punitive in times of decreased support. The imagery in this dialogue draws upon the classic struggle of the "dark side versus the force," from the *Star Wars Trilogy.*

YOU: That Carl is really tickin' me off!

OBSERVING EGO: Relax. You've had a tough few weeks and have worked a long shift with no assistance. You're run down.

YOU: Don't give me that support theory mumbo-jumbo. I'm mad and I want this kid to pay!

OBSERVING EGO [*simulating the voice of Obi-Wan Kenobi*]: Use the "force," Luke. Stretch . . . out . . . your feelings.

YOU: No, that kid—

OBSERVING EGO: Let the force guide you. The force is always with you.

YOU: Okay, I hear you. I'm being drawn to the "dark side." I've got to do what's right.

CARL [*entering through the back door in a flush of emotion*]: Am I in trouble!

YOU: Carl, we need to have a good talk and figure out what happened so you can make better decisions next time a delicate situation arises.

If the "force" image does not work for you, find one that does. Some people rely on religion or a more personal understanding of spirituality to stop them from being pulled toward punitive thinking. The imagery you use does not matter. What matters is that in the midst of rising anger and waning support you know you are at *great risk* for saying and doing things that will not be in your best interest or the child's.

The Way of Empathy

Would you be terribly upset with a disruptive child if you knew he had been picked on unmercifully at school that day, or denied dinner the night before? Probably not. You would most likely respond *empathically* to his side of the situation—and rightly so. As important as it is to be in touch with our own emotions, we need to empathize with what is going on for the child and, if only for a moment, walk in his shoes.

Empathy helps us see past negative behaviors and feel for the youngster. Here is how it works: Any time a child begins to raise our blood pressure, we try being him for a while. We think long and hard about the messages he is sending and about the factors contributing to his behavior. Then we check in and see how *that* makes us feel.

During workshops, I often have professionals reflect on the child who ticks them off the most. "What's the first word that comes to mind when you think about this kid?" I ask.

The answers range from "frustrating" and "provocative" to "exhausting," "manipulative," "jerk," and "ruination."

I then present the following scenario: "Say that tomorrow morning when you arrive at work, you go directly to the office to watch a video of the worst ten minutes of that child's life. You see him being neglected and abused, and crying out for help. After viewing this tape, how do you think you would respond to the kid as the day unfolds?"

"With a lot more compassion," some will say, or "I don't think I'd be as rough with him," or "I probably wouldn't be able to yell at him."

While working with troubled children who have had tough lives, view the tapes before you act. Every kid has one.

The tapes of Jody were vivid. This rambunctious, auburn-haired seven year old—one of a group of abused and neglected girls at a large residential treatment center—required physical restraint two to four times a day to avoid hurting herself and others. Most staff members were exhausted from dealing with this master of provocation. Entering the unit for the first time as the new supervisor, I quickly spotted her standing in front of a full-length mirror, staring intently at her reflection. She eyed me with a look of impending doom.

I mentally reviewed her history. Jody was reportedly a victim of gross neglect who had been sexually abused by her stepfather. She had been kicked out of three foster homes before coming to the center. I tried to imagine what life must be like for her and, given her history of sexual abuse, how she might react to a new male on the unit.

Five minutes after my arrival, the child-care worker on duty gave Jody a time-out for making a rude comment. She immediately began to yell and throw objects around the room. Because she was not responding to verbal interventions and because her aggressive behavior was escalating dangerously, I knew she would need help to regain control. Using physical management techniques designed to keep kids safe, I escorted her to a part of the building where she would be out of range of the other residents. Once there, she screamed and thrashed with intensity, requiring ongoing physical restraint. Struggling mightily, she screamed at the top of her lungs, "Leave me alone!" over and over again.

While continuing to restrain her, I thought to myself, "Oh boy, you've got some heavy work ahead of you with *this* gal." I tried to imagine how badly she must have been treated, the rage she harbored, the pain she carried. Wave upon wave of empathy helped me stay in control as she called me every name in the book and attempted to bite me.

After about ten minutes with no appreciable drop in decibel levels or intensity, I decided to try an experiment. The next time she screamed, "Leave me alone!" I reached in my pocket, retrieved a ten-dollar bill, and placed it in her view. I waited for a break in her wailing and then spoke: "You said to *leave you a loan*. All I have is a ten. Is that enough of a loan?"

The wailing stopped abruptly. Then ever so slowly, Jody turned to look at me. I was smiling. Soon she was, too. Hardly ever did I need to hold her again.

Six months later, several of us were at the beach. I was standing about five feet out in the ocean watching the children swim. Jody glided over and looked at me with an innocence only a kid can muster. Then she spoke, "You know, I thought you were going to yell at me like everyone else. But you made me laugh."

I knew instantly what she was referring to. "Was it better that way?"

"Yeah," she replied, giggling.

I picked her up and threw her into the water. She was laughing as she splashed down. It was good to hear.

Steering Clear of Labels

Responding sensitively also requires us to refrain from negative labeling. Why? Because when we attach a pejorative label to a child and it sticks, we—and everyone we have spoken to—begin to see the child for what he *does* rather than who he *is*.

Suppose you are deciding between two children who are on a waiting list for admission to your group. The first child has lived in four foster homes and has burn marks on his hands, which have been traced to abuses by his father; he is portrayed as a sad and lonely boy who has never had a friend and does not trust adults. The second youngster is described as self-absorbed, manipulative, incapable of following directions, in constant need of attention, and willing to do anything to get it. Which child would you choose? Most people I ask select kid number one.

In actuality, these descriptions are from two profiles of *the same child;* only the wording is different. Describe a child's painful history and people want to reach out to him; label his annoying behaviors and people are less willing to help.

Translating Negative Terms

Any time you are about to apply a negative description to a child, or are listening to someone else who is using one, stop yourself and mentally translate the term. Try to find the painful emotions and unmet needs it refers to.

Listed below are pejorative labels commonly applied to troubled children. Following each one are points to ponder as you seek out the underlying realities.

"Babyish"—Is the child developmentally behind? Has he perhaps missed out on the nurturing and attention he should have received years ago?

"Dishonest"—Is this child afraid to tell the truth for fear of suffering serious consequences? Is he lying to win approval from his peers?

"Egocentric"—Does the "me, me, me" attitude suggest that the child has to put extra time into looking out for himself because he does not trust that others will do the job? If so, egocentrism is his way of ensuring that his needs will be met.

"Just looking for attention"—Has this child failed to receive the attention he needed earlier in life? If so, is it reasonable to think he could be happy with a little bit of regard when what he craves is a mountain of it? Adults often become frustrated when troubled kids clamor for excessive attention; in reality, the time to be distressed is when they *stop* seeking extra attention, for then they may have given up.

Most troubled children are attention deprived. As a result, they are rarely satisfied with even our best efforts at attentiveness, or with the great sacrifices we make for them. Angry, we are apt to lash out at them, when in actuality we should be upset not with them but with the lack of resources that have been available to them.

"Lazy"—Is the child withdrawn, or depressed? Does he have a learning difficulty, or a history of failure? If not, perhaps he has previously invested in someone or something, and proceeded to "go broke." Or maybe he simply has no reason to be ambitious.

"Manipulative"—Could this child be manipulating his environment for safety purposes? Many children learn to survive by subtly controlling others; for them, manipulation is a form of self-preservation.

"Obnoxious"—Is the child drawing a boundary around himself so that adults will keep their distance from him? Children who have been hurt by adults and are therefore unable to tolerate intimacy with them will often use obnoxious behavior to push grown-ups away from them.

"Provocative"—Is this child feeling a need for attention? Some children, expecting to be rejected, will provoke an adult in order to be in control of when and where it happens. To eliminate their anxiety, they will set up the rejection through skillful provocation.

Other youngsters, having been mistreated by adults, harbor a great deal of anger toward them. To displace their anger, they will behave provocatively toward *any* adult who stands in their way.

The Impact of Negative Labeling

Given that misbehavior is a child's way of sending a message, negative labeling is nothing short of "shooting the messenger." It can both infuriate a child and impair your interactions with him.

Consider the case of seven-year-old Teddy, a warmhearted child full of spunk and humor. The product of a chaotic upbringing, Teddy possessed negligible self-esteem and had trouble trusting adults. He also lied—a lot! Any time he was caught in a lie and confronted with the "L word," he would go ballistic. "I'm not a *liar!*" he would scream. Teddy equated the L word with being a bad kid. He simply could not tolerate being labeled a liar; he was too fragile.

The third time Teddy was caught telling an obvious lie, his residential counselor tried a new approach.

COUNSELOR: Teddy, it looks like we have a problem here.

TEDDY: I didn't lie! I'm not a liar!

COUNSELOR: Hey, I didn't call you a liar. I just want us to have a little talk.

TEDDY: I didn't lie!

COUNSELOR: I hear what you're saying, and I know what I saw. Let me ask you something: Do you think it's very slightly possible [*putting thumb and forefinger together so that they were almost touching*] that what you are saying happened is [*again putting thumb and forefinger together*] a little less correct than what really happened?

TEDDY [*pondering the question, then smiling*]: It's possible that I was a little less correct.

COUNSELOR: Well, thank you for admitting this to me. I know it wasn't easy.

The next day, the entire staff began to use the "a little less correct" phrase with Teddy. As a result, his lying soon diminished and they were able to talk with him in greater depth each time a deep-seated issue surfaced.

If you tend to negatively label kids like Teddy, you might not be wrong—just a little less correct. Give it up and you will vastly improve your chances of communicating with the children *behind* the labels.

Avoiding the Misuse of Power and Control

One of the most challenging yet effective ways to respond meaningfully to provocative situations is by exercising caution in how we use our influence over children. Reacting forcefully to disruptive behavior will often interfere with our ability to get to the heart of the child's message. Worse yet, such misapplications of power and control will usually prompt more misbehavior. Why? Because children tend to experience these actions as hurtful, belittling, and infuriating, and acting out may be their only means of staging a protest.

Common Misuses of Power and Control
The path of good intentions is teeming with pitfalls. The following four count among the most insidious of them all.

• Abusing one's authority

CHILD: Why?

ADULT [*angrily*]: Because I told you to!

If this dialogue took place between you and your boss, you would no doubt walk away from it feeling furious and plotting your revenge. Why should a child feel any less angry when someone in authority says these words to him?

When people in positions of authority abuse their power in this way, they shut down conversations, all the while defining who is in charge and who is not. The effects can be disastrous. Many young children who have had the power of authority repeatedly misused against them undergo a stormy, retaliatory adolescence.

Emotional intensity was already evident in a fourth grade class that was nearing the end of a year-long conflict resolution program.

A fight had broken out on the playground, after which their some-what beleaguered teacher asked, "How can you kids talk about these skills so well in class but not use them outside?"

A few students offered feeble responses. Then Alex spoke, say-ing: "Maybe it's hard to use this stuff because we don't see much of it at home. My family is into joking about power. My grandmother laughs and says, 'We've got all the power.' Why can't adults just tell us that they are older and need to *take care of us* instead of say-ing that they've got the power? Why can't they give us *reasons* for things? My mother is using this new program. She says, 'One, two, three,' and then I'm grounded. Most of the time I don't even know what I've done wrong!"

At this point, one child after another started describing authori-tative powers that had been used against them. "My ballet teacher tells us we can't wear shirts over our leotards, but she *does*. When we ask her why she gets to wear one, she says, 'Because I'm the teacher!'"

"My parents never explain why I'm not allowed to do things they do. It's always, 'Because I'm the parent!'"

"My coach says it's his way or the highway!"

Nearly every child had a story to tell. Their emotions were raw, their anger real, and their memories sure to linger.

• Yelling

How do you feel when someone yells at you? Belittled, most likely, as well as not respected, intimidated, and angry. Moreover, you may want to get even with the person. Children feel the same way.

Yelling not only reinforces a child's negative self-image but can send a frightening message: *This adult is losing control of his emo-tions*. A child who discovers that the adults in his world have trouble controlling their emotions comes to view his interactions with them as uncertain and precarious.

Is there a distinction between yelling and raising one's voice? In one sense, there is: yelling serves the adult's need to discharge anger, whereas raising one's voice may serve the child's need for discipline. Children, however, have a hard time distinguishing between the two, particularly troubled children who are *hypersensitive to abuses of power.* In reality, the more we raise our voices, the greater the likelihood that tensions will ensue.

When yelling is reduced, children's behavior improves. In one residential program in Massachusetts where the staff significantly reduced their yelling, the use of physical restraints reportedly decreased by more than 50 percent. In other group situations in which yelling has been reduced, adults say they are relieved to spend their time listening to the children rather than forcing the children to listen to them. A five-minute time-out, they note, has more impact when it is announced in a calm, supportive tone of voice than when it is ordered in an angry "Sit down for five minutes!" command.

If you sometimes yell, do not feel guilty about it. Instead, strive to decrease your yelling over the next few months. Take it one step at a time and see how it feels. Notice, too, how the children respond to your quieter approach. You will certainly be rewarded for your efforts.

• Spanking

How would you feel if you were late handing in a report to your boss and he suddenly spanked you? No adult would tolerate such an egregious act; it is too demeaning and disrespectful. Imagine, then, what it is like for a child.

Spanking—including swatting, hitting, and tapping—is a maneuver in power and intimidation. Physically, it hurts. Emotionally, it makes kids angry. The reason we get away with it is that the children we spank are small, powerless, and unable to strike us back.

Not only do we save spanking for the young and defenseless but we often fail to see how counterproductive this angry, desperate act usually is. Spanking informs children that *physical violence is an appropriate response to frustration.*

If in a moment of anger you strike a child, remember that the good care you have been offering him will far outweigh the ramifications of one spanking. Even so, recognize what you have done, search for more effective responses, and apologize for having lost control. An apology will help to repair your relationship and will model productive behavior.

• Making decisions without consulting the child

Adults frequently make decisions that impact on children's lives without warning them or asking them to assist with the change. Teachers alter seating arrangements; group-home counselors switch the residents' roommates; foster parents amend house rules. Although any one of these moves may be in the children's best interests, if they are not properly prepared—especially for big changes—they may feel overwhelmed and devalued.

Imagine that you go to work tomorrow and your boss orders you to stay late to finish a report. Extending your workday will interfere with your evening plans—which may annoy you, if not cause you to act out a bit. Kids feel the same way when we take them for granted and arbitrarily change the rules on them. To help troubled kids, leave your lines of communication open, keep the children well informed, and whenever possible, let them make choices about issues that affect their lives.

If you have no choice but to suddenly alter a plan, explain your reasoning to the child and empathize with his reaction. An occasional change in plans without involving the child will not have disastrous effects; to the contrary, although children require predictability to enhance their sense of control, they also need to learn that life is sometimes unpredictable, that unforeseen developments do arise.

Any time you are about to unleash your power by abusing your authority, yelling, spanking, or making a unilateral decision, catch yourself before you begin, take a deep breath, and reflect on the ramifications of your action. Is there a more effective way to exercise your power and control? Yes, there is: *Interact with children the way you want people to interact with you.*

The Role of Past Abuses

Many children who chronically misbehave have histories replete with serious abuses of power and control. Those who have been sexually abused harbor tremendous anger; those who have been repeatedly yelled at, spanked, or responded to inconsistently also feel tremendous rage toward the world. No child—or adult, for that matter—likes to be unfairly controlled or intimidated.

Jody, who is described on pages 17–18, came to the residential treatment center with a tragic history of sexual and physical abuse. She arrived expecting to be treated unfairly, because that was all she had known. On some level, she also wanted power to be used against her, so she tried to provoke staff members to yell at her or physically restrain her. With each provocation, a little voice inside her chimed out: "See I *am* a bad kid. My parents had good reason to abuse and abandon me. I drove them crazy. Look around—I drive *everyone* crazy."

Yet, even though Jody's parents treated her unfairly, she loved them—they were all she had. She therefore believed that she *deserved* their mistreatment, that she was somehow bad, that the abuse she experienced was all her fault. In provoking adults to misuse their power against her, she was both protecting her parents and affirming her negative self-image. In addition, she was taking control of the situation by setting up the abuse so she would know when and where it would transpire.

The clinical term used to describe the actions of people who, like Jody, bring on the situations they are most afraid of is *counterphobic behavior*. This type of behavior is readily exhibited by students who, assuming they will be kicked out of class, provoke the teacher into "excusing" them from the room. They do not want to be sent out; they simply cannot stand not knowing when it will occur.

Over the years, many kids have screamed at me, "Go ahead, hit me!" They, too, were attempting to control the situation. They wanted me to prove that they were bad kids who deserved to be hit. They were testing me as well, to see if I would be like the other adults who had mistreated them.

Setting the Record Straight

Our job with children who exhibit counterphobic behavior is to set the record straight, to get them to believe that they are good kids. Our first task toward this end is to help them understand why their parents mistreated them. We might explain, for example, that their parents are good people who made some serious mistakes, probably due to a combination of bad luck and problems of their own. This explanation gives troubled kids a way of still loving their parents without blaming themselves for the destructive and abusive actions they experienced. Our second mission is to comfort the children as they deal with the resulting sadness and anger that inevitably emerge.

Mike, for example, spent two hours restraining Jonas, a two-hundred-pound adolescent with arms like tree trunks, who had just blown up over a minor incident. Although he hardly knew Jonas, he quickly surmised that he was a very troubled young man. After the restraint, Mike therefore spent one-on-one time with him, for he was still quite upset. At this point, Jonas began to direct a torrent of rage toward his mother. He talked about how she had repeatedly looked the other way as one of his uncles sexually abused him. After letting Jonas vent for a while, Mike commented, "I'll bet your mother loves you, and I'll bet she's had a tough life, too."

Jonas looked up at Mike with a how-did-you-know kind of look. "She was sexually abused as a kid," he volunteered, then related some of the details, including information about his own abuse. Suddenly, he began to sob. Mike put his arm on Jonas's shoulder, and they sat in silence for a while.

When we misuse our adult power, even in subtle ways, we risk reinforcing a child's negative self-image by fueling his belief that he is a bad kid who deserves to be mistreated. By calmly dealing with the child in a respectful manner, we can help him see that he is an inherently good kid who simply made a bad decision.

CHAPTER 3

DEVELOPMENTAL CONSIDERATIONS

DEVELOPMENTAL PSYCHOLOGY OFFERS AN ESPECIALLY HELPFUL LENS FOR viewing challenging behavior. One reason is that it fosters realistic expectations. Because the majority of troubled children are functioning years behind their chronological age, adults who respond to misbehavior on the basis of age alone end up expecting too much, leading to miscommunication and conflict. By contrast, adults who recognize a child's developmental level are able to realign their assumptions and avoid needless strife.

A second reason for a developmental perspective is that children who have difficulty relating to others are often displaying unmet basic needs. At such times, the message behind their misbehavior is: "I'm stuck at an earlier developmental stage and need help moving through it. Give me *now* what I should have received *then*." The better we are at recognizing the developmental messages behind misconduct, the more effective our response will be.

Volumes of developmental literature address healthy maturation in depth. The purpose of this chapter is to focus on some of the *key tasks* of the first five years of life, ways in which children function later in life if these tasks have not been accomplished, and what you can do to help.

The Foundation Years

The beginning of a child's life, like the earliest phases of house building, sets the stage for all that is to come. To withstand the elements
over the passage of time, a house needs a strong foundation; otherwise, it is at risk of crumbling. In a child's life, the foundation is set
during the first five years. Children whose needs are met in a "good
enough"[1] fashion during these years will have beneath them a sound
foundation and will experience comfort and security in knowing
that the world is an okay place in which to live.

Theorists say that such children have attained "object constancy," a
"cohesive sense of self," and most importantly, healthy "attachments" to
the significant adults in their lives.[2,3,4,5] Simply put, the children's depen-
dency needs have been met and development can proceed. Youngsters
who emerge from their first five years without a solid foundation, on the
other hand, are at risk for periodic "crumbling" and a generally troubled
life. The first three years are the most critical.

The First Year

In the first year of life, children are entirely dependent on their parents. To survive, they need food, clothing, shelter, bathing, cuddling,
rocking, conversation, sensory and tactile stimulation, protection, and
above all, love.[6,7] As they begin to navigate their surroundings, they
also require guidance and limits.

When parents meet these early needs, children form attachments
to them. Those who are well attached eventually embark on a "separation individuation" process.[8,9] In other words, through strong
attachment to their parents, children develop enough confidence
and skill to venture out into the world as separate individuals,
always knowing that mom and dad are behind them—in thought
if not in deed.

When the needs of the first year are not met—if, for example,
parents are chronically unresponsive, uncaring, or too punitive—
children come to view the world as a cold and unwelcoming place.
In time their personalities become molded by this perspective. They
experience encounters with adults as ungratifying and unsafe; and
having learned that depending on others is unreliable, they are con-

vinced that they must fend for themselves. The message they project is, "I must do it all by myself."

Children whose first-year needs are not adequately met tend to grow up extremely egocentric and incapable of sustaining social relationships. Because they have never fully attached to a significant adult, they often view adults more as objects than as human beings. As a result, they tend to feel isolated and alone in a world they regard as treacherous.

Any time you are working with a child who has antisocial tendencies—such as a disregard for rules, extreme self-centeredness, hostility, or a propensity for abusing animals or hurting peers without feeling remorse—understand that she may be developmentally blocked. Her behavior is most likely a way of saying: "I didn't get what I needed during my first year of life," "I'm unable to be kind to you, because no one in my immediate family has been kind to me," or "I am an unconnected kid. It's me against the world!"

What can you do for a child who is "stuck" at the one-year-old stage of life? You can address her unmet needs. Give her unconditional love and support; make sure she receives ample nourishment and clear instructions in personal hygiene; keep her environment safe, neat, and organized; set reasonable limits; and provide firm structure. In addition, strive to sustain a trusting relationship that will allow her to attach to *you* as a significant adult.

The Second Year

Around the beginning of the second year, many well-cared-for children are starting to walk, talk, and make better sense of their surroundings. As a result, the world opens up exponentially. What an exciting and scary predicament *this* is. Young toddlers, overwhelmed with feelings and impulses, cannot contain them all within their little bodies. They laugh, shriek, pout, and by the age of two, declare with predictable regularity, "No!"

The second year is a time for self-expression. The well-behaved "Queen of the Universe," who was previously the center of her parents' world, is now flinging her cereal bowl across the room with cunning adeptness, smacking an innocent playmate on the head, dissembling a cherished family heirloom, and deftly stowing away the TV clicker.

What accounts for this abrupt change in personality? The child's newly acquired abilities to influence her environment are generating waves of *frustration* and *anxiety*. Navigating an ever-expanding and increasingly uncertain domain is *nothing* like going for a free ride in the arms of mom or dad! Her parents' role, too, has changed: to allow for the unfolding of her separation-individuation process, they have formed a home base for her to return to, and to protect her, they have established parameters of safety—her first consistent exposure to limits.

Mounting frustration over this state of affairs is one of the triggers for the resounding "no" of the young toddler. "No" is her vehicle for obtaining control over an environment that is no longer safe and reliable. It is also a way of letting others know that she can make a difference. Each time she says no, she is staking her claim as a separate individual who wants recognition and validation: "Take notice, I am *somebody!*"

In the child's eyes, the individuals responsible for her increased anxiety are mom and dad. Who else is there to blame? These tender-hearted people seduced her into thinking that life was a warm, fuzzy joyride; but no, life is not so hunky-dory anymore. It's filled with uncertainty and restrictions, and the culprits must pay!

With the no's comes the birth of a fascinating psychological process. It all begins when the toddler first hears the word, which enters her consciousness as a rude "slap in the face," a fine "How do you do"—in short, an utter shock.

"No, Amanda."

"Whoa, Mom. Do you know who you're talking to? This is your little Amanda, your pride and joy. You can't say no to *me*."

"No, Amanda."

"I think my ears are clogged. Remember, little tykes like me have terrible ear problems. Let's go see that ear doctor."

"No, Amanda."

"Are you blind? Have you lost your senses? This is me, Amanda, Queen of the Universe—ruler of her parents. You can't say no to me. Off with your heads!"

"No, Amanda."

Certain at last that her hearing is intact, the child wonders,

"How can these people love me and still say no to me?" To cope with this stress-laden quandary, she "splits" both her mother and her father into "good" and "bad" parent figures.[10] The split helps her handle what feels like contradictory perceptions: the accepting (good) parent and the rejecting (bad) parent. "There must be two people inside my mommy and daddy," she says to herself. "When they are being nice to me and saying yes, they are the *good* parents; when they are mean and saying no, they are the *bad* ones."

Many young toddlers also split themselves. "When I'm behaving well," they think, "it's the *good* me. When I act devilish, it's the *bad* me." Splitting, whether it is directed outward toward their parents or inward toward themselves, helps two year olds adapt to the stress of parental limit-setting and to their own battles with impulses, both of which invariably interfere with their pursuit of pleasure.

A parent's job at this stage is to demonstrate *balance* by complementing firm and predictable limits with ongoing nurturance and affection. A serious imbalance between limit setting and nurturance can negatively affect the child's behavior and social functioning, causing her to become developmentally arrested at age two. Children raised by loving parents who refuse to set firm and predictable limits continue to split themselves into "good" and "bad" parts, never integrating them into a cohesive self. As they mature, they may have difficulty tolerating feelings of frustration and may become disorganized and angry in response to discomfort and stress. Children raised by parents who draw boundaries but do not provide appropriate affection are likewise unable to feel whole. Such kids will tend to regard discipline and limit setting as forms of rejection, and adults as "good" only when they gratify the child's wishes. Anyone who stands in the way of their pursuit of pleasure is apt to be viewed as "bad."

Splitting, which begins the moment we humans encounter stress, becomes a lifelong dynamic. Adults, too, split while anxious, mentally assigning people to "good" and "bad" boxes. Stressed-out child-welfare workers seen huddling in the lounge, for example, are often verbally splitting their associates into boxes. "That supervisor is a jerk. If only we had more supervisors like Helen!" they will say, or "That new worker is horrible. Why can't he start out like Ralph did?" Usually, someone in the crowd will observe that much as they may want to allay their anxiety, quick-and-easy splitting will not do the trick—that efforts must be made to balance their black-and-white perceptions with more true-to-life shades of gray. "Maybe the supervisor is not all that bad," he will suggest, "and perhaps Helen and Ralph were not so saintly after all."

Troubled teenagers who split under stress can be approached in much the same way. The only difference is that having missed out on the needed modeling in their second year of life, they require demonstrations rather than suggestions. Firm limit-setting and offerings of love will enable them to experience *you* not as either "good" or "bad" but as able to offer both nurturance and discipline. In acknowledging the coexistence of opposites in you, they will learn to accept the "good" and "bad" within themselves and take a giant step toward wholeness. The sooner they experience this integrated sense of self, the sooner they will temper their rage and stop converting frustration into hostility.

The Third Year

A well-nurtured child entering her third year of life begins to reconcile the "good" and "bad," and as a result arrives at a new sense of comfort and security. Consequently, she starts to regard her parents as supportive and available, even when they are disciplining her. This successful merging of the "good" and "bad" allows the child to advance developmentally, setting the stage for productive social relations.

Any time you encounter a youngster who regularly plays one adult against another and succeeds in getting them to quarrel over the best way to deal with her, be aware that she may be stuck at the two-to three-year-old stage of development. In such instances the child's greatest need is to complete the developmental task of merging the good and bad aspects she perceives in adults, as well as in herself.

What can you do? First, stop the splitting! Encourage the adults in her life to *set their egos aside and act in a unified manner;* help them realize that there is not *one* "correct" way to care for the child. Also let her see that the adults in her life are working together. Above all, provide her with a healthy balance of limit setting and unconditional love.

Children who have been deprived of adequate parenting during their first three years of life tend to engage in frequent splitting and display persistent behavioral difficulties. These children are at risk for developing a chronic *personality disorder* or *character disorder.* Although the diagnosis of "personality disorder" is not utilized with young children since their personalities are still forming, the behaviors they exhibit are considered *precursors* to this disorder.

Several types of personality disorders exist—among them, borderline, narcissistic, and antisocial—each of which is distinguished by a particular set of criteria. In all instances, the individual's personality reflects the chaos, neglect, and instability suffered in early life, which sets her at odds with the world. She will exhibit, among other characteristics, excessive self-indulgence, impulsivity, difficulty in managing emotions, and an inability to relate appropriately to others.

Working with teenagers who have a personality or character disorder is a challenge, and the risk of burnout is high. The good news is that although the condition cannot be *cured,* it can be *modified* by adults who set realistic expectations based on development as opposed to chronology; who maintain a firm balance between limit setting and nurturing; and who avoid being split by the teens. Adults who work with seriously impaired teenagers have a special mission to keep all involved parties on the "same side of the net."

The Fourth Year
Youngsters entering their fourth year of life are remarkably inquisitive, often displaying an insatiable thirst for knowledge. They want to touch, smell, taste, and in general interface with everything they see. In addition, they yearn to explore new territory whenever possible.

New experiences of this sort can elicit considerable anxiety. Sensory overload, combined with the lack of experience and expertise, often prompts feelings of uncertainty, fear, and confusion. To mitigate these uncomfortable feelings, many three to four year olds develop imaginary friends—unconditional buddies who can be summoned at will to offer companionship, comfort, and support.

Children of this age seem to know that to surmount obstacles and become capable of functioning competently in their surroundings, they must *practice.* While building with blocks, stirring cookie dough, hammering, painting, planting seeds, or playing with dolls or action figures, they devise effective ways to interact with the many facets of their environment. Dressing up like adults, they rehearse their prospective roles. In effect, youngsters between the ages of three and four are attempting to master the complexities of life by engaging in activities they can control and succeed at. This pursuit of mastery is the child's *link with her future.*

Four year olds who are hindered in this quest, or who fail to experience proficiency in an area of personal interest, tend to carry a deep sense of inadequacy and insecurity into their later years. Indeed, many troubled children who exhibit insecurity and anxiety about the road ahead have never had the opportunity to acquire mastery in early childhood. Some were discouraged from exploring their surroundings; others were dissuaded from playing with an imaginary friend; and still others were never permitted to bring their "play" to fruition.

Whenever you suspect that children in your care may have missed out on these developmental immersions, help them find projects, hobbies, or work endeavors that will infuse them with a sense of proficiency. Encourage them to build or fix furniture; request their help in the kitchen; ask them to organize cans and bottles for recycling. In the teenage years, see if they would like to tutor elementary school kids. In short, let them practice for adulthood.

The Fifth Year

Between the ages of four and five, most children begin formal education and more complex interactions with their peers and the world at large. A child who has attached well to her parents will have the confidence needed to navigate beyond the family cocoon. It is exciting to play with other children and share special moments with them. At times it is intoxicating!

Soon after entering the social arena, a developmentally on-course child makes a remarkable discovery: "No one is going to play with me if I always insist on getting my way." To be accepted by her peers, she quickly begins to *accommodate* to their desires and *subordinate* her own impulses.[11] Establishing friendships thus becomes a landmark event that serves to diminish egocentrism and launch a child into enriched social relations.

Children who enter school developmentally delayed are often *unable* to make friends, because they cannot surrender their egocentrism. They feel a need to be in control at all times, and they have little trust, for they have learned that it is unsafe to depend on others. Their self-esteem, already compromised by the psychologically impoverished environments of their earlier years, suffers yet another blow over their inability to relate well with their peers. Both the lack of friends and the impaired self-esteem follow these children into maturity.

For years I have been asking child-care professionals if they have ever worked with a troubled kid who had a best friend. Only *three* out of the five thousand people I surveyed said yes. The vast majority of troubled children, it seems, have no one their age to laugh with, explore with, share feelings with, feel supported by, or keep company with. Imagine what life would be like without a best friend!

The greatest service you can offer troubled children who have become imprisoned in loneliness is to help them link up with friends—or better yet, make a best friend. When two kids are arguing, override the impulse to dash in and separate them; instead, help them resolve the problem. Be a chauffeur: drive prospective friends to your home or center, and take the children to see them. Refrain from limiting their time with friends or classmates as a consequence for misconduct, unless a child's safety is at stake. After observing a troubled child at play, help her improve her social skills. Making a real friend is an exhilarating landmark experience for a child with diminished self-esteem.

Seeing it happen is equally gratifying. I remember conducting duo therapy—a relatively new treatment method involving the pairing of two children with one therapist—with Buster and Elliot, eleven year olds who met with me once a week to improve their social skills. Buster, who was rambunctious and impulsive, had a history of physical abuse, teased his peers, was continually getting into fights, and frequently required physical restraint. Like most abused kids, he was unpopular and quite egocentric.

Elliot was quiet and easygoing. Although he, too, had a history of abuse, he was more masochistic. He would welcome teasing until he could take no more of it, then he would act. Twice, he had set serious fires. Like Buster, he was self-centered and had never had a best friend.

During our first two sessions together, Buster frequently teased Elliot. "Is it okay if he teases you?" I would ask.

"Yeah, I like it," Elliot would reply.

The third session was different. This time when I asked him if he liked being teased by Buster, he replied, "No, I don't." I advised him to let Buster know the truth. At first, he refused; but toward the end of the session, he confronted Buster and asked him to stop the teasing.

Buster agreed! He was evidently willing to give up some of his antagonistic behaviors in order to make a friend. Elliot, for his part, had begun standing up for himself.

By the time of their twelfth session, the boys had become good friends. The following year they asked to be roommates. As the months unfolded, each boy modified more and more of his problematic ways of relating and learned to become more social. For Buster and Elliot, making a friend opened the floodgates to improved social functioning and more positive self-perceptions.

Laying Bricks on Shaky Foundations

Most children who have had inadequate parenting in their earliest years perceive the world as unsafe, inconsistent, and unloving. Because they have not developed strong attachments to their parents, they live with unrelenting anxiety and fearfulness—and are apt to carry these emotions into adulthood unless their relationships with their parents improve significantly or *they learn to "attach" to other significant adults*. Attachments of this sort can help stabilize the faulty foundations on which their development rests. The trusted adult, in such instances, can then begin taking over where the parents left off.

That is what happened for Henry, a seven year old who had experienced extreme abandonment during his first two years of life.

As a baby, Henry was rarely held or nurtured. Soon afterward, he was placed in a poorly run orphanage where he spent hours each day howling in a bassinet. To muffle his screams, orphanage workers reportedly covered the bassinet with sheets of plastic containing little slits for air holes. In response, according to Henry's adoptive mother, he learned to scream loudly.

Although Henry was seven years old when we first met, he acted more like a one year old. He focused on whatever was in front of him, trusted no one, had no internal sense of security, and lived in constant fear of abandonment. Each time his adoptive mother left him off at the treatment center, he feared he would never see her again.

Eventually, Henry and I began to venture off the property—usually by car, as he liked to ride in my Jeep. Shortly after we set off on our third outing, he spotted workers laying a foundation for a large house and asked if we could stop to watch. The work proceeded at a snail's pace, but even so, Henry was captivated. We stayed for about half an hour, and returned many times in the months to come. We watched the men pour the concrete and set the foundation; frame the walls; and complete the carpentry, siding, roofing, and landscaping. Henry was enthralled.

I was, too. In fact, it was at that construction site that I first recognized the correlation between laying a foundation for a building and laying a foundation for a child's life. I saw how in each case internal integrity depends on the solidity of the foundation, on each brick being laid carefully in place. And I decided that the most I

Figure 3–1

could do for Henry was help compensate for the deficits he experienced in his first years of life.

Henry's adoptive parents, the residential caretakers, and I agreed to collaborate in the task of filling in the "bricks" missing from his foundation. Our goal was to help him attach to adults and, over time, progress developmentally. Our plan of action: to provide at age seven what he never received at age one—namely, nurturing, safety, and structure.

People who work with seriously troubled children like Henry are dealing primarily with *deficits,* as opposed to *conflicts.* The adult's role is therefore not so much to *talk* as to *fill.* Although these children seem to be in and out of conflict on a regular basis, the behavioral eruptions we see are announcements that the *foundation needs some filling.* This cry is far different from that of a healthier child attempting to resolve a conflict.

Have you ever had a great talk with a troubled child and felt so good about finally "getting through" to her that you returned home exhilarated—only to find out the next day that you made no apparent difference in her life? You drive to work the next morning, looking forward to building upon the positive interaction you had, but the girl, now acting out big time, looks your way and behaves as if the talk never occurred. You are crushed, perhaps even angry at the kid. Your self-esteem plummets, and you are no longer at your best to deal with her, or anyone else for that matter.

Feelings of frustration and uselessness often arise when we have fooled ourselves into thinking that a good heart-to-heart talk will significantly alter a troubled child's life. The reality is that a good talk, an effective time-out, or any other positive interaction, although capable of setting in place a brick that will last forever, is not going to instantly eradicate the effects of years of inadequate caretaking. A child who has rocky attachments and little sense of trust[12] is not about to change overnight. Stabilizing a shaky foundation is a long, laborious process. Moreover, there is no guarantee that a child lacking those early bricks will *ever* function normally. Henry, for example, who progressed dramatically at the residential center, remains an emotionally impaired child who will probably never function at an age-appropriate level.

In short, positive interactions are vitally important, but they need to occur *over and over again*. There are no quick fixes for children who have experienced inadequate care in their first five years of life.

When dealing with tough kids, we also need a fresh perspective on talking. Among those who were psychologically deprived in their first years of life, actions generally speak louder than words. Why? Because the holding, feeding, rocking, loving, and limit setting they never received left a void that no amount of talking can fill. They respond to their environments much like babies do, and are not quite ready to work through difficulties verbally. What is needed above all is nurturing and structure.

Shifting our perspective from discourse to bricklaying can go a long way toward reducing our frustration levels and preventing feelings of failure. Indeed, it can help us feel *wonderful* about each caring intervention we provide, large or small, for we are filling in another needed brick.

Ultimately, with developmentally impaired kids, we are *fillers*, not *talkers*. In fact, from the day we start working with them until the day they "graduate" from our care or tutelage, our purpose is to add as many bricks as we can to help fortify their foundations. Although we may not see the immediate effects of our pain and labor—indeed, the kids may continue to act out their unfulfilled needs through adolescence—we can know in our hearts that the bricks we have set in place will never be dislodged. We can know, too, that the more bricks we have furnished, the more we have increased the children's chances of having a better life.

CHAPTER 4

THE QUEST FOR SELF-ESTEEM

MOST TROUBLED CHILDREN SUFFER FROM LOW SELF-ESTEEM. THEY want to feel better about themselves, and as soon as they begin to, their behavior improves. What can you do to help? More than you can imagine.

The Praise Connection

When I first started working with children at risk, I praised them continuously to bolster their self-esteem. No matter what they did, I was there with a compliment. When Sally drew a picture in twenty seconds, I would croon with admiration, as if Pablo Picasso himself had drawn it. When Albert sharpened his pencil, I would compliment his technique. I was convinced that these children needed enormous amounts of positive feedback to make up for the lack of praise and encouragement they had no doubt experienced. I wanted them to feel special, to know *someone* believed they were important.

After a while, I realized I was overdoing it. My excessive unconditional praise began to appear less meaningful to the children and seemed to keep some of them from working harder. Rather than feeling good about themselves, they were learning that very little effort could bring torrents of applause, which was not a helpful message to convey.

I then decided to let the children know that praise had to be earned. The next time Sally presented me with a quickly executed sketch, I politely thanked her and asked her how much time she had spent on it. When she told me, I suggested that devoting more time and care to her artwork might earn her a great deal of praise. Responses such as this conveyed a different message, and a valuable lesson: *With effort comes results.* At that point, my compliments began promoting self-esteem *and* competency.

Weeks later, I expanded my understanding of "effort" from the time and care invested in a project to the gesture made with it. One afternoon, a child who had never before extended himself to me suddenly drew me a picture. I praised him enthusiastically, explaining how meaningful it was that he would create such a beautiful image for me. His history of faulty attachments to adults had impressed upon me the importance of complimenting not only his artwork but, perhaps more importantly, his effort to connect.

Our first job in elevating the self-worth of troubled kids who have learned to keep their distance from adults is to *honor the links they make with us.* In these tender moments of reaching out, we need to think more about their inability to appropriately relate to adults than about the laziness that unconditional praise may spawn. Only after *engaging* such a child is it wise to become gradually more discriminating in the praise we bestow.

Our second job in elevating the self-regard of children who chronically act out is to reward them when they *improve* their behavior. Sometimes this means praising a child whose actions still fall short of our expectations. A second grader who was sent out of the classroom ten times last week, for example, should be complimented for being sent out only seven times this week.

Such advice often confounds child-care professionals. "Why praise a kid who is still screwing up?" they wonder. The answer is, because he is *working harder.* When we acknowledge a child's efforts to improve, we support his earliest strivings, affirming him for where he *is,* not where he *should be.* In response, the child will feel better about himself and be more motivated to take responsibility for his actions.

Universal Opportunities for Individual Success

Many at-risk children with low self-esteem are reluctant to engage in unfamiliar activities. Fear of failing yet again prevents them from trying out new games, sports, academic pursuits, or social interactions, all of which raise the specter of further emotional pain and embarrassment. "Why play softball if I'm gonna strike out?" a child may wonder, or "Why try hard in science? I'm stupid—I'll never get it right!" or "I don't like to draw; I'm no good at it," or "Why talk to that kid? He'll just brush me off. He knows I'm a loser."

Most troubled children, having suffered enough, prefer to play it safe and return to activites they are "good" at. In their spare time they will gravitate toward computer games, TV viewing, gang involvement, or other activities that present little emotional risk. Dwelling in a narrow comfort zone, they will be wary about venturing beyond its confines. For many of those who are not happy about their lot in life, taking even small chances is tantamount to suffering defeat.

Our task is to help these children relax their resistances, stretch the boundaries of their comfort zones, and experience a sense of accomplishment. How do we do this? By creating *universal opportunities for individual success.*

We create these opportunities first by viewing resistance as a defense mechanism rather than a display of dislike toward an activity or pursuit. For example, a troubled child who "hates" sports and never wants to play may in fact love sports but be mortified of making a fool of himself on the field. Having changed our perspective, we proceed to invent new activities—or modify old ones—that will lead naturally to success. A softball game, for instance, can be proposed with all-new rules: "There's no striking out today. It's spring training!"

This was the approach taken by a staff determined to start an intramural softball league at a large residential treatment center for abused and neglected children where only a few residents were turning up for softball on any given day. The announcement of the newly formed league was accompanied by two provisions: a trusted adult would pitch and there would be no striking out. About sixty kids signed up, many of whom had never played before and some of whom turned out to be outstanding athletes. All the players seemed to enjoy themselves—which was not surprising considering that the modified rules had created a chance for each one to succeed.

A staff "under siege" at a nearby juvenile detention center took a similar approach. Here, personal safety had been compromised, morale was down, and tension was palpable everywhere. To address the safety concerns and enhance relationships between the adults and juveniles, the staff, in addition to implementing more equitable disciplinary measures, introduced two evenings a week of Bingo and other activities that promoted individual success. Initially, most kids were reluctant to play Bingo—"It's corny!" they wailed—but as the weeks went by, more and more showed up, eager to play a game anyone could win. In response to all the changes, the residents soon began feeling better about themselves and started discussing some of their personal issues, all the while heeding the advice and counseling that came their way. Although appropriate consequences were still administered for disruptive incidents, the residents were at last showing signs of believing in themselves.

Opportunities for success are well received not only by groups of children but also by individual youngsters. Justin, at the age of seven, acted more like a two year old. He had limited impulse control, negligible tolerance for frustration, and extremely low self-esteem. These characteristics were all in full force the day I decided to take him bowling along with two other boys. They were fairly good bowlers, but Justin was not; he could not roll the ball down the lane without falling over. When I tried to teach him how to release the ball, he brushed me off, preferring to figure it out himself.

Midway through the first game, I could see that Justin was in agony. While the other boys were playing well, he was scoring ones and twos. To make matters worse, our scores were posted in overhead lights that everyone could see. Upset about this public display of his poor bowling skills, Justin began cursing under his breath, putting himself down, and acting rudely toward me as well.

Clearly, something had to be done. After the fifth frame, I called him over and said, "Justin, from now on, score yourself. Whatever you think you deserve, mark it in."

He stared at me incredulously, then bowled his sixth frame. This time Justin did not fall down; in fact, he scored a four. Slowly returning to the scorer's table, he looked around and then proceeded to give himself a strike. The huge X appeared overhead, whereupon he laughed uproariously. The other kids complained, but when I explained that we were just having fun, they stopped.

Justin then bowled his seventh and eighth frames, each time knocking down three pins and returning to the scorer's table to give himself another strike. He was in ecstasy—his score was "improving" and he could sense success.

His excitement continued throughout the second game. Each time someone walked past our lane, Justin would point gleefully at the overhead score sheet. At the end of the tenth frame, he tallied a three hundred—a perfect score!

He brought his "perfect game" score sheet back to the treatment center, where the staff agreed to use this unique score-keeping approach on future bowling trips. Within three months Justin, liberated from the fear of failing, had become a pretty good bowler and was slowly transitioning back into traditional scoring procedures. Soon afterward, he qualified to enter a Saturday morning bowling league.

Occasionally, people question the lowering of standards for kids who have trouble functioning within established parameters. The truth is that some kids need their academic and social pursuits modified in order to *play the game;* if they do not play, they may never know their capabilities. Other kids, however, need to be pushed and held accountable for making the grade. The modification decision ultimately hinges on assessment. You must know what motivates the children in your care so that you can decide how to foster their success. As a general guideline, *troubled children with low self-esteem need to experience more success in their lives.* Hence, if you are going to err, it is best to do so on the side of helping them feel better about themselves. The more you can help at-risk children discover success, the more they will engage you in their efforts, and the better they will do.

As for Justin, abandoning normal scoring procedures gave him a chance to succeed at a game from which he would have otherwise shied away. The eventual outcome was a kid who not only could bowl but had improved self-esteem. Not surprisingly, he was ready for a foster home more quickly than anyone at the center had anticipated, showing us all that improved self-esteem can open *many* new doors.

Twenty Tips for Promoting a Child's Self-Esteem

Listed below are tried-and-true methods to help boost a child's self-esteem. Incorporate them into your day; invent some of your own; and see what happens. Invariably, as a child begins to feel better about himself, he risks changing his approach to the world.

1. Trumpet success.
Show enthusiasm for work well done. Display the child's school papers on the refrigerator or bulletin board. Mount his artwork. Keep a scrapbook of his triumphant experiences. Over dinner, talk about his achievements.

In class, hang worksheets that show improvement and banners that recognize accomplishments. Talk about successes. Trophies, plaques, ribbons, certificates, and handshakes also boost confidence levels. Photographs keep successes alive.

2. Schedule one-on-one time on a regular basis.
Even five minutes a day of uninterrupted time together can let the child know you care.

3. Spend leisure time together.
Showing the child that you like being in his company will help him feel good about himself. If you are a foster parent, play board games together, hang out together in the kitchen, or work side by side in the yard. If you are a teacher, eat lunch with the child every now and then. In either case, attend his sporting events, art exhibits, and musical performances. Cheer loudly if appropriate. Being there counts.

4. Compliment the child on his appearance.
Say, "You look terrific today!" or "My, you are handsome," or "You look pretty sharp in that outfit!" or "Hey, that's one heck of a vest." Admiring the child's appearance will serve as a reminder to stop comparing himself unfavorably with his peers—a dynamic common among at-risk children.

5. Engage the child in work that needs to be done.
Requesting the child's assistance lets him know that he is trusted and has recognizable competencies. Invite the child to help feed a younger sibling, weed the garden, chop wood, paint a table, prepare a meal, clean the car and give it an oil change, deliver a message in person or by phone, make a bank transaction, tutor a younger student, read announcements, clean the blackboard, collect empty milk cartons, or send a fax.

6. Let the child take responsibility for chores.
Chores teach children about being accountable, helping others, and working as a team. Start by setting expectations in self-care, including personal hygiene and grooming. Then gradually extend the realm of responsibility to household maintenance, such as making the bed, setting the table, washing dishes, dusting, feeding the pets, walking the dog, vacuuming, clearing the yard, and taking out the garbage. Even very young children can pitch in; encouraging a four year old to sweep with a dust broom, for example, while you use a full-size broom can instill the value of helping and dispel the myth that chores are cause for an adult-versus-kid battle.

In elementary school, construct weekly "chore charts" to help students keep the classroom clean and orderly. Invite junior and senior high school students to help with building maintenance or office work.

7. Encourage volunteerism.
Assisting others helps children feel important and valued, and paves the way to new skills and areas of personal strength. Check the local paper for community volunteer projects, such as reading to an elderly person, working at a soup kitchen, participating in a vacant lot cleanup, tutoring younger students through a school assignment,

tending a neighborhood garden, picking up litter, recycling newspapers and other goods, and organizing town festivals.

8. Write the child a note of gratitude. Then mail it, or leave it on his bed or desk.
A simple note can make a world of difference. The following are two examples:

> *Joan,*
>
> *Thanks for helping me out yesterday. I really needed you. You're a great daughter.*
>
> > *Love,*
> > *Mom*

> *Hank,*
>
> *Nice job on your math quiz. You're doing excellent work in my class!*
>
> > *Mrs. Robinson*

9. Help navigate the job market.
Cultivate relationships with the managers of local restaurants and other businesses. Tell them as much as you can about your teenager and help them understand significant personality issues. Managers introduced to youths in this way are more likely to hire and retain them.

Many teens with emotional challenges tend to leave their first few jobs, either voluntarily or under duress. If this occurs, try not to overreact. Instead, hang in there and gently push your teen toward a new job. Success at a job is likely to greatly enhance his self-esteem as well as his ability to find and hold a job in adulthood.

10. Hug the child several times a day.
Showing affection through physical touch can reinforce a child's sense of self-worth. Such individual recognition also facilitates relationship building. (*A word of caution:* In our litigious society, childcare professionals need to be careful about the physical contact they

engage in with children. If you work in a child-care setting, find out what is acceptable and, within the limits, offer as much age- and context-appropriate physical outreach as possible. At the same time, because most children with abusive histories are anxious about being touched by an adult, be sure to respect the child's boundaries. Avoid touching a child who is not ready for tactile nurturing.)

11. Have friends and family members call or write to celebrate the child's birthday as well as his noteworthy accomplishments.
The staff at one residential center had ten kids call a lonely resident on her birthday, and as a result, the phone never stopped ringing. She was ecstatic.

12. Ask the child for advice.
Give the child choices and request his input whenever possible. Let him see that you value his opinions. Empowering children in this way helps them feel respected and trusted.

13. Encourage the child to play with animals.
Relating to animals is often easier than relating to people. An uncon- ditional furry "friend" can serve as a loyal ally, reminding the child of how lovable he is.

14. Be spontaneous with your generosity!
From time to time surprise the child with a special treat he has not had to "earn." If he asks why, tell him, *"Because you are you!"*

15. Affirm the child's unique strengths and talents.
Help find a hobby, interest, or sport in which the child can excel, then acknowledge him as he "shines." Recognized success in one area will often generalize to other areas.

16. Facilitate friendships for the child.
Go the extra mile to help the child relate positively to peers. Because reaching out to make friends may be difficult, your assistance can remind him that he deserves friendships in his life and is capable of sustaining them.

17. Initiate traditions.
Every year on the child's birthday let him select the dinner menu.
On Thanksgiving, ask him to give a few words of thanks before the
meal. On the Fourth of July, take him swimming, out for ice cream,
then to the park to watch fireworks.

Traditions bind together families, as well as classes and groups,
often infusing them with a sense of spirit. Best of all, they inspire
troubled children to look forward with predictability to occasions in
which they will play a warm, familiar part.

18. Honor hellos and good-byes.
Heartily welcome the child upon his arrival at your foster home,
school, or residential center. Posted signs and formal introductions
will let him know, "We're happy you've joined us. We think you're
special!"

Similarly, when the child leaves your setting, organize a formal
ceremony, such as a "good-bye circle" in which staff members and
children form a ring and express a few words of appreciation, recall-
ing funny anecdotes, sharing sentiments, or simply letting the child
know how valued he is; at the end, the child himself can say a few
words. The good-bye circle may be followed by a farewell party.

19. Respect the child's need for autonomy.
Exercise acceptable means of nurturing the child's growing sense
of independence. Children as well as teens like to experiment with
self-reliance, often wondering, "How much can I do without assistance?" The more supported they are in this quest, the more self-
confident they will feel, and the better prepared they will be for
adulthood.

20. Promote sound values.
Teach and model the importance of respect, honesty, nondiscrimina-
tion, generosity, and other qualities you believe in. Good values not
only foster a sense of self-worth but also help children make better
decisions and derive more satisfaction from their accomplishments.

CHAPTER 5

THE NEED FOR CONSEQUENCES

MOST WELL-INTENTIONED PEOPLE WHO TRY TO "LOVE" TROUBLED children into behaving appropriately find that nurturing is not enough and that *consequences* are necessary, too. Children who repeatedly act out need to have their behavior addressed because even if they have good reasons to be confused and angry, they do not have the right to break rules, hurt others, or wreak havoc on their surroundings.

If the staff had not issued consequences the first time Jody hit one of her peers, for example, the implied message would have been: "Since you've had it rough, it's okay to act out your anger. The heck with rules and respect—you're entitled to an occasional rampage." When adults allow children like Jody to *continually* act out, the inference is even more debilitating: "Because of what you've been through, you can't control your behavior." In response to this message, a child will think, "Hey, I can't help myself!"—a belief that is likely to increase the frequency of problem behaviors.

Ignoring a troubled child's ongoing negative behaviors, even seemingly innocuous ones, can send another message as well: "You are such a terror that adults are afraid to deal with you." This notion, once internalized, may reinforce the youngster's negative self-image and increase the intensity of her disruptive behavior.

When inappropriate behavior is ignored, it tends to be repeated on a larger scale because the children are feeling unsafe and seeking help in controlling their impulses. Many kids actually cry out for consequences; they long for the structure and boundaries that rules provide.

At-risk children, like other children, have a right to their *feelings,* not their *actions.* When you treat troubled children with compassion and understanding yet hold them *accountable* for their actions, the message you send is: "You are in control of your behavior, and you, like anyone else, will be held responsible for inappropriate conduct." This is a message of normalcy.

The Cry for Structure

Some time ago, while working at a residential treatment facility, I took three eleven-year-old girls to *Never Cry Wolf,* a Parental Guidance-rated movie billed as a nature film. Everything was going along fine until suddenly the main character, who was living in the wild, began running naked with the wolves.

"Oh, no!" I thought to myself, worried that at least one of the girls, probably Trish, would be pushed to the limit by the evocative scene.

Sure enough, Trish began to jump in her seat, waving her hands, making weird noises, and generally causing a ruckus.

I quietly asked her to try to control herself, whereupon she yelled back, with a wild gleam in her eyes, "I can't help myself. I'm *hyperactive!"*

"I'm sorry," I told her. Then quickly determining that she could probably handle this brief scene, I added, "I can't help myself either. If you don't stop in about three seconds, you'll be *hyper-in-the-car-going-home!"*

She smiled, settled down, and stayed relatively calm throughout the remainder of the movie.

Trish was indeed hyperactive. Yet she seemed capable of more self-control than she had initially exhibited, which is why I refused to let her use her diagnostic condition as an excuse to continue misbehaving. This story has two morals. One is, think twice about letting children use a condition as a crutch. The second is, avoid placing children in situations that are likely to provoke a disturbance. Matching youngsters to settings decreases the need for consequences.

Alfred's cry for boundaries was even more pronounced. Horribly abused at age four, he eventually landed in the foster care system, where he was bounced from one home to another. Although he was bright and humorous and longed desperately to be like other kids, his rage toward the world persistently erupted in uncontrollable behavior. He would throw objects, hit people, and scream incessantly. At age nine, he ended up in a short-term residential treatment facility.

Asked to serve as Alfred's therapeutic mentor, I began to meet with him on a weekly basis. Soon afterward, he was placed with Gertrude, an elderly, single foster mother who, although warm and loving, provided inadequate supervision. Alfred quickly attached to her, yet every time I met with him, he seemed worried about the lack of house rules and afraid of his own impulses. "Get her to make up some rules," he would plead.

I tried to help Gertrude devise rules and consequences for breaking them, but she did not have the energy to take on such a task. Consequently, Alfred was removed from her home and later placed in a foster home that provided a healthy balance of nurturing and structure. At last report, he was doing well.

Troubled kids like Trish and Alfred need affection, empathy, self-esteem reinforcement, and *rules*. Knowing where the lines will be drawn gives them, like developmentally healthy one year olds, a feeling of safety. Without clearly defined boundaries, on the other hand, they may begin searching behaviorally for the limits of acceptability.

Responding to the Cry

How should adults respond when kids act out? In the *best possible* manner.

Math problems have clear-cut answers; for example, 2 + 2 = 4. Behavioral problems, on the other hand, do not. Even so, contextual considerations can always be used to arrive at "best possible" responses to the challenges posed by misconduct.

Contextual Considerations

The first step in responding to problematic behavior is to assess the circumstances. The second step is to formulate an intervention that coincides with the *context* of the situation. In general, the more serious a misbehavior is, the more prompt and direct the response should be. A child who punches someone, for example, requires immediate attention and consequences that are commensurate with the severity of her actions.

The most serious forms of misconduct are those that threaten safety and stability. As a rule, the more out of control a misbehaving child appears, the more *appropriately* controlling you will need to be to help restore her sense of security. In settings such as classrooms and treatment facilities, where one child's escalating behavior can negatively affect an entire group, consequences often need to be even more immediate and directive.

Here are ten key questions to keep in mind when formulating a context-sensitive response to a situation:

✔ **Are safety issues at stake?**
   If anyone's safety has been compromised, firm limits need to be set. Strive for less talk and more action. In a group setting, *prompt* action is a must. At home, if no other children are around, the response need not be as immediate.

✔ **Is this really a problem?**
   Kids sometimes do things that set our hair on edge yet fall within the parameters of acceptable behavior, such as teens using crude language, wearing garish clothing, or covering their walls with offensive posters. In such instances, consequences are not always needed, and in fact can be counterproductive. Be sure to assess whether the child's actions are acceptable in terms of current norms, rules, and values so that you will not react solely out of personal discomfort.

✔ **Why is this behavior occurring?**
   Remember that acting out is a signal of distress. Once you decode the underlying whys, the what-to-dos will most likely

follow. In many instances, getting to the source of the problem is itself the solution.

✔ **How much responsibility should I assume for this incident?**
If you have contributed to the problem—through poor planning, for example, or an oversight of some sort—it is best to admit quickly to the mistake and work hard to avoid repeating it. A consequence may or may not be appropriate in such an instance. The point to remember is that the more accountable you are for your actions, the more responsibility the child will take for hers.

✔ **Who else is available to help?**
Are there people on hand to assist you? Are there accessible and affordable resources you can call upon? Outreach is often the intervention of choice.

✔ **Has this behavior occurred before? If so, does it appear to follow a pattern?**
If the behavior is recurrent and adhering to a *pattern*—occurring, for example, at the same time of the day, week, or month—look for possible precipitating factors (see Pattern Identification, on pages 83–85). Is the child experiencing anxiety over an upcoming visit, or math class, or bedtime? An effective response to an anxiety-based pattern of misbehavior is to refrain from reacting each time it surfaces; instead, respond with a comprehensive *plan* for exploring the pattern, together with a behavioral approach entailing an incentive system that will motivate the child to improve, all the while progressively increasing the severity of preannounced consequences. Exercise caution, however, so as to prevent consequences from becoming too extreme. Overly tough consequences may only frustrate the child and lock you into administering needlessly harsh disciplinary measures.

✔ **How strong is my relationship with this child?**
The stronger your relationship is, the more flexibility you will have in formulating an effective response. Because children at risk tend to test adults to see who can keep them safe, any time

your relationship with a child is not well established, you will need to set strong, consistent limits to prove you can be trusted. Softening limits over time is easier than firming them up.

✔ **What do I know about this child's developmental, social, medical, and psychological histories? What do I know about her current issues?**
The better informed you are in these areas, the more beneficial your response will be. Each hour spent exploring a child's history can reveal important information and eliminate untold hours of strategizing.

✔ **Which approaches have worked in the past, and which have not?**
To avoid relying solely on trial and error, reflect on previous responses to the child's misconduct; after discarding those that did not lead to behavioral changes, repeat one that did. If you have no history to call upon, begin collecting data for the future. Remember that your worst interventions can give you the best information.

✔ **What personal characteristics—such as age, height, weight, family customs, physical appearance, hygiene, coordination—could be influencing the child's behavior as well as my understanding of it?**
Factors such as these are often linked with low self-esteem, hence empathy is of the essence. A boy who acts out in gym class, for example, may require additional sensitivity if he is chubby and uncoordinated. Also *be mindful of your own prejudices,* and refuse to let them influence your response.

Is it possible to reflect on all ten of these questions in the precious few seconds that pass before you must act? Yes, it is; the human brain is capable of factoring in copious amounts of information and triggering an appropriate response in a relatively brief time span. Give it a try. You will soon find that the more experienced you are at assessing these issues, the more helpful your interventions will be.

Case Examples

Although behavior is the culprit, circumstances provide the corrective insight. The following examples illustrate how and why context determines the best possible response *regardless of the behavior at hand.*

Carol, while driving her troubled seven-year-old foster child Mark to his dentist appointment, noticed that he was growing increasingly anxious and restless. When they were about five blocks from the dentist's office, he swore at her. How did she respond? She knew that Mark was terrified of the dentist and that his fear, combined with his heightened state of agitation, might cause him to physically overreact to a harsh intervention on her part. To avoid compromising their safety while on the road, she decided to ignore the swearing until after his appointment.

When they returned home, Carol discussed the swearing incident with Mark, empathizing with his anxiety. She helped him see that he had hurt her feelings and that even in times of great anxiety there are better ways to respond. Mark apologized for swearing, whereupon Carol explained that there would be no consequence, given how nervous he was; that in the future she would expect a little more from him; and that swearing would warrant a five-minute time-out.

Four hours later, Mark became upset when Carol reminded him to complete his assigned chore of clearing the dinner table. Again he swore at her. Carol calmly asked him to take a five-minute time-out and to think about better ways of expressing his anger.

This time, the *same behavior* (swearing) elicited a *different response.* Because their safety was not at stake, Carol was free to act in a therapeutically ideal manner. Both her first and second responses, in light of their different contexts, were the best possible solutions.

Here is a second example of context-driven interventions. A staff member named George was left alone to cover a group home for troubled adolescents while his coworker, Stan, had gone to pick up a video. Manny, one of the largest and strongest residents, suddenly lost control and, swinging his fists in horizontal arcs, began moving toward George. No amount of verbal redirection halted his advance. George, acutely aware of the risk to his personal safety, headed for a nearby office, shut the door, and called the police.

The arrival of the squad car prompted Manny to cease his aggression. When the officer left, George and Manny processed the event and jointly determined the consequence: due to the seriousness of the incident, Manny was grounded to the house for two weeks.

Soon after the video ended, a resident named Larry began shouting obscenities and advancing in a threatening way toward George. This time, Stan was available to intervene. Together, they physically restrained Larry and led him to a quiet room. After helping him regain control, they reviewed the incident and, with his assistance, set the consequences: Larry was separated from the other residents until bedtime, grounded to the house for three days, and asked to write about the episode, identifying better choices he could have made.

As before, two similar forms of aggression elicited different responses, each of which was needed to preserve safety. In the first incident, entailing inadequate staffing, the kids needed to know that extremely stiff consequences would be levied for violent behavior; when understaffing was not an issue, the consequences were less severe and more therapeutically ideal.

A third example involves Mr. Nickerson, a sixth grade teacher with thirty students and, due to budget cutbacks, no full-time aide. One day Samuel, from his seat in the back row of class, hurled a spitball across the room. Muffled giggles erupted from the other students. In response, Mr. Nickerson calmly asked Samuel to report to the principal's office.

This teacher knew he could not afford to devote too much attention to one student at the expense of the other thirty-four. Yet he also knew that ignoring the behavior would identify him as a weak limit-setter who approved of inappropriate behavior, which would open the door to more misconduct. Considering the lack of human resources available to him, Mr. Nickerson provided the best possible intervention.

Even so, he felt frustrated. At the end of the school day, he told one of his colleagues that his preferred response would have been much different. If blessed with a full-time aide and only twenty students—as he had been the year before—he would have sat with Samuel at the back of the room and quietly talked with him. He might have found out that the boy was being scapegoated by other students, in which case they would have devised a plan incorporating a special signal, changed seating, and regular check-ins, as well as a consequence for throwing spitballs.

The Best Possible Response versus the Therapeutic Ideal
Dwindling resources is a growing problem in child welfare and public education. Because of the diminishing availability of support systems, foster parents, teachers, child-care workers, social workers, and detention counselors are often forced to respond to situations in ways that challenge conventional wisdom.

Chuck discovered this reality for himself while counseling Fred and Shannon Cartright—a couple about to adopt two foster sisters—Ashley, age nine, and Brandy, age five—who had been living with them for six months. Things were not going smoothly: the sisters, having come from a highly dysfunctional biological family and then an abusive foster family, spoke rudely to others, stayed up into the early-morning hours, refused to accept limits, and were at times physically aggressive toward each other as well as the Cartrights. By the time Chuck was asked to intervene, Fred and Shannon were at their wits' end and about ready to give up on their adoption plans.

It was clear to Chuck that the Cartrights loved these girls and that, despite the turmoil, meaningful bonding had taken place. To help restore order and buy time till more resources could be set in place—namely, individual therapy for the girls, family counseling, and some respite opportunities—he recommended behavioral incentive charts for Ashley and Brandy. Improved conduct would be indicated on the charts and would earn the girls stickers that they could trade in for material rewards. He also instructed the Cartrights in other behavioral strategies to enhance their interactions with the girls.

Ashley and Brandy responded well to the structure the sticker charts provided. Before long, more and more outside supports were set in place, during which time the home climate continued to improve. Two months after the first sticker charts were hung, they were taken down; the girls did not need them anymore.

Chuck, however, had second thoughts about the intervention. Aware that certain schools of thought disparage such forms of behavior modification, he began to ponder the negative effects of "bribing" children. His hope had been that the girls would modify their behavior not in exchange for material rewards, but to improve their relationship with the Cartrights and thereby "earn" their foster parents' ongoing love and nurturing. Concerned that he may have misled the family, Chuck went on to review the situation from a context perspective: the girls had been close to being removed from the home, no one was happy, and something immediate had to be done. The charts, he concluded, had provided an incentive for more harmonious family relations and were indeed the best possible solution to offer until more therapeutic measures could be set in place.

The cold truth is that we *cannot always respond in ways that are therapeutically ideal* for children. Due to lack of resources, as well as safety concerns, we are often forced to intervene instead with measures that fall within a range of best possible responses.

Any time that you, like Chuck, begin to doubt the value of an intervention you have recommended, remember the following guidelines. Your first obligation is to provide the best possible *context-sensitive* response to challenging behavior; your second is to advocate for better resources so that in the future your best possible response can more closely approximate the therapeutic ideal.

Good behavior management, in effect, occurs on two levels: *micro* and *macro*. While performing micro-level work, you are doing the very best you can with the resources you possess. While performing macro-level work, you are looking at the broader picture of behavioral change and advocating for additional support.

Is it feasible to operate on both levels simultaneously? Yes, it is. At the end of each day, think about your interactions with the children. Ask yourself, "Did I respond in the *best possible* manner?" If the answer is yes, then you did the job! Rather than worry that you may have failed to give the kids enough, look in the mirror and say, *"I did the best I could today with what I had . . . and I must fight for more!"*

PART II

PREVENTING CHALLENGING BEHAVIOR

CHAPTER 6

ASKING THE RIGHT QUESTIONS

THE BEST WAY TO APPROACH PROBLEM BEHAVIOR IS TO PREVENT IT through *proactive thinking*. Proactive thinkers prepare for the future by reflecting on the present. Any time a child acts out, for example, they will step back and ask, "What could I have done to avert this situation?" They will then pose a series of questions in order to arrive at a productive answer.

Proactive Thinking in Action

At a behavior management workshop for elementary school parents, a visibly worn-out foster mother named Stephanie raised her hand and commented: "Weekday mornings are awful at our house. We start off each one tense and argumentative, then the kids fight in the car on the way to school. If it's not about who sits in the front seat or which radio station we listen to, they'll find something else to bicker over. I spend the entire trip yelling at them. What can I do?"

What Stephanie could do, I reasoned, depended on the particular triggers for the children's misbehavior. Exploring the whys, in other words, would help us figure out the what-to-dos. Consequently, over the next fifteen minutes, I asked her a series of questions to help her view the problem proactively:

- What do the kids eat in the morning? Is it hot or cold? Do they make it themselves or is it made for them?

- What does the interior of the car look like? What about the inside of the house?

- Are the children physically and emotionally prepared for school? Does anyone make sure they are properly dressed, clean, well-groomed, and carrying their homework as well as other school essentials?

- Is there an established routine in the morning—a set time to get up, shower, and so forth?

- What do the children do before entering the car? Do they enjoy a somewhat relaxed breakfast or do they quickly gulp it down? Do they quietly watch a favorite video or do they play loud music and horse around?

- Does anyone give each child a hug or warm words of farewell before they leave for school?

- Do the kids run to the car or do they walk calmly?

- How do the children act at school? Are they getting along with classmates? Do they have one or two good friends? How would you describe their relationships with teachers and their academic performance?

- How well do the adults in the children's lives communicate with one another? With the children?

- Have you explored psychological issues related to the children's histories, such as family dynamics, sexual identity, abuse and neglect?

After contemplating Stephanie's answers to these questions, I strove to help her see the value in tightening the children's morning routine and in structuring their transition to school by jointly preparing a weekly car-seating chart. A week or so later, I received a note from her explaining that our proactive plans had significantly defused the morning chaos.

The Key Areas of Inquiry

When we play detective and ask the right questions, the answers often inspire a remedial course of action. The questions I asked Stephanie were drawn from the following nine areas of investigation. Each discussion contains tips and techniques that can help prevent many of the problem behaviors you, too, are grappling with.

Are Basic Needs Being Met?

Because most troubled children missed out on having basic needs fulfilled in their earliest years of life, they yearn desperately to have them met as they mature. Subsumed under "basic needs" are two key aspects of healthy development—nutrition and safety—each of which must be addressed independently to help prevent troublesome behavior.

Are Nutritional Needs Being Met? A good breakfast in the morning increases the likelihood of a successful day, especially if it is prepared by a significant adult. Why? Because such a meal will be physically as well as emotionally nurturing. With teenagers who prefer to make breakfast themselves, you can still stress the importance of eating a solid meal at the start of the day, thereby conveying the message that you care. In addition to breakfast, troubled children need ample snacks, sufficient portions of food, and regular mealtimes—requirements which, if met, will enable them to function at their highest potential socially, emotionally, behaviorally, and cognitively.

The need for food *should be held sacred and met unconditionally.* Withholding food, in other words, should never be used as a consequence for misbehavior; it if is, it will most likely interfere with learning and spark more serious transgressions. Youngsters who head off to school hungry or who skip lunch are less apt to learn and more likely to act out, as are children who live with uncertainty about their next meal. Many group-home kids with histories of neglect and deprivation secretly take food from the kitchen to hoard in their bedrooms because they do not trust that adults will furnish them with enough to sustain their growth. Showing such kids your pantry may help eradicate this behavior by assuring them that food is in plentiful supply.

Does the Physical Environment Feel Safe? A disorganized, messy setting intimates, "Things are out of place here," "Life is unpredictable," "We don't take pride in our possessions," or even "We don't care about you." For troubled children, who require a high degree of structure, predictability, and safety, such chaos is a behavioral hazard.

Three hours into my first shift as senior counselor at a residential treatment center for abused and neglected children, the place was crazy. Twelve girls, ranging in age from seven to fourteen, were misbehaving big-time, and my requests for peace and quiet were falling on deaf ears. The other staff members looked worried, for we had lost control of the group.

Humbly, I dialed the home number of our unit director, Ellen.

She answered on the first ring. "Hello."

"Ellen, this is Charlie. You've gotta get in here. The girls are wild. They're not listening to anything I'm saying."

"I'll be right in."

I could hardly wait for Ellen's arrival. I pictured her, brilliant and directive, charging through the doors and immediately putting the kids in their place. Minutes later, I heard rumbling in the stairwell. "*Yes,*" I thought to myself, "*revenge is at hand.*"

The heavy doors creaked open. Ellen walked up the long carpeted hallway and into the fray. With eyes like lasers, she scanned the large living room, and then she spoke: "Cathy and Joan, get the mop and head into the bathroom. I want to see that floor shinin'! Ellie, Rhonda, Becky, take the laundry into the dorm and start folding. Mavis, get a cloth and some Windex, and hit the mirrors; I'll

help you out in a minute. Lisa, Jill—get the two vacuum cleaners.
Jill, you do the hallway; Lisa, the living room and dorm."

Within two minutes the unit was serene. These girls, all of whom
had come from chaotic environments, relied on order and consistency; I, however, inexperienced and naive, had let the state of the unit
slip by prioritizing talking over doing. Now I know better. Whenever
I enter a facility that serves children at risk, I remove papers from the
floor, return chairs to their proper places, and straighten the pictures
on the walls. Why? Because I have learned that troubled kids with
underdeveloped internal structures require intensive external structure to experience a sense of order, organization, and safety.

If you work with a child who smashes holes in doors, writes on
walls, or breaks furniture, think twice about letting him live amid
the devastation, for he will soon feel like a messy kid living a messy
life. Although an appropriate consequence is to let him repair the
damage, if he does not do so within a reasonable period of time, find
another way to hold him responsible for his actions and consider
restoring the environment yourself. Think of it as adding bricks to
his foundation.

In addition to cleanliness and order, focus on warmth, color, and
stimulation. In many classrooms and residential units, the rules are
posted prominently on the main wall whereas the others contain faded,
torn, and sometimes defaced posters of dreary scenes hung so long ago
that few of the children notice them anymore. If your setting is anything
like these, think about a fresh coat of paint as well as vibrant artwork,
festive curtains, captivating posters, and perhaps a plant or two. A
spruced-up environment sends a message of safety and caring.

Consider each piece of furniture a deterrent to misbehavior, too.
Move coatracks; make key supplies more readily available; convert
two beds to a bunk bed; move the TV and stereo away from walls that
back onto a bedroom; reserve an old TV exclusively for video games;
and strategically reposition bookshelves. Designate one shelf for toys,
another for books, a third for art supplies, and perhaps a separate set of
shelves for videos and recorded music. Such arrangements let children
know where to find the items they are looking for and where to *return
them to*.

Well-placed furniture offers protection by creating clear boundaries, which in turn decreases anxiety levels. When designing the layout for a common room, let chairs, tables, and couches partition off areas for different purposes. Include small, semiprivate gathering places as well as a large communal space. A special bench or couch set along one wall of the large living area can serve as the site for a transition ritual, marking the place that children leave from and return to as they pass from one activity to the next.

Good telephone placement is equally critical. The best locations for telephones are in areas within sight of the children, for then they will not feel abandoned each time you receive a call and they will be less likely to act out as soon as the phone rings. While reading a child a story or eating dinner together, let the answering machine take over. Monitor the length of your calls as well, to avoid giving the impression that your phone time is more important than your time with the children.

When deciding on the placement of furniture and equipment, be sure to allow for unobstructed supervision sight-lines that will offer you direct visual access to the children in your care. If you are a foster parent, is your outdoor play area visible from the kitchen window, front or back porch, or living room? If you are a teacher, when you are seated at your desk, are all the children's desks within view? Two or three rows of desks arranged in a semicircle around the teacher's provides better sight lines than a linear arrangement of six rows of desks with the teacher's up front. If you work in a residential unit, can you unobtrusively observe what is happening in the quiet room? The easier it is to see the children, the better you will be at anticipating potential difficulties and quickly responding to problems that arise.

Another feature essential to a safe environment is *time-out spaces*. Troubled kids need a place to retreat to when they are upset or are taking a time-out for misbehavior. To avoid needless disruptions, the place of retreat should be a quiet spot away from the "action" yet readily accessible to the children. Ensure that it is situated far enough away from stairways, fire alarms, glass windows, and stoves.

Time-out sites vary according to the setting. Many children in foster care do well retreating to their bedrooms; others need to be in plain view of an adult. In some schools, teachers will send a misbehaving student to another teacher's room in lieu of "the office"—a place far less conducive to reflection—whereas in other schools, a behavior inclusion specialist will escort the child to a quiet setting down the hall to work through the incident. Programs that deal effectively with seriously disturbed youngsters create safe time-out rooms where children who are having difficulty can regain self-control. Mats are available in case a child needs to be physically restrained, and light fixtures as well as other potentially harmful objects are safely out of reach. The expectation in such environments is that angry kids will have trouble controlling their destructive impulses.

Regardless of the setting it is in, a time-out space should have a nonpunitive atmosphere, since its purpose is to assist children in regaining control, talking about their misdeeds, and exploring the underlying issues. Toward that end, chairs need to be comfortable and facing the center of the room rather than a corner. Lighting should be pleasant, and reading materials readily available.

Are the Children Physically and Emotionally Prepared for Each Endeavor?

Troubled children who are prepared for each segment of the day fare better than those who are not. One of the most critical facets of readiness is appearance. Because a child who looks dirty and disheveled on the outside is apt to feel the same way on the inside, it is important to emphasize the value of personal grooming and hygiene. A youngster who is expected to look neat and well-groomed will feel loved and cared for, and will think, "I'm a pretty important person. I'm worth fussing over!" Even children who cringe at such proclamations as "Time for a shower" or "Please wash your hands" are likely to feel better about themselves once the "ordeal" is over.

Years ago I was the unit director of a group of seven- to twelve-year-old boys at a large residential treatment center, all of whom had histories of abuse and neglect. Every morning as they lined up to go to school, I would scrutinize each one to make sure his belt was on, his hair was combed, his fingernails were clean, his clothes were free of holes and dirt, his shoes were tied, and his face was scrubbed. At times, the kids gave me quite a stink, saying, "I don't *care* how I look!" or "I don't *like* combing my hair!"

In response to their complaints, I would reply, "Let me get this straight—you're mad at me because I care about you and want you to look handsome for school. Is that what you're saying?" I also constructed a Peg-Board to hold twelve hairbrushes, and any time a kid messed up his hair at the last minute, I would have his brush in hand, ready to restore him to neatness. I wanted these kids to go off to school with the knowledge that someone valued them and thought they were good-looking dudes!

These are battles worth fighting. But what about clashes over colored hair, "fashionably" ripped clothing, or shorts in winter—where do we draw the line? Distinguishing between acceptable and unacceptable clothing for school is not always easy, but if we want kids to know that school is a place for behaving respectfully and learning, we need to inform them that the clothes they wear to the mall may not be appropriate for class. The point is to draw the line somewhere and stand by it!

If you are a foster parent, check out "appearance" norms and allow your child to be in style without going to extremes. Then discuss the matter with him, listening closely to his point of view, and negotiate mutually agreeable terms, such as, "Okay, can we agree to one earring, a small spike in your hair, and ripped jeans once a week—but no earring through your nose?"

If you work in a group home or residential center, remember that some kids overdo their appearance to broadcast their unhappiness about family dynamics or other serious issues. In such instances, you might try a more forthright approach: "I think the way you are dressing sends the world a message that you are not a happy kid, that you need help. Well, your message has been received. Since there's no longer a need for an SOS, let's decide on some details about your appearance. I'm not saying you have to look like a choirboy, but the rainbow hairdo and seven facial earrings are too much. What middle ground can we reach?"

In addition to hygiene and grooming, being prepared refers to gathering all the essentials needed for each upcoming event. A child who has not completed his homework, has forgotten to have a note signed, or is missing the right materials is likely to start off the school day in a state of anxiety, which may only intensify as the hours unfold.

To prevent such situations, consider establishing a regular "checking time" the night before to ensure that all necessities have been taken care of, then in the morning, quickly make sure everything the child will need is in his book bag.

The homework itself may require some attention on your part. Failure to complete an assignment may hinge on any number of factors—among them, the work is too difficult, the home environment is too chaotic, the child is preoccupied with personal issues, or the child forgot to bring it home. Your task is to seek out the cause of the problem and come up with reasonable solutions. Tackling homework as part of a structured routine—at 4 P.M. every day, for example—is a time-tested winner. It is also wise to have the child do his homework in the *same place,* preferably one that is quiet and free of distractions. Ultimately, your goal is is to encourage him to develop systems for making sure everything is in place before embarking on *any* new endeavor, be it school, an important visit, or a camping trip.

Are There Established Routines?

Set routines provide structure, predictability, and a sense of safety in the sometimes scary world of a troubled child. In fact, the more troubled a child is, the more critical is the need for routines, and the more tightly administered they should be. Parents of a healthy eight year old can afford to be far more relaxed about daily schedules than foster parents of an eight year old who has grown up the hard way. The same holds true for special education teachers and workers at a juvenile detention center.

Routines also delineate segments of the day, helping a child feel comfortable about stopping one activity and beginning another. Given a schedule, he can anticipate the end of playtime, for example, assured that it is time for another activity and that he can play again the next day.

"Okay," Frankie's foster father might say, "in ten minutes it will be time for dinner. Why don't you start putting away some of your trucks." If Frankie understands that dinner is usually served at the *same time* each evening, chances are that he will start cleaning up and come to the dinner table on time. However, if dinner is served at a different time each evening and if he is not given ample warning, he is more likely to procrastinate, be late for dinner, and misbehave during the meal.

A lack of structure to the day often precipitates power struggles. This phenomenon becomes highly visible among many troubled children just before a school vacation. Rather than being excited about their upcoming free time, they become increasingly anxious about its ill-defined structure and begin acting out more intensely.

One way to help troubled children feel more at ease about pending transitions is to post daily schedules. Foster parents can display upcoming events at the start of each morning so that all family members will know "the plan" for the day; home-to-school and school-to-home shifts, traditionally hectic interludes, can be calmed with a five-minute preview or catch-up meeting setting the stage for the next segment of the day. Similarly, elementary school teachers can post a class schedule on the bulletin board and review it aloud at the beginning of each day, whereas junior and high school teachers can inform students about the content of each class, explaining, for example, "We'll do independent work for the first twenty minutes, then we'll have the review quiz." Residential care workers, for their part, can hang a daily "What's Happening" sheet listing the staff members on duty, appointments, activities, medications, visits, chores, and even menus.

Are the Kids Kept Informed about Upcoming Transitions?

You can bet that if a child is rambunctious during a transition, his agitation will carry over to the next activity. To avoid these shake-ups, inform children of significant transitions *well before* they occur. Your announcement can be as simple as, "Kids, we'll be leaving for school in ten minutes. Please turn off the music, put the cards away, and sit quietly in the living room with your book bags. Thanks." Similar notification can be given before the next class, a meal, or bedtime.

Remember, troubled children usually have difficulty delaying gratification. If they are having fun, they are reluctant to stop for fear that more fun may be a long time coming. Because they live for the moment, they must often be *eased* out of pleasurable activities.

Many variables can be manipulated to reduce stimulation for a child about to transition to a new activity. Consider decreasing physical exertion levels, for example, as well as dimming the lights, lowering the volume on the TV or radio, and redirecting evocative conversations. The object is to be mindful of how *the current activity will impact on the next one.* If bedtime is rapidly approaching, do not plan on sending a child off to bed in the middle of a gripping movie, but rather choose a TV show that will end before bedtime— or better yet, read a story. In a group-home setting, do not allow phone conversations immediately before bedtime, for they may be overly stimulating.

Robert, the new director of a twelve-bed young boys' residential unit, worked with another variable to ease the transition to bedtime. The routine in place before his arrival proved to be a dismal failure: from 7:30 P.M. until "lights out," the boys were required to sit quietly and watch the large console TV in the common area. Because some of the boys had short attention spans and many others had poor social skills, the quiet-time routine lasted about fifteen minutes before dissolving into tantrums, boisterous acting out, and unfriendly staff-child interactions.

During his second day on the job, Robert purchased four wall lamps and hung them in different areas of the large living space. That night he told the boys that instead of watching TV, they could choose to spend their quiet time drawing, having fun with action figures, or playing games in any one of the newly designated areas. He also made the kitchen available, a room that had previously been off-limits after dinner.

Robert's "divide and conquer" strategy worked wonders. The kids loved having choices and adapted well to their new level of personal responsibility. Evenings soon became mellow—the frequency of misbehavior had dropped dramatically, and in turn, the adult-child relationships had improved.

How Are Transitions Managed?

The heart of proactive thinking comes into play when transitions are managed *as they occur.* In settings where children are allowed to scramble to a car or run wildly to a new class or activity, the probability for misbehavior increases with striking rapidity. The key to orderly conduct during such times of change is to ensure that children understand how they are to behave.

Emily, a beginning child-care worker at a residential treatment setting for abused and neglected children, was in charge of a rowdy group of seven- to twelve-year-old boys. The boys frequently misbehaved during meals and other group events, shouting and scattering about the room. The anxiety in the group was palpable long before each new activity began; the kids, it seemed, did not feel safe.

Aware of the problem, Emily decided to tighten the transitions. For the next two weeks, any time the boys strayed from the group, fooled around, became too loud, skipped stairs, or ran while en route to a new activity, she would take them back to their starting point and have them try again. As she walked them back, she respectfully let them know why it was important to proceed in a calm and orderly fashion. Once, on the way to dinner, she had the boys return to their living unit *four times* to "try it again," because they were not walking properly. Within a few weeks, Emily was conducting excellent transitions, and her group was far better behaved during the subsequent activities.

Is it also possible to line up *teenagers*—kids who do not like to conform, because they are carving out niches for themselves as separate and unique individuals? The answer is, yes and no. While it is important to keep teens feeling safe and secure, control measures must be tempered with respect for their autonomy. The level of structure to employ in transitions therefore needs to rise and fall in relation to the degree of acting out that is present. In other words, the more frequently problem behaviors occur, the more tightly monitored the youths must be.

Troubled teens in juvenile detention centers are expected to line up and walk quietly from one activity to the next. Those who do not perform up to par must suffer the consequences of their actions, often losing key privileges. At the other end of the spectrum are junior and senior high school students whose teachers report problem behaviors in the hallways. Increased adult supervision between classes has been shown to reduce such tumult. In all teenage settings, the challenge for adults in charge is to *maintain a safe environment without misusing power.*

Are You Aware of Significant Problem Areas?

Many children misbehave in anticipation of an emotionally charged encounter, such as an appointment with a therapist, a confrontation with an antagonistic peer, or a visit from a biological parent. The better you are at identifying the source of anxiety, the more effective your proactive interventions will be.

A child who misbehaves before school hours, for example, may be asking for academic assistance, saying, in essence: "School isn't much fun for me. Please help!" The message he is incapable of articulating directly may be something like: "Excuse me, Mrs. Stewart, but the math problems you have assigned are a bit too challenging given my cognitive development and inclination toward hyperactivity."

For a child struggling with academics, placement in appropriate classes, groupings, and levels is crucial. The longer this cry for help goes unheeded, the more severe the next one will be, which may well result in a call from the principal: "Your foster daughter, Geri, knocked over a couple of desks this afternoon and pushed a teacher. Could you please come in. We need to talk."

Having identified the source of Geri's anxiety, you can help her express her concerns in an *acceptable* manner, and also intervene on her behalf to reduce the stress. You could meet with her teacher to explain Geri's learning style, or schedule her therapy appointments at a more favorable time of day, or help her develop a script for resolving her conflict with a peer. Remember, *the smallest changes can have the greatest impact.*

Another way to prepare children for anxiety-producing events is by letting them know what to expect. One foster mother uses this approach: "Doug, you have an appointment with Dr. Sullivan after lunch. Remember the testing we talked about at your last conference? Well, Dr. Sullivan is going to give you three reading tests today, none of which will involve right-or-wrong answers. The results will help your teachers know how to teach you better. You should be finished by three o'clock—then we'll go to the arcade." A camp counselor uses a similar approach: "Sarah, we will be going to the infirmary after lunch. Dr. Harvey is just going to make sure your ear infection has cleared up. She'll probably look in your ears and throat."

A simple explanation of a dreaded encounter can help dissolve most negative fantasies about the future, especially among kids who often fear the worst. Knowing that things are under control gives them courage to face their fears without sending out more behavioral flares for help.

Are Hellos and Good-Byes Conducted Meaningfully?

Hellos and good-byes can make all the difference between an invigorating day and a traumatic one. A child who receives a big hug and smile from his foster dad as he is dropped off at school walks into his classroom ready to say hello to learning. A child whose parting message from dad is, "Stop picking on your brother or you'll be in big trouble after school!" enters his classroom burdened with unfinished business. It is hard for a child to greet experiences in a new setting if he has *not said good-bye to the old one.*

No matter how strained the early morning hours may be, your last encounter with a child calls for warmth and affection: "Craig, it's been a rough morning, but you're still my favorite little guy. Have a great day." Remember to follow up your parting words with a tender gesture. Young children need hugs; teens may prefer a pat on the shoulder.

A warm hello from a teacher is equally important. Whether the greeting comes in the form of a smile, a handshake, or a few words of welcome, the message it conveys is, "I'm glad you're here today."

Are Communication Systems in Place?

Caregivers who communicate well among themselves prevent and de-escalate challenging behavior far more effectively than those who do not. Why? Because ongoing communication within a child's inner network of providers—including foster parents, teachers, counselors, coaches, and clergy—keeps everyone informed each step of the way.

Following are five proactive guidelines you can use in developing a top-notch communication system. First, *keep all important tele-*

phone numbers and addresses on hand. Record the telephone numbers and addresses of key players in an easily accessible Rolodex, address book, or hand-held computer, and update this data as needed. Also post prominently beside your telephone the numbers for critical local contacts, such as the fire department, police department, poison control center, and for immediate refreshment, your favorite pizzeria.

Second, *identify roles, boundaries, and expectations.* Agree on whose job it should be to relay information; how frequently it should be transmitted; the sort of information that needs to be conveyed; the best medium for communicating, such as telephone, fax, mail, e-mail, or face-to-face conversations; and what constitutes an emergency situation.

Third, *establish crisis response procedures.* Whenever safety appears compromised and reactions are slow, confused, or nonexistent, uncertainty takes hold and tension levels rise in subtle yet destructive ways. Having a plan in place for such eventualities can instill caregivers with the confidence and assurance needed to set proper limits. The best team approach is to devise your own "911" communication system for securing behavioral help *fast.*

An elementary school in Massachusetts recently created a new position for a behavior inclusion specialist and hired Sean for the job. Before the school year began, however, the faculty realized that since each classroom was equipped with only a simple intercom, teachers would be unable to reach Sean quickly if one of their students was in serious trouble. To solve the problem, the school bought four walkie-talkies: one for Sean, one for the front-desk secretary, and one for each of the two teachers with the most challenging students.

When school opened in September, the faculty was delighted with the crisis response system they had created. Sean kept his walkie-talkie clipped to his belt at all times and arrived promptly on the scene whenever he was called. The teachers who had not been furnished with a device buzzed the office, whereupon the secretary would dispatch Sean to the proper class. In many instances, he was able to help a troubled student stay in class and work through the difficulty rather than take a time-out in the office and perhaps never examine the situation. At the end of the year, one of the teachers told him: "What a difference emergency back-up has made. We were more relaxed, more positive, and able to give the kids more attention and to set more effective limits."

A fourth recommendation for enhancing core-group contact is, *utilize written forms of communication.* Verbally conveyed information is often rushed, sketchy, easily distorted, and unlikely to reach the appropriate person. Writing down the facts, on the other hand, ensures that they will be properly relayed.

Written communication can take several forms. Child welfare agencies could post important information on walls and bulletin boards. Residential centers could require staff members to read key logs and initial the documents before starting a shift; such logs may be used to track behavior patterns, note important events, and store data for treatment planning. Some foster parents keep a daily journal of their children's progress, in which they record the frequency of misbehavior, times of day in which it occurred, precipitating factors, and duration of the episodes. Such entries are often personally enlightening as well as informative to counselors and teachers.

Lastly, *meet regularly*—both with group members and with the children in your care. Weekly core-group meetings can provide a forum for reviewing each child's progress, addressing logistics, and keeping your vision unified. Weekly meetings with the children in class, on the unit, or at home can keep your communication lines open regarding recent happenings, changes in rules, current issues, and upcoming events. Daily meetings, when needed, can release tension and enhance relationships. Children who are empowered to participate in such discussions, and are respected for doing so, tend to exhibit improved behavior. Why? Because regularly scheduled meetings of this sort foster connections and attachment.

In addition to meeting formally with the children, plan on more casual encounters with them. In fact, it is a good idea to check in with each child on a daily basis to see how things are going. A ritual of this sort, conducted at the same time of day, is sure to comfort many youngsters.

When communicating with a group of children, envision yourself as a pie with an equal slice of your best communication going to each one. Holding to this image, you will be less tempted to veer away from kids whose behavior *pushes* you away. They are, after all, the ones likely to need you the most.

Are You Aware of Any Underlying Psychological Issues?

A final consideration in developing a proactive viewpoint is understanding the psychological origins of misbehavior, particularly from a *systems* perspective. Sound clinical theory suggests that every family, school, or group-care setting is a system, and that members of a system will act out any time its leaders need help. Children's acting out, in other words, can be seen as an attempt to call attention to the leaders' problems, as opposed to their own. Help the leaders of the system and you help its members.

Thus, a child will sometimes misbehave to call attention to the problematic conduct of one or more of his caregivers, such as his parents, foster parents, a child-care provider, a teacher, or the staff at a residential facility. His acting out forces the adults into public view, exposing their issues and child-care practices, and thereby increasing the likelihood that these adults will receive the help they need.

To apply a systems approach, take a long, hard look at what a child's actions are attempting to tell you. Who is he trying to help—parents experiencing marital discord, a stressed single parent making poor decisions, a burned-out teacher, or perhaps residential staff members who are punitive or not communicating well? When an adult takes the time to find answers to these questions, problem behaviors often dissipate.

CHAPTER 7

TROUBLESHOOTING IN ADVANCE

THE GOOD NEWS ABOUT MISBEHAVIOR IS THAT IT IS OFTEN PREDICTABLE. It tends to be triggered by certain precipitants that, once detected, can be strategically controlled to eradicate or minimize problem behavior. Interestingly, most of these precipitants originate in one of the areas of investigation addressed in the previous chapter. A caregiver's task in cultivating a preventive mind-set is therefore not only to ask the right questions but to anticipate the trouble spots and plan accordingly, using the four approaches described below. Implementing these troubleshooting skills promotes staying power in the child welfare arena.

Pattern Identification

One reliable technique to use in forecasting troublesome behavior is pattern identification, or *looking for disruptions recurring at similar times or places and tracking them back to their source.* To develop expertise in pattern identification, each time you encounter a disruptive behavior ask yourself: "Do I see a *pattern* here? Is this behavior noticeable at the same time each day, week, or month? If so, what might be triggering it?" You may find, for instance, that a child in foster or residential care repeatedly acts out before visits with her biological parents; that a student with a stressful family life frequently misbehaves prior to school vacations; that a child who has been sexually abused tends to lose control at bedtime; or any number of other situations.

Once you have identified a problematic behavior pattern and detected its cause, a good way to change it is by *involving the child.* Begin by choosing a calm, nonepisodic moment in which to talk gently about the pattern you have observed. Or better yet, see if the child herself is able to recognize it. In either case, empathize with her feelings and together devise a plan that can help her manage her behavior during the difficult periods. Such a plan may call for more adult support, additional counseling, journaling, an incentive plan, a new activity, or the introduction of select self-management techniques. Collaboration is equally effective in group situations.

Cathy, an eleven-year-old resident of a group home, acted out frantically on Thursday nights, just before her Friday visits with her biological mother. The Thursday after I identified this pattern, I took Cathy aside and asked her, "What time should I take out the boxing gloves tonight?"

"What are you talking about?" she queried, with a puzzled look in her eyes.

"Every Thursday night we go round after round," I replied, pretending to spar with an imaginary figure. "You're given a short time-out for misconduct; you scream and yell; and after an hour or two of 'boxing,' you quiet down."

"Get out of here," she scoffed at me.

"Hey, I'm serious. I want to know what time the bout will start so I can have my gloves ready."

She laughed and walked away.

Around 7:15 P.M., Cathy was given a time-out for rudeness, whereupon she began to argue, gradually increasing the volume of her protests. Hearing her loud cry, I jumped in, saying, "Wait a second, Cathy. I think it's time to get the gloves from the staff room. Please hold your cool for two minutes until I get back."

She started laughing.

With the tension broken, Cathy was able to look at why Thursday nights were so difficult; then together we created a plan to help her work through her previsit anxieties. She agreed to do a voluntary chore on Thursday nights, stay in close proximity to staff members, and record her thoughts and feelings in a journal. She also consented to having staff members talk to her about her feelings, which ended up improving her relationships with them.

Did we eradicate her previsit jitters? A little. Could she understand why she had them? Absolutely. Did she begin managing them more appropriately? Very much so.

Victor called upon this pattern identification technique in a group situation. While conducting an activity/therapy group consisting of nine seventh graders who were having behavior problems in school, he began to notice that in the last ten minutes of each session the kids became restless and started teasing one another, roughhousing, and throwing pencils and pens through the air. He mentioned this pattern during a calm period early in the session. He told the students that although some of the problem was his fault, as he tended not to prepare for the final moments of their session, they were nevertheless responsible for their behavior. He then asked for suggestions on how to keep the last ten minutes of their time together running smoothly.

One of the boys proposed a game of Uno, which is precisely what solved the problem. Toward the end of their next session, Victor distributed three decks of Uno cards, and much to everyone's delight, the kids played well together, with no disruptions.

Proactive Exploration

Former world chess champion Bobby Fisher had to think twenty to thirty moves in advance in order to gain victory. Those who troubleshoot with challenging kids must conduct a similar exploration to prevent disruptive behaviors.

When left to your own devices for ameliorating a troublesome time period, consider trying the *Proactive Exploration Exercise.* Begin by writing across the top of a sheet of paper: "Factors that may be leading to behavioral difficulties at _____ (the troubling time period)." Then list every precipitating factor you can think of, no matter how trivial it may seem.

Imagine that you work at a residential treatment facility where dinnertime is consistently loud and hectic, and you complete this exercise by listing the twenty-five precipitating factors shown in figure 7–1.

Figure 7–1

Proactive Exploration Exercise 1

Factors that may be leading to behavioral difficulties at dinnertime:

1. The transition to dinnertime is mismanaged.
2. The dining room is unpleasant, due to its dim lighting, cold temperature, and drab decor.
3. The dining room is not cleaned before the kids arrive, nor is the table properly set.
4. The dining room is too small; the kids are eating elbow-to-elbow.
5. The time-out area is so poorly situated that each misbehaving child who is asked to leave the table disrupts others on his way out.
6. Dinner is served at a different time each day.
7. Dinner is poorly prepared: the food is cold, unappealing, and in short supply.
8. The seating arrangement fails to place a staff member between the most disruptive kids.
9. The group does not take a moment for silent gratitude at the start of the meal.
10. Rules and procedures for mealtime are unclear, and no "chore chart" is posted.
11. Staff members provide inadequate supervision.
12. Staff members fail to facilitate conversation or use humor.
13. The kitchen phone is answered during the meal, and is out of the diners' range of vision.
14. Because of a staff illness, an unfamiliar substitute is often present.
15. There is too much shuffling around during the meal, with kids getting up to refill their glasses, find their favorite salad dressings, and so forth.
16. Kids who experience conflict or disappointment prior to dinner receive inadequate attention.
17. The staff members on duty are inexperienced.
18. Some staff members on duty are not coping well with personal issues.

---

19. The staff members supervising dinner are not working as a team.
20. Staff members sometimes wear provocative clothing.
21. Unfamiliar visitors walk through the dining room during dinner.
22. Thunderstorms are common at dinnertime.
23. The kids are not properly warned about dinner coming to an end; some still have food on their plates when it is time to clear the table.
24. Staff members do not help the kids with mealtime cleanup.
25. The kids have no fun activities to look forward to after dinner.

Is it possible to be on top of all these factors? With practice, it is, depending on how well trained and dedicated your child-care staff is and on the resources at your disposal.

Having completed this Proactive Exploration Exercise, your next step is to bring your findings to a staff meeting and ensure that before every dinner, members do their best to have each factor under control. Whenever a thunderstorm is forecast, for example, you could talk about thunder and lightning before dinner and have the most frightened kids sit beside a staff member. Although you may not have a list with twenty-five boxes to check off, you will probably know, from your staff discussion and personal experience, what needs to be covered before, during, and after the meal.

Sometimes only a few simple changes can dramatically affect children's behavior. I remember spending huge chunks of time at staff meetings debating the most minuscule details, such as how a kid's pants should be folded, or whether we should use bar or liquid soap. I would think, "This is why I went to graduate school—to spend fifteen minutes arguing about soap?" Then invariably I would remind myself, "Yes, this is exactly why I went to graduate school, because the soap is an integral part of the larger dynamic inspiring behavioral change."

A child-care setting is, after all, much like the inside of a clock, where numerous gears and mechanisms work in sync to keep the proper time. Whenever one gear is not running well, the entire timepiece can malfunction.

Use of the Proactive Exploration Exercise is not limited to large groups of children. Ms. Padilla, a third grade teacher, wrote out every reason she could think of for recent class disruptions provoked by John, a student struggling to control his behavior (see figure 7–2).

Figure 7–2

Proactive Exploration Exercise 2

Factors that may be causing John to misbehave in class:

1. John is having trouble understanding the subject matter, which embarrasses him in front of his peers.
2. I have stopped breaking down his class assignments into sequential tasks. Because he has attention deficit hyperactivity disorder, he does not respond well when I simply say, "Do the worksheet."
3. He has been sitting between two students who often tease him and who may be egging him on.
4. He has been having a rough time at home and appears to have a lot on his mind.
5. I have been tired lately, which has decreased my tolerance for fooling around. Perhaps my tone, affect, and language are a bit too strong.
6. He forgets his assignments and is not prepared for class.
7. Because he has been acting out a lot, I am presently not fond of the kid. Actually, I don't like having him in my class! Perhaps I have been conveying that message to him.
8. He appears hungry as soon as he comes in the door.
9. The classroom has been in a state of disarray.
10. Lately, I have been changing the class routine without much warning.
11. John sometimes seems nervous about his lack of after-school plans.
12. He seems to enter the classroom on the verge of erupting. Perhaps he is having a hard time on the playground before the bell rings.
13. End-of-the-morning announcements over the loudspeaker have been interrupting our class discussions.

After looking over her list, Ms. Padilla decided to address each factor, beginning with those she could tackle right away. She immediately resumed her practice of giving John step-by-step assignments, tidied up the classroom, moved his seat, and initiated meaningful contact with his parents, then augmented additional changes as time went on. Over a period of weeks, John's behavior improved. In fact, the more his learning environment fulfilled his personal needs, the more self-control he asserted.

Any time you are confronted with difficult behaviors, it is a good idea to explore possible precipitating factors. You need not commit your list to paper, as Ms. Padilla did; mentally reviewing the items may work just as well. Then following your review, implement the needed changes. The extra energy invested in *preventing* future disruptions is minor compared with the energy expended in *grappling* with them. When responding to the behavior of challenging kids, always remember this axiom: Pay now or pay more later.

Resource Evaluation

A third mainstay in troubleshooting is an evaluation of the human and physical resources available. Here the operative law is: *A setting with many demands and limited resources is at increased risk for ongoing and episodic behavioral difficulties.*

With resource evaluation, as with pattern identification and proactive exploration, strategic interventions play a preventive role. You can bet that a parent aide in a second grade classroom with thirty-two students, for example, will have more positive impact than an increase in disciplinary measures. Similarly, a donated air conditioner is apt to improve summertime behavior at a group home for troubled adolescents far more than a new behavioral approach. The point is, never underestimate the importance of securing the human and physical resources you need.

Finding Human Resources

Many adults are martyrs when it comes to dealing with children at risk. Dedicated to "doing it all," they often fail to see that by not taking care of themselves they are less able to take care of the kids. A far saner and more preventive approach is to find other adults who can help support the children in our care.

The greatest untapped resource pool for schools and residential facilities is *parents*. Many employers now offer flextime, enabling mothers and fathers to participate in their children's school life. With appropriate training and support, parent helpers in schools can be asked to tutor students, monitor lunch and recess, and assist teachers in meeting curriculum needs. Participating parents who are clear about classroom rules, procedures, expectations, and responsibilities can enrich the school community by introducing not only extra hands but a multitude of talents as well.

Residential facilities also benefit from parent involvement in day-to-day operations. Increasingly, treatment providers are realizing that the advantages of family-centered care extend well beyond therapy sessions. Many residential centers are now inviting parents to spend large segments of time with their children—taking them clothes shopping, tutoring them, chauffeuring them to medical appointments, and simply "hanging out" with them in their living quarters. In some centers, parents are encouraged to interact with other residents as well, by cooking a favorite dish or organizing an activity. Such cooperative, empowering approaches give rise to win-win-win situations for the center, the parents, and most importantly, the children.

Another underutilized resource is *mentors*. Not only do numerous studies attest to the power that one "significant" adult can have in changing a child's life, but an adult who serves simultaneously as coach, ally, and confidant can spell the difference between a troubled child "making it" and failing miserably.

Too often, however, lonely kids at risk are placed on a long Big Brother or Big Sister waiting list, never to be matched with a mentor. Some public schools are taking up the slack by asking teachers to mentor troubled kids. Caring volunteers electing to spend time each week in this capacity have inspired dramatic improvements in the children's behavior.

Child-care settings, too, are starting mentoring programs. A live-in facility in Nashua, New Hampshire, upon learning that the local Big Brother agency had too many other children to match, managed to find adult mentors for nearly 75 percent of its residents. Staff members conducted the interviews, screening, and reference checks; paid for the criminal records check; made the matches; and provided training as well as ongoing supervision. The center's success in attracting willing mentors was due, in part, to its relaxed visiting schedule: mentors were allowed to visit every other week in lieu of the standard once-a-week commitment. The staff's belief was that securing special relationships for as many kids as possible outweighed the need for more frequent visits. Interestingly, most of the mentors who committed to biweekly visits ended up coming more often.

Many foster parents who are unable to engage the services of Big Brothers or Big Sisters, and even some who do, develop a *network of caring adults* to support them in decreasing problem behaviors at home. Friends, relatives, or neighbors come to watch the kids for an afternoon, or agencies such as Boys and Girls Clubs provide them with more structured activities—all of which give foster parents an opportunity to run errands or simply take a break when they need one.

Some foster parents, by contrast, are reluctant to let others care for their children. "I'm the only adult this kid trusts," they will say. "I could never leave her with someone else." Such a mind-set can lead to unbearable stress, exhaustion, yelling, and overly severe consequences. The reason for the fallout is that being a foster parent to troubled kids is similar to running a marathon: by the time you experience great thirst, you are already dehydrated and in serious trouble. Just as a marathon runner must drink plenty of water *before* the marathon, so must a foster parent avail herself of replenishment *before* the need arises.

If you are a foster parent, do not let yourself reach the point at which you cannot stand another second of child rearing. Why? Because it may be too late. Instead, seek relief each step of the way. Call a friend for encouragement or advice. Visit a neighbor or family member who can validate your feelings of guilt, shame, or isolation—feelings that each of us has at times experienced. Plan a once-a-week dinner with good friends and show up regardless of what is going on at home. Look for support groups through your agency, local schools, or nearby clinics. In short, begin now to develop a support network that can sustain you in times to come. Think prevention!

Volunteers and student interns are also great resources. They are often willing to work with child welfare program administrators, teachers, and foster parents alike. *Volunteers*—available through local newspapers, religious organizations, word of mouth, radio, and television—may include woodworkers, artists, musicians, landscapers, and tutors, as well as other individuals with special talents. For troubled kids, contact of this sort can open doors to creativity and competence. Although it may take "a whole village to raise a child," a few volunteers from the village can make a world of difference.

Student interns are becoming increasingly visible now that more high schools are encouraging, if not requiring, their students to volunteer in the community. Undergraduate and graduate schools, too, are often in need of field placements for their students. Taking on a student intern will necessitate training and supervision—a small time-investment reaping enormous returns.

In addition to securing human resources, it is a good idea to *creatively reutilize* those already on hand. As noted earlier, some public schools solicit teacher volunteers to provide one-on-one attention on a daily or weekly basis to children with learning or emotional difficulties. Others divert funding for teacher aides to a clinical behaviorist who not only works with troubled students but presents training sessions to the teachers, parents, and support staff. Such effective reutilization of on-site human resources can prevent students from slipping through the cracks and teachers from throwing up their hands in despair.

Many child welfare settings are reutilizing their resources as well. Several residential centers for troubled kids are training their support staff—including maintenance workers, secretaries, cooks, and nurses—to take a more active role with the children. Others are teaching their child-care workers to conduct individual and group therapy for the youngsters, thereby freeing up program therapists to work with the families, perform collateral tasks, and in some instances, provide aftercare. Such institutions, spurred on by the current climate of dwindling resources, are reexamining every staff position in an effort to do the best they can with what they've got.

Increasing Physical Resources

Although troubleshooting in the realm of physical resources is often grueling, it can ultimately avert behavioral flare-ups. One way to refill depleted coffers is by *seeking donations and gift certificates,* especially between November 1 and December 25, when people are inclined to help needy children. If you work in residential or foster care, and your facility or home is not in need of toys, you can always ask instead for gift certificates to a local bowling alley, movie theater, or clothing store. A large supply of certificates can be used *year round* to augment an inadequate budget.

Another way to reduce the stress imposed by limited resources is through *fund-raising.* Organizing a fund-raiser can be as simple as sending pledge cards to twenty corporations or making ten solicitation calls.

A third promising way to increase physical resources is by *enlisting help from local businesses.* Bowling alleys, miniature golf courses, martial arts academies, music schools, health clubs, hair salons, fast-food restaurants, outdoor adventure firms, video stores, and wilderness supply shops are often willing to offer services, products, or space at reduced rates, if not free of charge. In addition, some office supply stores offer teachers substantial discounts on classroom supplies.

Because troubled children tend to experience heightened anxiety in anticipation of summer vacation—a long period of unstructured time—a fourth avenue to explore is *implementing summertime activities.* Camps frequently offer discounts or scholarships; low-cost or no-cost structured opportunities may also be available through swimming facilities, country clubs, youth clubs, libraries, activity groups, and municipal parks and recreation departments. An imaginative winter and spring search for enjoyable scheduled activities can lead to less acting out during May and June, and a more delightful summer for everyone.

Relief is also available by *creating transportation options.* Troubled children often lose their desire to go places when they have no way of getting there. To overcome such deficits, make sure the kids you care for know how to use public transportation; let them earn bus passes (or have the passes donated); buy used bicycles at garage sales; form carpools; or seek out volunteers to provide rides at prearranged times of the week.

Agencies that work with families having limited access to transportation can consider providing them with rides, bus schedules, or gas money. Such efforts are often rewarded by improved relationships with the families and more optimally functioning children.

Tony Brown, a distinguished African American author and advocate for minority families, once said on his television show, *Tony Brown's Journal,* that every family, rich or poor, should have a computer at home, and that poverty should never be used as an excuse not to have one. "Find a way," he urged his viewers, convinced that a personal computer could help young children learn and thereby give them a more advantageous start in school. In addition to computers, children need books, bicycles, book bags, school supplies, recreational items, as well as many other physical resources, and our job as caregivers is to "find a way" to ensure that they have them.

Preparing for Change

Troubleshooting also requires us to devise strategies for difficulties that might arise in the wake of change. Altering life-as-we-know-it can be extremely unsettling, not only to kids but also to adults.

For adults, changes often result in narcissistic injury. "Wasn't I doing things right before?" they may wonder, or "Are you saying the old way wasn't good enough?" Those of us seeking to help troubled children need to take our egos off the line—a feat best accomplished by acknowledging change as a recurring part of life.

For the children, changes may be more threatening. Kids who frequently misbehave have become accustomed to this style of relating. In a sense, they have come to rely on it; convinced that they are bad kids, they interpret the angry responses they evoke from adults as confirmation of their negative self-image. When we install preventive measures against acting-out behaviors, these children are apt to find themselves in unfamiliar territory and, in response, to put up fierce resistance.

The monologue running through eleven-year-old Andrew's head two weeks after Mr. Johnson, his unit director, created a new behavior modification chart and taught him a series of self-management techniques probably went something like this: "Hey, it feels pretty good getting along with people. I like what they're saying about me.

Mr. Johnson has really gone out of his way to help me. But . . . this isn't going to last. Adults are always turning on me. At some point, they're going to abandon the chart and start getting on my case again. Why don't I get the waiting over with and act out—go back to how things were."

By the third week, Andrew was growing increasingly anxious, perhaps thinking: "It feels weird being polite and getting all this positive attention. I'm not used to this. Plus, they're expecting more from me now! And wait till they see the real me. No, this dude was more comfortable before . . . Hey, Mr. Johnson, you're a jerk!" Andrew subsequently reverted to some of his earlier behaviors for a while, but finding that Mr. Johnson was not one to wilt under pressure, he soon stopped fighting the changes in his environment and accepted a more positive self-image.

One good way to stay the course through periods of sustained change is to think two to three months into the future. Tell yourself: "I can take all the acting out this child may throw at me for the next two and a half months. It will be worth it if in ten weeks he is functioning far better, with relatively few relapses." In other words, pump yourself up by looking down the road.

Moving down that road is generally a "two steps forward, one step back" journey, as illustrated in figure 7–3. In fact, rarely does a child change for the better without some *positive regression*—designed to "test" whether the adults in charge will stay with the new plan or

Figure 7–3

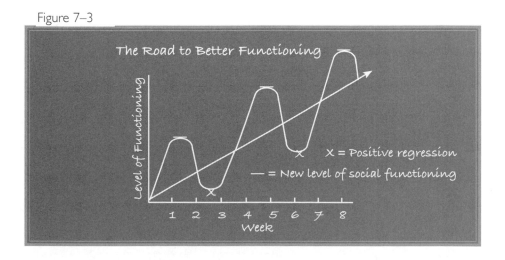

return to their old, less therapeutic ways of relating.

To sustain long-term behavioral gains during positive regressions, we need to resist the temptation to overreact or vent our disappointment. In other words, you would not want to say, "Bobby, you were doing so well. Why are you misbehaving again? I thought you learned to stop acting that way!" or "This new program isn't working anymore. The kids are worse than before!" Instead, it is far better to anticipate positive regressions and know that with your ongoing support the children will eventually get back on the track to improved functioning.

Such a mind-set, however, is not always easy to maintain. In a coed juvenile detention center that had recently instituted new rules pertaining to violence and aggression, male-female relationships, and the earning of privileges, we encountered a momentary calm followed by serious acting out requiring the need for a number of physical restraints. When on several occasions the residents were close to rioting, I began to wonder if we would ever improve the functioning of the unit. Yet throughout the tumult, the direct-care workers did not overreact to the positive regressions by abandoning or sabotaging the new approaches; and as a result, we did indeed create real, sustainable change. That, for me, reaffirmed lesson number one in how to become a successful agent of change: *If you truly believe there is no such thing as a bad kid, and if you appreciate how people react to change, then you do what it takes to hang in there, aware that resistance is a normal part of the change process.*

Lesson number two came while reading Robert Crichton's *The Great Imposter*, a true-to-life biographical account of Frederick Demara.[1] A genius who roamed the world taking on other people's identities, Demara went from forging the credentials of a prison administrator and subsequently reforming a southern penitentiary to posing as a navy doctor during the Korean war and performing surgery on several Koreans, saving their lives. The mind-set he adopted upon entering each situation in which he had had no prior experience was this: he would walk in with a supreme sense of initiative and purpose. This man who seemed to will himself into pulling off miracles inspired people to believe in him by exuding confidence and hope *no matter how insecure he felt.*

That is the attitude I strive for in my work with severely troubled children. When I hear that there is a crisis in the recreation room and that staff members need help, I sprint over as fast as I can, but just before reaching the room, I take a deep breath, slow my pace, and enter with a nonchalant, relaxed air, as if to say, "I'm not worried. I'm in control, so don't panic. Things will be okay!"

Whether beset by a momentary crisis or a program in dire need of restructuring, you, too, can be an agent of change. The secret is to adopt a positive, upbeat attitude; radiate confidence; and smile a lot despite the apprehension you may feel inside. In other words, be an actor—don't let them see you sweat! And remember, you get better with practice and success, no matter how small or fleeting it may at first appear.

CHAPTER **8**

THE POWER OF HUMOR

HUMOR—A LONG-OVERLOOKED COMPONENT OF CHILD CARE—NEEDS to be taken more seriously. Troubled kids want to laugh, and adults who care for them are often delighted when they do. Indeed, studies of endorphins suggest that suffering subsides with laughter, and with the suffering, the inclination to act out. "But I'm not funny," many teachers and caregivers protest upon first learning of the healing power of humor. The truth is that *anyone* can be funny. Although some people are inherently sillier than others, many forms of humor do not require a predisposition toward the lighter side. For instance, you do not have to be a bona fide comedian to read puns from a joke book after the noonday meal. Try it once and not only will you have the kids in stitches but, as they warm up to you, your not-so-funny self-image will wither. The point is that whether you are funny by nature or by intent, you can help children laugh themselves out of chronic misbehavior.

The Preventive Action of Mirth

In the all-too-sobering business of child welfare, lightheartedness plays a unique de-escalating role. Among its many special behind-the-scenes effects, humor does the following:

- **Sheds light on darkened landscapes**

  "I thought you were gonna yell at me like everyone else. But you made me laugh," Jody said six months after I restrained her, as described in chapter 2. For her, one moment of playfulness illuminated months, perhaps years, of living.

  Kids like Jody lead hard, foreboding lives. Over the next hill they see no lush green valley, but rather a desolate and treacherous terrain. Humor, to them, is like sunshine, radiating warmth and vitality, hope for the future, and endearing links with others. In short, the energizing and uplifting power of humor's light will brighten a darkened soul.

  We who deal with children at risk are grappling not so much with troubling behaviors as with overcast minds. Because this is so, our task is to shed lots of sunshine.

- **Memorializes acts of love**

  Ask me to recall my teenage years and I think of my cousin Jon. Five of us were playing poker one afternoon before heading over to the local ice cream parlor, where Jon ordered a thick chocolate milkshake—so thick that he kept tilting the glass for a sip until its entire contents splashed onto his face! We all laughed uncontrollably, and I will never forget the spectacle of his eyelids, nose, and chin engulfed in chocolate. Every time I reflect on this uproarious image now frozen in time, I remember the many crazy things we did and the intoxicating camaraderie we felt as we made our way through adolescence. This milkshake incident is far more than a memory; it forms the gateway to a *reservoir* of meaningful moments that buoy me through tough times.

  Troubled children, however, have few such gateways and, worse yet, reservoirs devoid of fun memories. Kids returning to visit a residential center that once served as their home often like to reminisce with a staff member. "Remember the time you restrained me on the playground?" they will ask, or "Remember when I broke the chapel window?" Disgrace and defiance often color the memories they carry.

  When we make it our mission to fill the children's memory

banks with laughter rather than humiliation, we offer a *pleasantly* enduring gift: kindling for years of smiles and for a lifetime of recapturing that feeling of love. At the same time, we convey the message that we want to please the children, that we like them, that we want them to feel good—so much so that we are willing to look foolish in front of them—all of which help restore their faith in adults as well as themselves. Love fortified by such faith is the best deterrent there is to misbehavior.

- **Engages resistant children**
  Every Wednesday, Derek and Jane conducted group therapy for eight teenagers who had been before Boston's juvenile courts. Midway through the year, fourteen-year-old Wesley was ordered to join the group. Week after week, despite all attempts to help him open up, Wesley sat there in stone silence. Not until he entered the clinic for his seventh session did he speak up, asking, "What are those metal gates for on top of the building?"

  Derek, having no idea why the gray, fifteen-story stone building that housed the clinic bore metal gates on its roof, was not about to pass up an opportunity for fun. He responded, "That's where we lock up kids who don't talk during group therapy."

  Although Jane turned white and nearly choked on the pretzel she was eating, Derek smiled. Then Wesley grinned. Engaged at last, he became an active participant in the group.

- **Demystifies the power of authority figures**
  Because of their difficult histories, many troubled children are wary of authority figures. A good chuckle, however, can clear the air of past associations and create a more balanced setting by suggesting, "It's not me against you; it's *us together.*"

  Upon meeting a new group of children, barriers will crumble if you begin on a positive, humorous note. Icebreakers such as jokes and magic tricks are likely to help kids see you as a caring adult rather than a commander in chief. Remember, initial impressions set the tone for future communications.

- **Enhances relationship building**

  My eighth grade math teacher, Mr. Burns, was the classiest person
  I had ever met. Dressed impeccably in a three-piece suit, he spoke
  perfect English with a slight British accent, had a dry wit, and frequently replied in axioms, such as A rolling stone gathers no moss,
  A penny saved is a penny earned, and A stitch in time saves nine.
  When he asked me for the answer to a trick question one Friday
  afternoon, I fell for the bait—hook, line, and sinker, as he would
  have said. Mr. Burns smiled, looked me right in the eyes, and
  declared, "Mr. Appelstein, there is a sucker born every minute."

  I stared back at him and replied, as if on cue, "Mr. Burns, it
  takes one to know one." The class erupted in laughter, then fell
  into a quiet hush, wondering how he would respond.

  He turned and solemnly strode to the front of the room,
  where he picked up a piece of chalk and etched a small vertical
  line on the upper right corner of the blackboard. "That is one
  for you, Mr. Appelstein," he said in proper English.

  It was a moment I will never forget. Although Mr. Burns
  did not spend extra time with me, the humor ingrained in his
  teaching inspired me to make it through math and to deepen my
  relationship with him.

- **Reduces tension**

  In a troubled-child–oriented milieu, tension often permeates the
  atmosphere. A teacher addressing a restless class experiences it.
  A foster parent confronting his potential runaway teen feels it. A
  residential counselor trying to maintain composure as her group
  escalates out of control could write a book about it.

  Amid mounting tension, adrenaline starts to flow and we
  can soar to the top of our game. When our actions do *not* reflect
  our best efforts, however, it is often time to turn to levity. The
  following three approaches can be used to evoke chuckles and
  diffuse the stress.

  "Mission accomplished." When a group or a child's behavior
  disturbs you, one good retort is: "You seem to be trying very
  hard to upset me. And do you know what? You're doing a
  fabulous (said humorously) job. I *am* upset." Use of this tension

reducer can model good affect control while giving you a few seconds to regain composure before addressing the issue.

"You're my bodyguards." When two children are squabbling and you are unable to help them resolve the conflict, consider inviting them to be your bodyguards. This approach can serve as a promising alternative to the "divide and conquer" option of separating them, especially if you have a good relationship with each child.

Imagine that Ellie and Judy are not getting along and have been unable to resolve their differences. You can bring them together and say something like this: "Okay, Ellie, I know you and Judy have refused to make up. I also know you have hated Judy all your life. You even hate the name Judy. In fact, you hate words that start with the letter *J*. When we go outside, we ask you to play on the 'ungle gym' so you won't get mad. And Judy, I know you've hated Ellie all your life. Every time it rains, you blame her for the downpour. Each time you break a fingernail, it's Ellie's fault!"

At this point, Ellie and Judy may burst out laughing and willingly resolve their conflict. If tensions persist, however, it is a good idea to inform them that they will both need to be by your side like bodyguards until they work through the problems. It is best to utilize this technique only when you sense that a quarrel is due to a minor misunderstanding and that intervening in this way is not likely to exacerbate the situation.

Mirroring the mimic. Luther, a bright, angry thirteen year old, lived at a residential center. One afternoon, Luther was in a particularly foul mood as he, five other kids, and I were in the unit's large living room. All my attempts to get him out of his funk had failed, so when he spoke disrespectfully to another kid, I asked Luther to please take a five-minute time-out.

"I didn't *do* anything!" he quipped.

"I know you're upset. Please take the time-out, and after that we'll talk," I replied.

"Go to hell," Luther shot back.

"If you don't start the time-out within a minute or so, you'll need to take a ten-minute time-out," I politely informed him.

Luther's defiance continued to escalate, whereupon he

received a ten-minute time-out, refused to take it, and was asked to cool off in the hallway. I followed him out of the room.

Standing ten feet away from Luther, I could feel his rage. He began pacing back and forth, and cursing under his breath. To break the tension, and simultaneously appear calm and collected, I called out to three kids playing at the far end of the hallway, "John, Chuck, and Joey, you've got twenty minutes before we go outside."

Luther snidely mimicked me, calling out, "John, Chuckie, and Joey, you've got twenty minutes before we go outside."

I ignored his remark and a few minutes later tried another diversionary ploy: "Hey, Ethan, make sure to pick up your Matchbox cars before dinner. You can't leave them out like that."

Again Luther echoed my words.

He was starting to get under my skin. My observing ego kicked into overdrive, and I began coaching myself to stay calm. Desperately attempting a third maneuver, I called out, "You guys in the bathroom, you need to be out of there soon," well aware that no one was in the bathroom.

Luther repeated the sentence before the last word had left my mouth.

I was approaching the end of my rope and knew I had to try something new. Although looking eye-to-eye with a kid who is escalating his rebellion is usually not a good practice, it was time for action. I turned, took a step toward Luther, then looking him straight in the eyes, said, "Okay, I'm ready to do my time now."

Without blinking, Luther shot back, "Okay, I'm ready to do my time now."

A slight grin eased onto my face. "Well, go ahead," I replied. Luther stood silent, pondering the volley that had just taken place. He then shuffled into the living room for his time-out.

As I walked past him, we smiled at each other. Drawing an imaginary vertical line in the air, similar to Mr. Burns's etching on the blackboard twenty years earlier, I remarked, "One for me." From then on, Luther and I enjoyed a special relationship.

- **Fosters identity formation**

Kids who exhibit chronic behavior problems often struggle with identity issues. "Who am I?" they wonder. "Am I good or bad?" Funny times can help them improve their grasp of who they are and, better yet, what they can become.

Will and Artie Bender were brothers, though you would not know it by looking at them: eight-year-old Will wanted nothing to do with five-year-old Artie. They had been brought to the residential center after being abandoned in an automobile and left to eat out of trash bins. Although Will had done his best to take care of Artie, the burden of caregiving had taken its toll. By the time he arrived at the center, Will was filled with rage—at Artie and at the world. Artie, too, was angry; moreover, he was deeply hurt by Will's rejection of him.

The staff went to work restoring the brothers' relationship by administering large doses of physical nurturing, which the boys craved. Hugs soon turned to wrestling matches. Stan, the unit director, let them win each match with him, and then one day he had a brainstorm: he would agree to tangle with Will only if Artie was around, and this time he would *not* let him win. When Will and Stan began their next bout, Stan took the lead; you could see the frustration on Will's face. After a few minutes, Stan said, "It's a good thing your brother isn't helping you. I wouldn't want to take on the *two* of you!"

As if on cue, Artie jumped in, whereupon Stan yelled, "Oh no, it's the Bender brothers. Put 'em together and you have Bender power!"

"Bender power!" they cried out with each new maneuver. Delighted that they had joined forces, Stan let them destroy him.

In time, Will and Artie moved into the same bedroom. A month later Will, who had previously referred to Artie by name, was calling him "my brother." Having reclaimed their identity as siblings, the two deepened their relationship and two years later found a home together with a warm, caring adoptive family.

Six Rules for Using Humor

Listed below are six cardinal rules for achieving comic relief. If observed, these principles are guaranteed to make humor an indispensable tool in your work with troubled children.

1. Be willing to give up quickly.
Any time a child does not respond positively to an attempt at humor, it is wise to abandon the approach. Prolonging the intervention may only convince the child that you are making fun of her, or that you are not taking the situation seriously. As you get to know the kids in your care, you will learn who responds well to levity, who does not, and who can be gently nudged into a chuckle.

2. Avoid the use of sarcasm and nicknames.
Sarcasm, no matter how funny it may seem, masks feelings of hostility and is perceived for what it is—namely, a put-down. Most troubled children have experienced copious amounts of humiliation in their lives, and another pernicious blow to their self-esteem does nothing more than reaffirm an already poor self-image.

Nicknames, too, are belittling. Scott, a fifteen-year-old detention center resident with severe cognitive and emotional impairments, picked up the nickname of Dog. Almost all the residents and staff members called him by this name, unaware that he consequently saw himself as having animal-like impulses, further devaluing his sense of self-worth. Only after his nickname was dropped did Scott begin to feel better about himself. The moral of this true story is that humor should be administered at your own expense, not anyone else's—and certainly not a child's.

3. Let familiarity be your guide.
Before using humor in situations involving heightened tension, it is best to establish a trusting relationship with the youngsters. Why? Because troubled children need to see that the adults in their lives can be counted on. Once the kids are confident that you care for them and will not intentionally hurt them, it is safe to begin clowning around.

4. Integrate caprice into everyday interactions.

There is no need to reserve silliness for special occasions. On the contrary, it is wise to let laughter join hands with discipline. A light touch at the end of a discordant day is sometimes a powerful teaching tool.

5. Be versatile.

The humor that works today is not likely to have the same impact tomorrow. To activate the magnetism of infectious laughter, seek counsel with your intuition.

6. Avoid worrying about overstimulation.

A popular decree in the child welfare arena is, "Don't get the kids going! If you do, they'll be giddy and disruptive." While humor *can* cause children to break out of patterns of obedience, our task is not to ensure compliance but rather to build character. The secret to generating jovial moments is to develop skills that will assist the children in regaining control. In other words, instead of fretting about the possibility of overstimulation, *give structure to the chaos.*

Moments of silliness can be structured in any number of ways. One is to plan ahead for a wind-down period. Build in time for soothing showers, for example, or for lowering your voice and dimming the lights before proceeding to the next activity. A second method is to set limits in advance, letting the kids know what will happen if they go "too far." A third means of reining in the chaos is to let the kids know that funny times will come again—and again—provided that they are capable of settling down afterward. Structure transforms the stimulation of humor into a lesson in self-discipline.

Developing a Repertoire of Humor

To create a jovial atmosphere at the drop of a hat, it is best to have a bag of potent tricks at your disposal. Toss into this bag forms of silliness ranging from a revered pun to unexpected or incongruous attire—anything that is likely to extract an infectious giggle. The path of humor offers limitless possibilities, such as the following staples, all of which can be modified to suit any age group or setting.

Jokes and Riddles

Kids love jokes and riddles. You need not come up with new material all the time; instead, memorize a few one-liners and spout them out as the need arises. Or write them on numbered slips of paper, and give one or two to each child in your group. Have the children clap five times, then ask the child holding joke number one to stand and read it aloud. When he is finished, have the kids clap five times before requesting joke number two, and so on. You can also buy a few corny joke-books and let the children take turns reading the entries out loud.

Joan Embry, a fourth grade teacher, was sure she had been born without a funny bone. Then Alex, an extremely challenging student, joined her class, and she knew it was time to lighten up. At the beginning of his second day of class, she marched up to his desk and asked him to say the word *stock* five times fast.

He looked confused, then said, "Stock, stock, stock, stock, stock."

Joan immediately asked him, "What do you do at a green light?"

"Stop," Alex replied.

"So, Alex, you stop at green lights. That's a funny way to drive!" Everyone laughed, including Alex.

Slapstick and Physical Humor

Farce and horseplay can be downright hysterical. Following are three motifs that are sure to arouse ripples of laughter.

Costumes and Sight Gags. A goofy costume can set a happy tone for the day. If you are a teacher, consider dressing in period garb to illustrate a history lesson. Or just for fun, don an outlandish hat, a strange tie, or a plastic nose and black glasses. Young kids, especially, love to wear costumes and will be thrilled to see that you do, too.

Water or Shaving Cream Fights. Indoors or out, water fights can provide hours of joyous abandon, provided that they are governed by ground rules, such as "Aim only for grown-ups" and "Steer clear of electronic equipment." Shaving cream requires a bit more cleanup, but is well worth the effort.

Props and Gizmos. Wind-up toys extract instant chuckles. Sending a plastic squirrel across the table during a serious talk with a child is apt to immediately eradicate gloom. Card and magic tricks, available at most toy stores, also add a frivolous touch, as do plastic eyeglasses with motorized windshield wipers.

Amusing Games

The more innovative a game is, the more likely it is to captivate a tough group of children. For unequivocal enticement, try embellishing on an old favorite or, calling upon the kids' powers of observation, inventing a new one.

Bonkers Bingo. This game lends itself to at least three different renditions. One, Ognib—Bingo spelled backward—is a perfect option for kids with poor self-esteem who moan, "I never win" every time one of their peers yells, "Bingo!" In Ognib, the children each play with only one card, which they turn over once it is filled; the winner is the last child to do so. For added amusement the contestants, while turning over their cards, can moan, "I've got Bingo."

A second variation entails the ringing of a bell midway through the game to signal "ESP time," an interlude in which each child tries to guess the next number to be called. Those who guess correctly win a prize. In a third variation of Bonkers Bingo, designed especially to hold the attention of children who are easily distracted, the caller announces the numbers in a variety of tones and inflections.

To further assist kids who hate to lose, you could reward more than one winner. Tell the kids, for example, "Whoever gets up-and-down Bingo wins a prize, and so does the the kid to the left of him."

Simon Says . . . with a twist. Simon Says can be as zany as you wish, and the more descriptive you can be, the more laughter you will evoke. You could announce, "Simon says to walk like the Hunchback of Notre Dame," for instance, or "Simon says to jump like Michael Jordan," or perhaps, "Simon says to jump like Michael Jordan and hang in the air . . . Okay, come on down . . . Hey, Simon didn't say to come down!" Getting rid of Simon is another possibility, as in "Shaq says, 'Walk big like me.'"

Personalized Mad Libs. Prewritten silly stories known as Mad Libs, which allow participants to fill in the blanks, can be purchased at most gift shops. Many troubled children, however, quickly lose interest in prefabricated stories and prefer to contribute to more customized tales that ask for their own names as well as those of familiar adults, thereby enhancing their sense of togetherness. If you are a teacher, you could design Mad Libs related to class material. If you are a foster parent or youth worker, you may want to create a crazy Mad Libs adventure in which you all band together to save the day (see figure 8–1). Whatever you decide on, be sure to include a blank for the name of every child in your group, place the adults in hilarious self-deprecating situations, and be prepared to make a copy of the completed story for each of the participants.

Figure 8–1

An Invented Mad Lib

The (adjective) _____ Trip to Yankee Stadium

(Adjective) _____ (name of adult) _____ decided to take six kids to a New York Yankees baseball game. Before going, the kids made (adjective) _____ (deli meat) _____ sandwiches on slices of (number) _____ -day-old bread. (Name of kid) _____ wanted (condiment) _____ and fried (insect, plural) _____ on her/his sandwich, even though the (same insect, plural) _____ sometimes got caught between her/his teeth! (Name of kid) _____ liked her/his sandwich with a touch of (liquid) _____ . (Name of same adult) _____ rented a (adjective) _____ (color) _____ (unusual mode of transportation) _____ to get the children to the game. (Name of kid) _____ wanted to drive, but (name of same adult) _____ reminded her/him that she/he only had a license to drive (adjective) _____ (color) _____ (same mode of transportation, plural) _____ .

On the way to the game, a (adjective) _____ (noun) _____ -shaped object suddenly dropped from the sky and landed in front of the group. "It's a UFO!" cried (name of kid) _____ . Instantly, a door opened and (number between 5 and 50) _____ (adjective) _____ (color) _____ aliens emerged from the ship. Incredibly, they all looked like (funny cartoon character) _____.

(Name of kid) _____ called to them, "Aliens who look like (same cartoon character) _____, do you come in peace?"

"We come to see Yankee game. Where is Yankee game?"

"Follow us," yelled (name of kid) _____.

Together, the aliens and the kids from (foster home address or name of facility) _____ saw a great game. The aliens caught all the foul balls with their (adjective) _____ (noun, plural) _____ and they gave the balls to the kids in return for a bite of (first kid's name, possessive) _____ sandwich.

Aliens, it turns out, love fried _____ (previous insect, plural)!

The Memory Game. This comical game will delight kids between the ages of five and thirteen. The instructions are as follows: One child sits comfortably in a chair without moving while another child is asked to study him and, after a few minutes, leave the room. The seated child then changes five aspects of his appearance; he may decide, among other things, to untuck his shirt, switch his left and right shoes, untie one shoe or both, roll up one sleeve, cross his legs, comb his hair in the opposite direction, take off or put on glasses, or take off or put on a watch. The child who has left the room then returns and tries to guess the five changes.

When playing the memory game, have the children take turns as changers and guessers. Be sure that *you* rotate in as well.

Loony Tunes

The universal language of music is an unsurpassed medium for self-expression. Indeed, an amazing mood shift can take place when troubled children gather together with simple "instruments" and a shared desire to "ham it up." Following are only a couple of euphonious possibilities.

Kazoo Time. Start your own kazoo band. One fourth grade class in New England boasts a five-member kazoo band that plays in talent shows and for birthday celebrations, dressing up and entering the room with their kazoos packed in violin or guitar cases. For effect, the band leader will announce a guest soloist, who generally steps forward and plays one note—usually, the last one of a song.

A Pots 'n' Pans Rhythm Band. If your pots and pans hang from Peg-board hooks, you are probably aware that each of the vessels has a distinct sound when drummed with a large utensil, such as a wooden spoon. These "metal drums," together with two large pot covers for cymbals, and barrel-shaped or tapered pots for bongos and congas, add up to a rib-tickling ensemble. Show tunes such as the theme songs from *Hello Dolly* and *Mame* are highly conducive to pots 'n' pans band jamming.

Whimsical Poems

When writing poems to kids, a little self-disparagement will add a pleasing touch. More importantly, be sure to end with a line of appreciation. When it comes to children at risk, gratitude cannot be expressed often enough.

Howard, a therapist assigned to a unit at a large residential center, never missed a child's birthday dinner. After the meal, he would read a funny poem he had written in the child's honor. The kids could not wait for him to start reading. Perhaps what they enjoyed more than anything else was the fact that he had taken time to do something special for them. See figure 8–2 for a birthday poem he wrote for thirteen-year-old Mike, a resident known for his unkempt room and remarkable artwork.

Grandiose Praise

When challenging kids do something noteworthy, the door separating them from the world begins to open. If we stick a foot in that opening, the door is less likely to slam shut. A cosmic tickle that holds open such doors, indelibly imprinting a moment of victory on the child's mind, is exaggerated praise. Following are some examples:

"Sarah, that is a *wonderful* picture! I'm calling the art muse-

Figure 8–2

Mike's Birthday Poem

Today you hear my poem, and it will be very good.
Tomorrow we will eat pizza—and watch *Robin Hood*.
On Sunday you will definitely need time to rest
But the staff won't let you . . .
'Cause your room will be messed!

Face it, Mike, you and I aren't very neat
But at least we're both handsome and sweet.
And we both love spicy chicken wings, and we're both incredibly smart
And we both love stoppin' at Dunkin Donuts
After Art!

Hey, all kidding aside, I think of you with
Tremendous pride!
You're bright, strong, and witty—
And if we eat too much pizza
It won't be a pity!

Happy Birthday

um right away and that painting's going in. Picasso, Rembrandt, Sarah—the names fit together like salt and pepper!"

"Ezra, I really like the way you solved that problem. Are you trying to take over my job? Aren't you satisfied with being a kid for a few more years?"

"Sam, you got a 90 on the math quiz. I've got to scream that out the window. [*Opening the window and yelling*] *Sam got a 90 on his math quiz!*"

"This is a great class. I'd like to thank you all for being such outstanding students!" Then, pointing at the kids one by one, "Thank you, thank you, thank you . . ."

Frivolous Standbys

Any collection of humor is incomplete without a few reliable narratives. Here are two all-time favorites to hold at the tip of your tongue for use in emergency situations.

The Escaping Smile. When your intuition gives you the go-ahead, try to elicit an escaping smile. In many circumstances, this intervention is a reliable way to turn a solemn face into a cheerful one.

Twelve-year-old Abby was looking dejected and refused to talk. Larry, her foster father, said: "It's in there, I can see it. There's a smile at the bottom of your throat and it's trying to get out! Ah, it's climbing up your windpipe, slowly but surely making its way to the top. Oh, it's jumped onto your tonsils and has begun swinging back and forth. Now I can see it better—it's a *big* smile. Hey, it just flew onto the back of your tongue; do you feel a little tickle there? Whatever you do, don't swallow or burp. Good, 'cause now it's taking out a hammer and chisel, and chipping away at your front teeth. Yes, it's come through your teeth and is pushing against your lips; they're starting to quiver. You can't hold it back any longer. It's coming. *There it is.* What a smile!"

The Gorilla Story. This tale can be told in five to twenty-five minutes, depending on the needs of the situation and your willingness to embellish on the basic premise. The premise is as follows:

A downtrodden janitor, after spending his last dollar on a lottery ticket, wins the largest payoff in lottery history. With his winnings he buys a gigantic mansion. After living there a few days, he realizes he needs a maid, but every housekeeping agency he visits has booked all its service personnel. Calling on the last agency in town, the man pleads with the owner to send him some help. Although this agency, too, is fully booked, the owner reluctantly offers him an "experimental" maid—who turns out to be an 800-pound gorilla!

Upon seeing a demonstration of the gorilla's extraordinary cleaning skills, the man agrees to engage its services, whereupon the owner sternly cautions him not to touch the gorilla. The man, promising to heed this advice, takes the gorilla home and assigns it thousands of difficult cleaning tasks around the mansion.

After three months the man, who can no longer resist touching his new maid, taps the giant creature on the shoulder. The gorilla immediately goes berserk and begins chasing the man—by skateboard, sports car, and private jet—at last trapping him in a cave at the Grand Canyon. Unable to escape, the man crouches against the wall of the cave and stares at the creature's silhouette as it passes back and forth beyond the entrance. From the dark interior of the cave, the gorilla appears to weigh 1,600 pounds! Terrified, the man's heart begins beating out of control.

As if this weren't bad enough, the gorilla slowly advances toward him, its mouth and huge protruding fangs dripping saliva, and its powerful forearms raised in the air. Paralyzed by fear, the man can only watch as the gorilla's huge forearms extend even further, then swing violently downward to crush the man's scalp. Within one-half inch of his head, the hands freeze. The gorilla smiles, gently pats the man's head, and says, "Tag—you're it."

PART III

RESPONDING TO CHALLENGING BEHAVIOR

CHAPTER **9**

THE ESSENCE OF COMMUNICATION

UNDERSTANDING AND PREVENTING CHALLENGING BEHAVIOR ARE STEPS one and two in working effectively with troubled children; the third step is *responding* to the behavior. The most successful responses arise from adults who, consciously or unconsciously, inspire change through their interactions with the children.

To consciously promote healthier behavior in the children entrusted to our care, we need to pay close attention to our patterns of communication—not only our verbalized messages but the many subtleties that underlie them. *What* we say is certainly important; but *when* and *how* we say it often determines whether or not it will make a positive difference. Coloring our every interaction, in other words, are cues that either strengthen or dilute the impact of our words. These are the factors that form the essence of our communication with troubled children.

Our most helpful responses are those accompanied by an affect, tone, word choice, and body language that are respectful of a child's *emotional needs* and *sense of dignity*. All four of these communication dynamics are within our realm of control and are compelling influences regardless of the child's age, history, biological makeup, and temperament.

Affect

The responses most likely to inspire at-risk children to alter their trouble-some behaviors are those delivered with an affect, or emotional expression, that meets their needs for safety, support, control, and respect. Naturally, the affect displayed will vary depending on circumstances. For instance, when a child begins to lose control, the adults in charge must demonstrate that they are in control and able to maintain an atmosphere of safety. The guiding principle at such times is to establish an *inverse relationship* between the child's level of agitation and our own expressiveness. Simply put, *the louder and more out of control a child appears, the quieter and more controlled we need to be.*

Figure 9–1

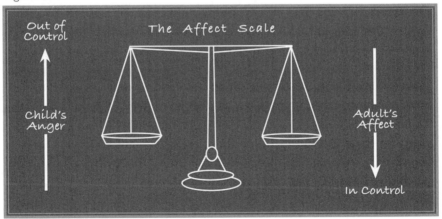

The Affect Scale

A good way to gauge the affect most appropriate to a volatile situation is to imagine an affect scale similar to the one shown in figure 9–1. Here, as a child "loses her cool" and the left side of the scale rises, the adult must respond by becoming that much more subdued, proportionately muting his affect. In other words, the degree to which the child is out of control determines the degree to which the adult must show that he is *in* control, as illustrated in figure 9–2. As one of my supervisors used to say, "The professionals most respected in child-care settings are those who don't yell at the kids but rather stay *calm* in the face of emotional outbursts."

If both sides of the scale go up—that is, if both child and adult lose control of their emotions—communication becomes seriously threatened, and the child, hypersensitive to misuses of power, will invariably strike back in anger, if not fear. An unfortunate predicament of this sort unfolded for George during an afternoon gym trip at a residential center where he had recently started out as a new child-care worker. After he had taken three kids to shoot hoops with him in the gym, one of the boys, ten-year-old Luke, immediately ran to retrieve a ball at the far end of the room. When George ordered him to come back and sit in the bleachers, Luke ignored the request and picked up the loose ball. George marched over and commanded him to drop the ball and sit on the bleachers, but Luke refused.

Figure 9–2

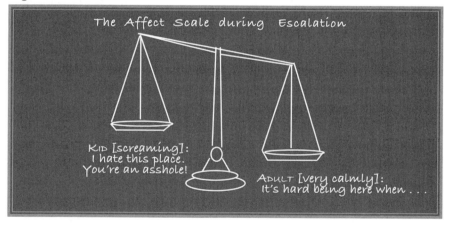

"Take a five-minute time-out for not listening to me," George yelled.

"Fuck you!" Luke shouted.

"Now you've got ten minutes!" George shot back.

"Fuck you!"

"Fifteen minutes."

The verbal volley continued until Dave, a more experienced staff worker, intervened; at this point, Luke was on the verge of violence, the time-out was approaching forty minutes, both sides of the affect scale were rising dangerously, and the balance beam across the top was about to break! Dave quietly reminded George that time-outs were usually capped at ten minutes, whereupon George sighed, realizing that he had been as out of control as Luke.

Considerable self-discipline is required to stay calm and suppress the impulse to yell at or speak negatively to a child whose behavior is growing more extreme. Suppressing these natural impulses, as discussed in chapter 2, is not as difficult as it may at first appear. The calm demeanor you are seeking to maintain comes not by bottling up your feelings, but rather by appreciating the needs of the child and by practicing *patience,* knowing that your emotions can be expressed at a later, more appropriate time.

The Level Zone

When the beam across the top of the affect scale is relatively balanced, both you and the child are in the *level zone,* where troubled children are apt to be receptive to emotional give-and-take. Now the time is ripe for revealing your feelings by saying, for example, "Jeb, you're starting to get me angry. What can we do to make this a better day?" or "Sarah, I'm upset with how you're acting. We need to talk about your behavior."

As the beam tilts, this window of opportunity slowly closes. In the following dialogue between nine-year-old Carl and his teacher, Carl's opening statement suggests that he has exited the level zone and that any affect-laden response is likely to provoke more anger, which is exactly what happens.

CARL: I really hate this class. *You never help me!*

TEACHER [*animatedly*]: Carl, it upsets me when you say that. I do spend a lot of time with you.

CARL [*more angrily*]: I don't care if you're upset. You're a jerk like all the rest!

Expressing emotions to a highly agitated child like Carl is apt to cause him to feel worse and to retaliate, because he is most likely in a self-protective mode thinking only about his *own* needs and feelings. Later—after he has calmed down and the balance beam has leveled off—you can express your feelings and work through the incident together.

Always keep an image of the affect scale in the back of your mind. You may well find it to be among your most effective tools in your work with troubled children.

Tone

Even when a statement is expressed with little affect, emotionally fragile children can infer a negative message. Why? Because many such kids who are accustomed to having power and control used against them are prewired to pick up on disempowering messages. While talking to troubled kids, it is therefore critically important to monitor your tone of voice.

Monitoring is essential because your intonation converts the *content* of your statements into *messages* they convey, based on how they are perceived. Whereas the statement "The house is pink" informs the listener about the color of the house, accentuating the word *pink,* as in "The house is *pink,*" relays the message "Why on earth did you paint the house *pink?*" And whereas "You look *great* today!" promotes good feelings in the listener, "You look great . . . *today!*" does not.

Said angrily to a child at risk, a seemingly nonthreatening statement like "You need to knock it off" may be interpreted as ominous. She may conclude that the speaker is angry and does not like her anymore, will not want to hear her side of the story, is verbally attacking her, and is treating her like all adults do. Her natural reaction will most likely be to argue, refuse to accept responsibility for the problem, and fight back.

A nonsupportive tone of voice can lead to any number of problematic reactions. Imagine that you are a teacher and that Eli, one of your most challenging students, has just destroyed his math book in class. The *message* he receives will depend on the tone in which the *content* is expressed, as illustrated in the following scenarios.

Scenario #1: "I am really upset with you, Eli!" delivered in an angry tone of voice.

Possible messages—The teacher is angry and I'm in big trouble. This stinks. Who the hell is she? What's going to happen next? Angry messages often evoke angry reactions, especially if your anger is intended to intimidate. Children who hold in their resulting anger are likely to release it in a later, perhaps unrelated context.

Scenario #2: "Iamreallyupsetwithyou, Eli!" delivered in a rushed, almost hysterical tone.

> *Possible messages*—The teacher is very angry and doesn't seem to be in control of her emotions. This is scary. I hope nothing worse happens.

Blurting out irate remarks can shake a child's confidence in your ability to manage him. This loss of confidence can provoke an angry reaction and increased acting out.

Scenario #3: "*I am really upset* with *you*, Eli!" delivered in a loud, furious tone with a negative emphasis on key words.

> *Possible messages*—The teacher is ticked off and needs to drive her point home.

When a statement starts out loud and furious, it immediately raises the defenses of a troubled child, increasing the likelihood that he will overreact and fail to hear the rest of the words. If you catch yourself beginning your response in a loud and angry voice, try pausing and radically altering your tone. For example, "*I am really upset* . . . with you, Eli!" A shift in tone can add humor to the situation, helping to lower the child's defenses.

Scenario #4: "I am really upset with you, Eli," delivered in a firm, yet controlled manner.

> *Possible messages*—The teacher is upset, yet is calm and still cares about me. It isn't the end of the world.

Describing your feelings in a firm, supportive manner is the best way to communicate with a challenging child. Why? In part, because the child's reaction is apt to mirror the calm, controlled tone of your statement; and also because in refusing to verbally attack the child, you have not activated his defenses—all shields are still down and the message can come through.

To be sure the content of your message is properly received, use a supportive tone of voice; speak in a steady, unhurried cadence; and avoid emphasizing power words. The more closely you adhere to these guidelines, the better your relationships with the children will be—and as a result, the more behavioral changes you will eventually see.

Word Choice

Effective communication also relies on a wise choice of words. To begin with, when giving a child directions, it is *essential* to always say "please" and "thanks." For example, "Could you please go to your room—thanks" is far more encouraging than "Go to your room." Similarly, "Hey, John, would you please take out the trash—thanks" is much more likely to yield the desired result than "Take out the trash."

In addition to saying "please" and "thank you," avoid utilizing a disparaging "you," as in "You better knock it off!" "You need to stop that," "You cut that out, you" (double jeopardy), and "You come here right now!" The perceived hostility underlying such messages is apt to prompt an adverse reaction, whereas substituting you-statements with I- or we-statements can lead to increased rapport. This approach was popularized by Thomas Gordon in his 1970 book *P.E.T.: Parent Effectiveness Training.*[1]

The following examples illustrate a move toward more tolerable messages by changing just a few words.

Less effective: "*You* need to stop talking like that, John."
More effective: "John, *I*'m uncomfortable with that sort of language."

Less effective: "*You* need to stop running in the hallway."
More effective: "*We* don't want kids getting hurt, so *I*'m asking you to please not run in the hallway."

Children at risk have trouble tolerating power-laden content without overreacting, hence choosing your words carefully is well worth the effort it may at first take; after a while, supportive words will come naturally, and changed behaviors are likely to follow. Teachers and child-care workers alike report that adding "please" and "thank you" to their conversations with children, as well as replacing you-statements with I- or we-statements, has led to dramatic improvements in their behavior. Communicating respectfully with kids has another advantage too: they will soon begin communicating respectfully with *you*.

Body Language

Body language is equally significant. Because troubled kids are often hypersensitive to the nonverbal messages this language conveys, you will want to take extra care to use it strategically.

Facial Expressions

To be effective, facial expressions need to be in tune with a child's emotional state. The more in control a child appears, for example, the more expressive you may safely be. When a student has quietly added an interesting observation to a class discussion, feel free to extend your enthusiasm; "What a marvelous contribution!" you might declare, with a big smile and brightly shining eyes. Kids will cherish exaggerated facial expressions in response to their accomplishments as long as they do not feel you are being insincere or making fun of them.

Conversely, when a child appears distraught, facial expressions should become less animated. At such times, it is best to say, in a firm tone and with a composed appearance, "I'm getting frustrated, and rather than yell, I will step away for a few minutes. Then we can talk." In this case your subdued expression, by sparing the child further aggravation, is apt to help you get your point across.

Hand Gestures

Improper use of hand gestures tends to exacerbate anxiety. Finger pointing, for example, which often sends a negative message rippling with power, control, and often anger, can dampen a child's motivation to change her behavior. Effective use of hand signals, however, can keep the volume in the room at a reasonable level, facilitate the relaying of information, reduce stress, and help build self-esteem. Following are several examples.

Palms Up at Waist Level. This hand gesture gives the impression of asking for help, rather than demanding compliance.

The Okay Sign. This popular signal is formed by holding the palm outward and creating an O shape by touching forefinger to thumb and pointing the other three fingers upward. Saying, "That was great" is validating; saying, "That was great" while flashing the universal okay sign is even better.

Thumbs Up. The thumbs-up signal, like the okay sign, reinforces positive verbal messages, and in some instances is a perfect substitute. A child who has been having a rough time and is beginning to regain control will most likely benefit from a supportive thumbs-up signal, especially if she is not yet ready to converse with you.

The Good Old-Fashioned Handshake. Shaking hands makes use of touch to convey the message "I care about you." For a kid who craves physical attention, a handshake may be the best possible way of connecting.

An elementary school teacher I know in Texas makes a point of physically touching each student at least once a day during the school year. Whether it is a tap on the shoulder or a handshake, this physical contact, she is convinced, reinforces her emotional and intellectual ties with her students. Aware that some children may not want to be touched against their will, she starts off the year by asking each one individually for their permission.

Nonverbal Cuing. These nonverbal cues effectively deliver a message without interrupting an activity or calling attention to a particular child. Here are three of the many signals available:

- *Visual cues.* Pictures or diagrams can be posted on a wall to remind the children of proper conduct. That way, rather than stopping to address a misbehavior, you could point to a poster or simply glance in the direction of a word-card to communicate the needed message.

    A third grade teacher I know begins every school year by creating a mural of her students' handprints. Thereafter, whenever a student speaks without raising her hand, the teacher points to the mural. Moreover, when the class gets rowdy, she turns off the lights to restore peace and quiet. In most instances, her "quiet" messages are received.

Body gestures can be used in much the same way. When Audrey, a group home supervisor, grabs her earlobe, whoever she is looking at knows it is time to "stop, think, and act."

- *Sign language.* Some adults who work with troubled children design hand signals to relay such messages as "Please be quiet"; "That was great"; "We're a team"; "No, don't do that"; "Return to your seats"; "I need your attention"; "Five minutes till the next activity"; "I'm upset"; and "Thank you." A sign often used to restore quiet is a hand raised in the air, palm facing outward.

- *Auditory signals.* Sound is an excellent way to capture the attention of a group that has become scattered, unfocused, or loud. One auditory signal used frequently by elementary school teachers and youth-care workers is rhythmic clapping, or clapping loudly in a particular sequence—such as three slow claps followed by a short pause, two quick claps, another short pause, and four quick claps—which the children then repeat. This method is less intrusive, and far more productive, than shouting, "Pay attention . . . *now!*" Other auditory possibilities include ringing a small bell or playing music. Nonverbal cuing is an art form that invites as much creativity as you wish to give it.

Horizontal and Vertical Positioning

Physical proximity often sways the outcome of our interactions with troubled children. To begin with, an agitated child needs space around her in order to regain her composure. Unless she is on the verge of a tantrum, it is therefore best to avoid stepping too close to her until she has settled down. Staring at her or forcing eye contact with her can also be counterproductive. Because she is not ready for an "invasion" of the space surrounding her, and will therefore guard it with her defenses, your job is to respect those defenses and to make your approach only after they have been lowered.

In terms of vertical positioning, eye-level contact works best, particularly if the child is under stress. Whereas towering over her while she is seated is likely to provoke feelings of powerlessness and intimidation, crouching down so that your eyes are parallel with hers is not. If she is extremely agitated, an even lower position may be more helpful. I have had some of my best conversations while stretched out on the floor.

Physical positioning also includes circulating among the children rather than standing continuously at the front of the room or sitting behind a large desk. Teachers note that in response to varying their proximity to the students, both horizontally and vertically, the children's attention spans lengthen and kids in the back of the room are pulled into the day's lessons. If a student is tapping a pencil, just walking toward her will usually stop the disruptive behavior.

Physical Appearance

Because children are keen observers of adults, a teacher's or caregiver's physical appearance can evoke strong reactions. Inadequate attention given to hygiene, grooming, or dress may send the message "I don't care much about myself"—a statement that will invariably be interpreted as "If he doesn't care about himself, he certainly won't care about *me.*"

The appropriate clothing for a job depends on the nature of the job. In some instances a suit and tie, or a dress, can indicate that you take your occupation and the kids seriously. In other instances, such attire constitutes overkill. It is hard to play ball, for instance, in a three-piece suit and fancy shoes!

The single most important clothing guideline is, *never wear provocative attire.* Beer or cigarette insignias, or sexually suggestive clothing, may excessively stimulate troubled children. A youngster who has been abused by an alcoholic uncle, for example, might look at an adult wearing a Budweiser shirt and wonder, "Is this guy safe?" The shirt, after all, is likely to imply: "I like Budweiser. I like to drink. And I might hurt you just like your uncle did." In the context of a child-care setting, it may intimate, "The program is now hiring people who are unsafe to be with."

Emotional Appearance

When you are communicating with troubled children, emotional honesty can help cultivate trusting relationships. If you are in a bad mood and say, "You know what, kids, I'm in a really lousy mood today," they may even give you a break. Caution is advised, however, for they may take this comment personally, or may fear that your mood will negatively affect their day.

Any time a person's safety is at stake, honesty is unquestionably *not* the best policy. Indeed, such situations require top-notch acting. Your stage directions in times of peril call for taking charge and remaining in control. If a child asks, "Are you scared?" your best reply is, "I'm a little worried, but I know we'll be okay." Admitting to fear or showing alarm will only exacerbate tensions and out-of-control behaviors.

One night the teenagers at a detention center in New Hampshire seemed ready to riot. We were short-staffed and the tension was rising dramatically. A few of the residents, having committed acts of violence, were being physically restrained, and for the first time in twenty years, I feared for my own safety. While I was physically restraining one resident, others walked by hissing, "It's zooey tonight!" and "The place is bonkers!" and "This unit is gonna blow!" Each time my reply, masking extreme anxiety, was simple and reassuring: "It's loud now, but things will be okay. We've got a few people coming in. We'll be fine." By feigning some semblance of composure and control, my coworkers and I managed to quell a near revolt.

Caution: Avoid message discord. Although it will at times be necessary to disguise your feelings, always ensure that your verbal and nonverbal messages are in sync. If they are not, the resulting message discord will most likely intensify the problematic situation.

Message discord is what twelve-year-old Jon experienced when, in response to rude remarks he had made to classmates, his teacher said, without yelling, "Jon, please talk to the other kids more kindly."

"Get out of my face!" he barked in reply. The problem was that although the teacher's tone of voice and choice of words were basically respectful, she had walked quickly to his desk, peered down at him, and waved her hand near his face while speaking. Her supportive verbal statement did not mesh with the messages conveyed by her positioning and gestures.

Communicating is an art form. Conducted skillfully, it can richly color your relationships with troubled children; ill-used, it is apt to compromise even the hardiest attachments.

CHAPTER 10

BASIC VERBAL INTERVENTIONS

MANY PEOPLE WHO WORK PROFESSIONALLY WITH CHILDREN HAVE a natural ability to connect verbally with them. Relying solely on nature's gifts, however, is often inadequate when interacting with more complex and troubled children. Work of this nature requires sophisticated communication skills.

The first of the basic communication skills—developing a pretalk routine—comes into play long before uttering a word. Inaudible as it may be, such a routine is likely to have a resounding impact on any serious conversation you conduct with a troubled child.

The Pretalk Routine

Just as a professional golfer develops a preshot routine to improve his odds of hitting the ball straight and long, so can you establish a pretalk routine to maximize your potential as an effective communicator. Listed below are key questions to reflect on before responding to a disgruntled child. Included under each one is self-coaching advice that can be personalized while dialoguing with your observing ego, as described in chapter 2. All eight of these pretalk considerations may be adapted for use in responding to *groups* of children as well.

✔ **How can I engage this child?**
The first order of business is to connect with the child; otherwise, your words may go unheard. The more committed you are to creating an empathic bridge linking your feelings to his, the more receptive he is apt to be.

Self-coaching advice: "No matter what he says, *support his feelings*. Let him see that you empathize with his plight and are able to handle his anger without retaliating. Sit with him a while; don't be so quick to resolve the problem."

✔ **What is on my mind?**
The unwanted content you bring to the interaction—particularly your personal issues or professional pressures—may sabotage the intervention. The better you are at putting these concerns in check, the greater will be your chances for successful relating.

Self-coaching advice: "Sure you're mad because your car broke down this morning and it's going to cost a bundle to get it fixed. Of course you're worried about falling behind schedule and incurring the wrath of your supervisor. But remember, such concerns are peripheral to your relationship with the child. Let go of all pressures while talking to him; you can deal with them later."

✔ **How do I feel about this kid?**
It may be more tempting to speak harshly to an angry kid you do not like than to one you are fond of. To be fair, explore your personal feelings toward the child and, if they are negative, counter them with as much objectivity as possible.

Self-coaching advice: "Okay, you don't like this kid. But you have to deal with him the same as all the others. And if you do it right, you may end up liking him after all!"

✔ **What is the child's side of the story?**
Even when a child has obviously messed up, it is vital to *hear his point of view*. If you begin your conversation without listening to what he has to say, you are likely to risk shutting him down.

Self-coaching advice: "You saw the kid knock the desk over (fire the spitball across the room, cut a hole in the curtain). You're angry and want to deal with the offense right away. Instead, be patient and listen. Feel the kid out first; *then* get to the desk (spitball, curtain) situation."

✔ **What nonverbal messages will I send?**

Plan your nonverbal approach. The manner in which you advance toward the child, use your hands and arms, and demonstrate facial expressions will carry more meaning than the words you say.

Self-coaching advice: "Walk slowly. When you get to the kid, crouch down a bit; don't hover over him. Look calm and refrain from pointing at him."

✔ **How will I cope with a defensive reaction?**

Defensiveness is often a child's best means of protecting himself, whereas opening up may only increase his sense of vulnerability and fear of rejection. Therefore, as you approach the child, anticipate resistance, perhaps even a provocative word or two. All the while, use the "force" described in chapter 2 to avoid succumbing to the power of the "dark side." Plan to start your conversation in a lighthearted manner and, as the protest wanes, to move gradually toward more serious topics.

Self-coaching advice: "He's going to either deny the wrong-doing or blame it on someone else. He may even yell at you and hold *you* accountable for the incident. Although his accusations may hurt, do not take them personally. After he has vented for a while, slowly begin to work through the incident."

✔ **Are consequences necessary?**

If the situation calls for consequences, identify a few ahead of time. Then during your discussion, let the child help decide on the most appropriate ones.

Self-coaching advice: "Never before has the kid done something like this, so maybe you can cut him a little slack. See what he has to say. Also make sure you let him know that repeated offenses could result in stiffer consequences."

✔ **Was I responsible for this incident? If so, what could I have done to prevent it?**

Kids often act out when their calls for help have been ignored, or when they have been placed in precarious or threatening situations. For example, troubled elementary school students who act out during recess—a notoriously undersupervised time of day—are set up for disruptive behavior on a daily basis. Your task is to refrain from coming down too hard on the child for a situation beyond his control. Instead, you need to accept responsibility for the part you have played, openly admit to your error, and make plans to prevent a recurrence of the episode.

Self-coaching advice: "Had you been more involved, you might have prevented this incident. As a result, although the kid needs to assume responsibility for his actions, he also needs to hear that you let him down a bit. Collaborate on a better approach for the future."

Adults who work on the front lines with children at risk are often strapped for time, and as a result, good communication practices are frequently compromised. More often than not, taking time to go through a thoughtful pretalk routine seems impossible! In reality, however, this practice is a *preventive* discipline. Taking a little extra time for a pretalk routine can significantly reduce the amount of time spent reacting to behavioral issues.

Verbal Intervention Techniques

Have you ever watched skilled professionals intervene with a troubled child and wondered how they knew what to say and seemed able to anticipate each comment? Although such expertise comes from experience, anyone can jump-start successful verbal interventions by working with the twelve techniques described below, all of which meet the communication needs of challenging children. To add these techniques to your toolbox of effective responses, focus on one or two a week, practicing them whenever an opportunity arises until they come naturally.

By way of introduction to the techniques, here are three points to keep in mind. First, a meaningful conversation with a troubled child consists of a beginning, middle, and end phase. The *beginning phase* entails nonevocative dialogue intended to engage the child. Once signs of engagement have become evident, it is time to embark on the *middle phase,* which involves a gentle introduction of more serious topics. The *end phase* brings closure to the discussion, sheds light on the future, and makes way for good-byes. As outlined in figure 10–1, on page 154, the beginning phase consists of the first four interventions; the middle phase, the next seven; and the end phase, the final intervention.

Second, the interventions that follow do not necessarily appear in the order in which you will use them. In practice, the sequencing of interventions within the first two phases will vary as needed from conversation to conversation.

Third, to illustrate each technique, the following pages contain a running dialogue between a troubled twelve year old named Ned and his sixth grade teacher, Mr. Neil. Ned is the bright, rambunctious, and angry son of a hardworking single mother who loves him but is often unavailable and a father who visits him infrequently. As the dialogue opens, Mr. Neil is on his way to talk with Ned, who has been kept after school for throwing a pencil at him. Ned is sitting on a bench in the school office.

The techniques are as follows:

1. Supportive Comments
Supportive comments are nonjudgmental, empathic statements voiced to offer comfort in times of emotional unrest. Their purpose is to connect with a child by supporting his position.

Examples:

KID: I hate this place!
ADULT: Seems like you're pretty upset.

KID: Get out of here! I don't want to talk.
ADULT: Man, you seem mad.

KID: My mother is a jerk!
ADULT: It sounds like you're really mad at her. That's too bad.

KIDS: John was picking on us!
ADULT: No wonder you're so angry.

KID: I don't care.
ADULT: Seems like you're very discouraged.

TEACHER: Kids, I don't blame you for being upset. It's terrible
              when it rains and you can't go out. I'd be mad, too.

Mr. Neil and Ned

Mr. Neil approaches Ned, who is sitting anxiously in the school office. Mr. Neil sits on the same bench as Ned, about three feet away from him, and slouches down until he is almost at eye level with him.

MR. NEIL: How are you doing, Ned?

             (No reply)

MR. NEIL: It seems like you're still pretty angry. Who can blame you? It's been a hard day (*supportive comments*).

Mr. Neil is trying to connect with Ned. By establishing that he is not mad at Ned, and by supporting Ned's angry feelings, he creates an opening for further communication.

Because children who are agitated or angry are bound to say things they do not mean—that is, displace their feelings—it is important not to take their words too literally. In a classroom or other group setting, a good response to such venting is to provide a private place, such as an office or "think-time corner," for expressing frustration without jeopardizing the safety and stability of others.

2. Repeated Statements
Repeating back almost word for word what a youth has said will give him the feeling that he is being listened to. This technique should be used judiciously, however, because kids will often rile against any-

one who uses too much "psychology" on them or who engages in too much parroting.

Examples:

KID: I hate going to bed this early!
ADULT: So you're saying you hate going to bed this early.

KID: Get out of here—I don't feel like talking.
ADULT: I hear what you're saying: you don't feel like talking. I'll come back in a little while.

KID: I feel like running away.
ADULT: You feel like running away . . . Wow, you're really going through a lot right now. That's not fair.

NED: You never call on me! I know the answers, but you ignore me.

MR. NEIL: Ned, you're saying that I never call on you (*repeated statement*). No wonder you're so upset. *No* kid wants to be ignored (*supportive comments*) . . .

Mr. Neil, familiar with Ned's family dynamics, knows that he is hypersensitive to being ignored by adults—men in particular, because of his history with his father. Mr. Neil is gently trying to help Ned connect to these inner feelings.

---

3. Feelings Update

Periodically asking how a child is feeling and sharing your feelings as well can model ways to identify emotions and appropriately express them. Be careful not to report negative feelings too frequently, however, especially about the child or any child-related work you are doing, because too much negative reporting may reinforce the child's low self-esteem.

A feelings update needs to be conducted with sensitivity for

another reason as well: troubled children are often resistant to opening up and acknowledging how they feel, because doing so might
increase their vulnerability. It is therefore important to help the child
you are conversing with understand that *all* feelings are okay and
that *acting them out* is what causes trouble.

Examples:

KID: Sarah is always making fun of me. She does it every day.
ADULT: That's too bad (*supportive comment*). How do you feel
        when she teases you (*feelings update*)?
KID: It really makes me angry!
ADULT: Of course it does! I'd be angry, too (*supportive comments*).
        Thank you for letting me know that. Let's talk about it.

TEACHER: I'm feeling frustrated about our lack of effort today,
        kids. What will inspire you to try harder?

MR. NEIL: How does being ignored make you feel (*feelings update*)?

NED: It makes me feel terrible. I get really angry.

MR. NEIL: I don't blame you. I'd get angry, too, if I was ignored (*support-
        ive comments*). Thank you for sharing that. By the way, Ned,
        there's nothing wrong with anger. You just have to learn how
        to express it in a way that gets you the help you want.

Mr. Neil is helping Ned express his honest feelings. By quickly supporting and praising him for opening up, he is increasing the likelihood that
Ned will continue to be expressive. In addition to normalizing feelings of
anger, he is suggesting the need to channel them appropriately.

---

4. Animated Praise

Two forms of animated praise can be used to facilitate engagement.
The first is *basic animated praise,* or expressing approval in a spir-
ited manner.

Examples of basic animated praise:

KID: I got an A on my history report.
ADULT: That's *fantastic,* Ellie! I am so proud of you.

KID: I let Frankie go first.
ADULT: What a nice thing to do! It's not easy to let someone else go first.

TEACHER: This is the greatest class in the entire world! You kids are so smart that I expect you'll soon be teaching me.

The second form of praise is *balancing animated praise,* which focuses on what a child has done *right,* rather than *wrong.* Hearing only about his mistakes is likely to raise his defenses, whereas listening to positive words interjected at the beginning of the conversation is apt to lower them.

Examples of balancing animated praise:

ADULT: John, you made a big mistake by running away, but you made a *great* decision to return after an hour.

ADULT: Carla, you should not have pulled Mary's hair, though I *do* like the way you paid attention when I asked you to stop.

NED: I always get sent to the office. You teachers love screwin' kids. Are you going to call my mother? Am I going to get suspended?

MR. NEIL: Ned, you made a serious mistake by throwing the pencil; I could have been hurt. But you made a really good decision to walk calmly from class without making things worse. You've also been sitting here like a gentleman. You have shown a lot more control than usual today (*balancing animated praise*). I'm really proud of you for that (*basic animated praise*).

By praising Ned's self-control, Mr. Neil increases the probability that Ned will be able to handle the rest of the conversation, including a discussion of consequences. In addition, praising Ned gives a vital boost to his plummeting self-esteem and enhances his connection with his teacher.

5. Apologizing

Apologizing helps diffuse power struggles a child may be grappling with. Apologizing regularly—and thereby modeling honesty, humility, and vulnerability—can immeasurably enhance relationship formation.

Examples:

KID: You didn't have to yell at me.
ADULT: You're right—I apologize. I didn't need to talk to you that way.

KID: You said we would go to the movies tonight.
ADULT: I forgot that my mother was coming to visit. I'm really sorry—I know you were looking forward to going. We'll do it tomorrow night.

CHILD-CARE WORKER: I'm sorry, guys. I forgot to defrost the turkey. Dinner is going to be late. I really messed up this time.

When you are feeling defensive, or have been accused of something you did not do, try a *nonresponsibility apology.*

KID: You didn't have to yell at me.
ADULT: I'm sorry you think I yelled at you. I know you don't like people raising their voices at you. I'll be more careful in the future. Thanks.

NED: Why didn't you call on me?

MR. NEIL: I know how frustrating it is to have the answer and not be called on (*supportive comment*). I apologize for not calling on you as quickly as you would have liked (*apologizing*). I could have handled the situation differently.

Although Mr. Neil initially believed he had a good reason for not calling on Ned, after replaying the situation in his head, he came to think that he could have behaved more sensitively. His apology is genuine and likely to enhance his relationship with Ned.

6. Humor
Well-timed humor is effective medicine.

Example:

KID: You're a fat pig. Get out of here.
ADULT: Okay, so I eat too much ice cream. But man, I can't *stand* frozen yogurt. Give me a break!

NED: But why didn't you call on me?

MR. NEIL: Because even though you looked really interested in answering, you kept calling out without raising your hand. Maybe if you had said, "Mr. Neil, my arms don't work anymore—they're glued to the desk," I would have reacted differently (*humor*).

(NED smiles.)

MR. NEIL: I'm really glad you wanted to answer the questions (*balancing animated praise*), and I know it's hard to hold back (*supportive comment*), but we've talked about needing to sit more quietly . .
.

Mr. Neil, familiar enough with Ned, decides to interject some lightheartedness. Getting Ned to smile reduces his tension and increases their chances of arriving at a mutually agreeable resolution to the discussion.

7. Reasoning Responses

Reasoning responses usher in an explanation for decisions to come, thereby making a child's world safer and more predictable. Reasons increase relationship building,whereas authoritative statements such as "Because I told you so" increase stress. In reasoning responses, the key words are "What if . . ."

Examples:

KID: Why can't I go outside after eight at night?
ADULT: Because it's dark out and it's hard to see. *What if* all parents let their seven year olds play in the neighborhood after dark? I think we'd have a lot of kids getting hurt, don't you?

KID: Why am I grounded?
ADULT: Katie, you made a big mistake by taking the car without permission. *What if* your father or I had an important appointment to get to? We like letting you have the car—you just have to ask before using it.

MR. NEIL: *What if* all the students called out without raising their hands *(reasoning response)*?

NED: It would get pretty loud.

MR. NEIL: And I don't think I'd be able to teach as well.

By zooming in on the "big picture," Mr. Neil helps Ned see why it is inappropriate to call out impulsively. If instead, Mr. Neil's response was, "Because it's not right to call out" or "Because there's a class rule about speaking out of turn," Ned might see him as abusing his authority and be less likely to engage in meaningful discussion.

---

8. Connecting Statements

When adult and child are on opposing sides of an issue, connecting statements can bridge the two viewpoints. With the exception of supportive comments, connecting statements are the verbal intervention most capable of dissipating power struggles. These statements are often used in conjunction with reasoning responses.

Examples:

KID: Why can't I go out?

ADULT: Hey, it's not like I enjoy keeping you in. It's not *me against you* (*connecting statements*). But what if parents let their kids play all the time and never encouraged them to do their homework (*reasoning response*)?

KID: You *like* giving me time-outs!

ADULT: I'm sorry you see it that way (*supportive comment*), because it's *not* me against you. We're on the same side (*connecting statements*). In fact, I'm president of your fan club. We're having a rally tonight and I'm bringing the buttons (*humor*)!

TEACHER: Kids, I don't like the way this day is going. I'm feeling like a meanie. I'm not the enemy; I'm right with you (*connecting statement*). I love this class. Let's turn our day around.

NED: Is that why you didn't call on me—because I wasn't raising my hand?

MR. NEIL: Yes, but I made a mistake; I should have explained that to you (*apologizing*).
You were so excited about having the answers, I think you forgot about the right way to give them. I feel bad that I didn't remind you. It's not me against you—I'm on your side (*connecting statements*) . . .

Mr. Neil, realizing that he could have given Ned helpful feedback, accepts his portion of responsibility for the incident. He then apologizes to Ned and realigns with him. Having given more of himself, Mr. Neil will get more from Ned.

9. Empowering Messages

This intervention shifts power back to a child by asking for his opinion and giving him choices in areas related to his well-being. In one sense, empowering messages can gently nudge an insecure child to take more responsibility for his life. At the same time, they *entrust* him with the decision making, crediting him with competence—a message that a child with little self-confidence needs to hear repeatedly in order to believe it.

Examples:

KID: What's going to happen to me?
ADULT: What do you think should happen?

KID: What should I wear?
ADULT: Why don't you decide. You know what looks good.

KID: Bruce is bothering me!
ADULT: What can you do to get him to stop?

KID: What's my consequence?
ADULT: What do you think it should be?

TEACHER: These are the subjects we need to work on today. Can you kids come up with a schedule showing when each one should be covered?

CHILD-CARE WORKER: We'll go to the movies tonight if you all do your chores and the unit looks spiffy. It's up to you kids; it won't be my decision.

MR. NEIL: Even though I'll try to remind you in the future, can you think of ways to remember to raise your hand and to control your anger (*empowering message*)?

NED: I could try to look more often at the picture of the hand that's hanging on the wall. I could also try counting to five when I get mad; you've talked to us about *that.* Or maybe I could stand up and walk to the back of the room to cool off.

MR. NEIL: Those are *great* ideas (*basic animated praise*). Why don't you give them a try . . .

Mr. Neil empowers Ned to think of better ways to handle his frustration. In so doing he demonstrates confidence in Ned's ability to act on his own behalf.

10. Surface Clarifications

These interventions help gather missing pieces of information needed for spelling out in detail events leading to the troublesome situation. They also serve to eliminate confusion regarding the immediate cause of the problem. Of course, children sometimes get mad after deep-seated issues have been triggered, as described in chapter 1; other times, what we see on the surface is all there is!

Examples:

KID: John teased me so I hit him.
ADULT: What exactly did he say? Has he teased you before?

ADULT: So let's get this straight: what is making you the most upset is the fact that Bobby got more popcorn than you and got to sit in your favorite chair.
KID: Yeah—what is he, a king or something?

MR. NEIL: Ned, you're saying you threw the pencil because you were mad at me for not calling on you, right?

NED: Yeah.

MR. NEIL: So nothing else going on in the classroom was bothering you (*surface clarification*)?

NED: Well, every time you called on Ray, he looked at me and kind of rubbed it in. He was really tickin' me off.

MR. NEIL: Thanks for letting me know that. What do you think you should do about Ray's behavior (*empowering message*)?

NED: I should try to talk to him about it . . . let him know how I feel.

MR. NEIL: Excellent (*basic animated praise*)! That's exactly what we talked about in class last week.

NED: What about the pencil? Am I going to be sent home for that? Are you going to call my mother?

MR. NEIL: What do you think should happen (*empowering message*)?

NED: It was the first time I threw something. I don't think I should be kicked out of school for that, and I don't think my mother should be called.

MR. NEIL: Throwing an object at a person is a serious matter. I could have been hurt. What if we let all the kids throw pencils or other objects without issuing consequences for their actions (*reasoning response*)? They might get the message that throwing things is not a major safety problem, when in fact it is. I was pretty upset (*feelings update*).

NED: So you're going to kick me out?
MR. NEIL: Can you think of a different consequence (*empowering message*)?

NED: What about an in-school suspension?

MR. NEIL: I think that's fair. After all, as you've stated, this is the first time you've thrown something, and you've made a lot of good decisions recently (*balancing animated praise*). I will still need to call your mother, however. I'll give her the whole story, including what happened with Ray and how I made you mad. When safety is jeopardized, parents should be called.

Mr. Neil succeeds in accessing important information to help flesh out the cause of the problem. Due to his empowering responses to Ned's fears, Ned is ready to listen and contribute to the discussion about consequences. Mr. Neil, meanwhile, interjects how it felt to have the pencil thrown at him, showing Ned the ramifications of his act.

11. Explorative Response

An explorative response, which is best used during the mid to later stages of a conversation, helps a child open up and talk about difficult underlying issues, including any rage that has been displaced onto the current situation. Signs of redirected rage include little annoyances turning into major episodes, as well as displays of anger that are disproportionate to the circumstances. Although an explorative response can help identify such problematic displacement, care must be taken in using this technique. When encouraging a child to talk about sensitive issues, a trusting relationship needs to be in place, the child's defenses and boundaries must be respected, and overly aggressive questioning should be avoided.

Examples:

ADULT: Heather, it seems like you got pretty worked up about a rather small issue. You don't usually act this way. Is anything else bothering you?

ADULT: Hector, it seems like you've been upset all day. Is there something on your mind you'd like to talk about?

When a child's defenses are down, it is sometimes a good idea to gently suggest a possible reason for his discontent, or to lead him to a conclusion of his own. For example, eleven-year-old Matt, who becomes increasingly anxious as his weekly Friday dinner with his father approaches but does not understand the source of his anxiety, or is reluctant to talk about it, might benefit from an explorative response such as "Matt, tomorrow is Friday. Is anything happening tomorrow that might be making you a little nervous?"

NED: If you call my mother, she'll yell at me. She's been in a bad mood lately.

MR. NEIL: Are things okay at home (*explorative response*)? You seem more on edge these days.

NED: My mom's father is sick. She's spending a lot of time at his place helping out. She's tried to get my dad to come and stay with me, but he says he's too busy this time of year. Mom's real tired—I can see it. And when she's tired, she gets into bad moods and yells more.

MR. NEIL: Boy, it sounds like you and your mother are going through a really rough time. That's too bad. No kid should have to deal with that (*supportive comments*). I like your mom; she's a nice lady. It sounds like she's under a lot of pressure (*supportive comments*).

Mr. Neil, having opened a channel of honest communication with Ned, takes this opportunity to sensitively explore his underlying issues. When Ned opens up, Mr. Neil supports his feelings. He goes on to empathize with Ned's mother, letting him know why such a loving parent might be doing unloving things.

---

12. Plan Making

This intervention, which marks the end phase of a serious conversation, can help a child take more control of his life. Created collaboratively, a plan of action identifies steps the child will try to take to eliminate recurrences of the misbehavior. Plan making is also used as a proactive intervention to add more predictability and structure to an environment, as described in chapter 7.

Examples:

ADULT: Okay, Bob, I'm proud of the way you talked about this. I know it wasn't easy. Do you think we can draft a plan to help you avoid making the same mistake next time a similar situation arises?

TEACHER: This class didn't run as smoothly as I had hoped. Can we take a few minutes and come up with a plan for our next class?

NED: Maybe things will get better at home when my grandfather isn't sick anymore.

MR. NEIL: I hope you're right, and I want to thank you again for talking to me about this stuff (*basic animated praise*). You really have it rough right now (*supportive comment*). Do you think we could make a plan to help you get through the next few weeks (*plan making*)?

NED: That would be okay.

MR. NEIL: Can you think of ways to make better decisions in class (*empowering message*)?

NED: I could talk about the problem, or like I said before, I could walk away when I start to get upset.

MR. NEIL: Those are two good ideas (*basic animated praise*). Do you mind if I write down our plan?

NED: No.

MR. NEIL: So you'll try to talk more and take personal time-outs (*surface clar-ification, repeated statement*). What else (*empowering message*)? Earlier, you mentioned some other ideas.

NED: I could try counting to five when I'm mad, or thinking about what will happen if I misbehave.

MR. NEIL: Did you remember those two suggestions on your own or did you just read them off the wall (*humor*)?

NED: [*Smiling*] I just read them.

MR. NEIL: Well, we'll write them down anyway, because they are good suggestions and we've talked about them a lot.

NED: Hey, I could also try to do more chores around the house. I know my mom doesn't have much time anymore.

MR. NEIL: That's a wonderful idea (*basic animated praise*)! Do you think your grandfather might enjoy the issue of *National Geographic* that we've just studied in class? Maybe you could take it to him next time you visit. I want you to know that in addition to talking with your mom, I'll see if there are ways the school can help out—we do have some after-school programs. And what about you and me having a ten-second check-in before class each day so that we can see how things are going. Can that be part of our plan (*empowering message*)?

NED: Sure.

MR. NEIL: I have one last idea.

NED: What.

MR. NEIL: To help you get through the next month, I'll buy you one comic book a week if you show improved behavior.

NED: Really?

MR. NEIL: Really. But just for the next four weeks—I know they'll be tough ones.

NED: Thanks, Mr. Neil.

MR. NEIL: Oh, almost forgot—[*reproducing the plan, handing one copy to*

Ned, and adding notes to his own copy] I'm making my own plan to give you reminders if you call out in class.

NED: I'll give you one of *my* comic books if you do that.

MR. NEIL: Hey, where does it say, "Kid makes joke" (*humor*)?!

Mr. Neil and Ned conclude their discussion by making a plan to assist Ned in taking more control of his life. Mr. Neil encourages his input and writes down the plan, giving one copy to Ned as a reminder and keeping another for future reference, just in case Ned's misbehavior begins to escalate again. Documenting the plan in writing, although not a necessary step, models a good life skill—namely, writing down important information, which allows kids who mistrust adults to see their agreements in black and white.

Although Mr. Neil has taught his students self-management skills, he can see that Ned needs more individual attention; yet he also knows that human resources for classroom use are quite limited. Considering these circumstances, his comic book offer—a short-term positive reinforcement plan—represents a best possible response. Moreover, in addition to talking with Ned's mother, Mr. Neil plans to inquire about support services available through the school and to arrange an appointment for Ned with the school guidance counselor.

Interestingly, Mr. Neil feels ambivalent about the "social work" duties that seem to have been added to his classroom responsibilities. On the one hand, he resents them for taking time away from teaching, his true passion; on the other, he derives deep satisfaction from helping students like Ned. Now, as so often in the course of each school day, he reflects on these thoughts and feelings, aware that they influence his actions.

Figure 10–1

Summary of Verbal Intervention Techniques

Phase	Technique	Definition	Example	Key Principles
Beginning Phase	**Supportive Comments**	Statements that support a child's feelings	*I don't blame you for being so upset.*	Employ regularly to enhance the likelihood of engagement
	Repeated Statements	Remarks that echo back a child's previous comment	*So you're saying no one cares?*	Use sparingly to help the child feel listened to
	Feelings Update	A solicitation or verbal expression of feelings	*How does that make you feel?*	Conduct sensitively to facilitate the identification and expression of emotions
	Basic Animated Praise	Emphatic praise delivered with lively affect	*That was a really nice thing you said!*	Keep the animated approval coming!
	Balancing Animated Praise	Emphatic praise given to offset criticism	*You made a mistake by running off, but it was a great decision to come back.*	Express strategically to counteract defensiveness
Middle Phase	**Apologizing**	Openly admitting to mistakes	*I'm sorry I yelled at you. I apologize.*	Use regularly to model honesty, humility, and vulnerability
	Nonresponsibility Apology	Acknowledging false accusations without accepting blame	*I'm sorry you feel I yelled at you. I'll be more careful next time.*	Use to model sensitivity when you are not at fault
	Humor	The art of bringing on a smile	*If you don't want more home-work, then laugh at this joke.*	Time it well and take it seriously!
	Reasoning Responses	"What if" statements that explain a forthcoming decision	*What if we let every kid ...*	Employ readily to increase predictability and diffuse authority issues
	Connecting Statements	Reassurances that you are still in the child's corner	*Hey, it's not me against you. We're on the same side. I just don't like having to ...*	Utilize in times of tension to demonstrate care and bridge opposing points of view
	Empowering Messages	Solicitations for input, which instills confidence and autonomy	*What do you think ...*	Transmit generously to share the power
	Surface Clarifications	Questions asked to elucidate a situation	*What exactly happened?*	Conduct open-mindedly to hear the child's side of a story and avoid jumping to conclusions
	Explorative Response	An invitation to gently uncover underlying issues	*Is anything else bothering you?*	State sensitively to seek out the true sources of displacement
End Phase	**Plan Making**	Devising strategies to prevent recurring misbehaviors	*So we'll use a new "stop, think, and act" signal. This is a good plan.*	Conduct collaboratively to encourage appropriate functioning

Summary Vignettes

The vignettes that follow illustrate how the basic verbal intervention techniques can be artfully woven into a serious conversation. The first scenario takes place in a residential center; the second occurs in a foster home.

Scenario # 1

Nine-year-old Stu has been asked to leave the residential center's dining table for throwing food. He is sitting in the hallway with a disgruntled expression on his face as a staff member named Jeremy approaches.

JEREMY: Hey, what's up (*supportive comment*)?

STU: Get away from me!

JEREMY: Man, you seem pretty upset (*supportive comment*).

STU: This place really sucks!

JEREMY: It can be a pretty tough place to live. It's hard for kids to be here (*supportive comment*).

STU: You guys are all the same.

JEREMY: So you think we're all the same (*repeated statement*).

STU: Why did you give me a time-out and not Bobby? He was being silly, too.

JEREMY: I didn't see it that way, and I'm sorry if I missed it (*apologizing*). I know it really ticks kids off when we don't catch everything (*supportive comment*). I'll try to watch more closely.

STU: So do I still have to do this time-out?

JEREMY: Hey, it's not me against you. I don't like having to give time-outs (*connecting statements*). But you were being silly and flicked some food across the table. What if we let every kid flick food around (*reasoning response*)? It would look pretty wild in there.

STU: I don't care.

JEREMY: Yes, but I do. Your safety and well-being are important to me.

STU: How much time do I have?

JEREMY: Well, you made a mistake by flicking the food, but when asked, you left the table without difficulty (*balancing animated praise*). So what do you think the right amount of time should be (*empowering message*)?

STU: Fifteen minutes.

JEREMY: That sounds fair to me.

STU: Fine, I'll do fifteen minutes.

JEREMY: Hey, you don't usually get so silly and act that way. Could anything else be bothering you (*explorative response*)?

STU: No.

JEREMY: Today's Tuesday . . . Tomorrow's Wednesday. Is anything special happening tomorrow (*explorative response*)?

STU: We have group.

JEREMY: Oh yeah, that's right. Last week, some of the kids gave you a hard time during group (*supportive comment*). Are you perhaps a little nervous (*feelings update*)?

STU: A little.

JEREMY: A little, sure (*repeated statement*). Who can blame you for being nervous (*supportive comment*)? That was a rough day. Do you think your dinner problems might be related to worries about group (*explorative response*)?

STU: Maybe.

JEREMY: Thanks for sharing that with me. I'm really proud of you for that (*basic animated praise*). What could you have done differently to deal with your nervousness (*empowering message*)?

STU: I don't know.

JEREMY: Well, think about it for a second . . .

          (A twenty-second pause)

STU: Talk to a staff member, or take a personal time-out.

JEREMY: Those are two excellent ideas (*basic animated praise*). I
          knew you could think of a few ideas. Maybe we can make
          a plan to help you deal with your nervousness around the
          group (*plan making*), what do you think (*empowering
          mes-sage*)?

STU: Okay. But make sure you watch Bobby. He flicked food,
          too.

Scenario #2

Jane, sixteen years old and recently placed in her third foster home,
has a history of sexual abuse and has not seen her biological mother
in eight months. Because Jane has been sexually active for three
years, has pseudo-mature mannerisms, and likes to go out with
young men in their twenties, her social worker is concerned about
her safety. Ruth, Jane's new foster mother, has for years provided a
home for kids with similar histories. Aware that Jane returned an
hour past curfew the night before with a hickey on her neck, Ruth
has asked Jane to sit at the kitchen table for a talk.

RUTH: How are you today?

JANE: I'm fine.

RUTH: Did you sleep okay?

JANE: Not bad, but that pillow is lumpy.

RUTH: Oh, you should have told me. I don't want any of you kids
          sleeping on lumpy pillows (*supportive comment*). I think I
          have a better one for you.

JANE: Thanks, can I go now?

RUTH: What's your rush?

JANE: I'm meeting some kids later and need to shower.

RUTH: Well, it didn't take you long to make some friends. That's
          great (*basic animated praise*).

JANE: Can I go?

RUTH: I think we need to talk about last night.

JANE: About me coming in late? I said it won't happen again.

RUTH: I was really worried about you (*feelings update*). I care.

JANE: That's what my other foster mothers said. Shit, even my
          real mother said it. And look where I am now! I don't
          think you really care. That's a crock.

RUTH: So you don't think I really care (*repeated statement*). Why
          should you? You haven't had a whole lot of luck with adults
          (*supportive comment*), and you certainly don't know me
          very well.

JANE: Don't give me this shit.

RUTH: Jane, when it's just you and me talking, it's okay to swear,
          although I don't love it—but not when there are other
          people around, okay?

JANE: Fine, just don't give me this therapy crap. I've heard it a
          million times.

RUTH: Gee, and I thought I was using that therapy crap rather
          well (*humor*).

JANE: [*Smiling, then serious*] So what are you going to do?
          Ground me for coming in an hour late? Is that what you
          want to do?

RUTH: You came in an hour late and that was a mistake, but you
          also apologized and said it won't happen again. That meant
          a lot to me. It's never easy to apologize (*balancing animated
          praise*).

JANE: So what are you going to do?

RUTH: Actually, I'm less concerned about your being late than about who you were with and whether you were making good decisions. After all, you said it won't happen again (*empowering message*).

JANE: Hey, I can take care of myself.

RUTH: I'm sure you can. You've had to look out for yourself more than most kids your age (*supportive comments*). But I'm responsible for your safety, and I do care about you. What if every foster parent let their kids hang out with whomever they wanted (*reasoning response*)? We can't keep you safe if you hang with the wrong crowd.

JANE: You can't tell me who to hang out with. You guys get off on bossing kids around, but we don't always have to listen.

RUTH: Hey, I'm not the enemy—I'm on your side. I wanted you to come live with us (*connecting statement*)—you're a wonderful kid. I just need to know where you are and who you are with. We need to make a plan for accomplishing this (*plan making*).

JANE: Fuck you! No way am I making a plan. You can go to hell!

(JANE storms off to her room.)

Not every conversation that is conducted well ends well. The most we can do is honor the communication process and trust that each meaningful discussion paves the way to another one.

In this vignette, Ruth begins to establish a relationship with Jane by being genuinely supportive and caring while also being direct about her concerns and expectations. As an experienced foster parent, she surmises that under Jane's tough facade lies a scared and insecure kid who desperately wants Ruth to love her and to set appropriate limits. She knows that reaching kids like Jane, if they *can* be reached, takes time, patience, perseverance, and love.

CHAPTER 11

STRATEGIC VERBAL INTERVENTIONS

THE NEXT SET OF TOOLS NEEDED TO COMMUNICATE EFFECTIVELY WITH troubled children is strategic verbal interventions. More advanced than the basic verbal interventions described in chapter 10, these responses *validate* children for acting on their own behalf, even if such actions are deemed inappropriate. The youngsters, in response to being validated, begin to feel better about themselves and, as a result, are more likely to open to therapeutic insights into the origins of their behavior.

This chapter illustrates five strategic interventions, each of which is a bit more clinically complex than the approaches set forth in the previous chapter. Yet with practice and vigilance, their successful implementation is within reach of most people who work with children and youth at risk. The challenge in using these interventions is to match the most suitable one to a particular child's needs and circumstances. Intuition, creativity, and experience will guide your selection process.

Reframing

Reframing portrays a negative behavior in *positive* terms. Its action is twofold. First, praising a child's coping strategy can counter the ill effects of negative labeling—a practice that erodes a child's self-esteem and, along with it, the motivation to improve her level of functioning. In addition, it can help her understand *why* she acts the way she does. A youngster whose behavior has been reframed often discovers that her acting out has been serving a self-protective function.

Jennifer, a junior high school guidance counselor, recently used reframing with fourteen-year-old Julia, who often exhibits obnoxious behavior. "Julia, you seem *very good* at pushing people away," she said. "When you criticize your teachers, whine, and make disgusting comments about them, they don't want to get close to you—which is a shame, since you're a great kid. You really know how to keep adults at a distance."

A victim of repeated sexual abuse who was subsequently kicked out of four foster homes, Julia uses obnoxious behavior to keep people at a distance because for her, intimacy has become equated with pain. Considering her history, Julia is doing the best she can, and what she needs most is understanding and help. Jennifer's desire in reframing the obnoxious behavior was to loosen Julia's defensive posturing and enable the two of them to establish meaningful contact, thereby showing Julia that adults can indeed be trusted. Her long-term goal was to gently nudge Julia into connecting her "pushing away" behaviors with her childhood experiences of pain and rejection.

Although reframing casts acting out in a positive light, it in no way condones misbehavior. A child who hears her behavior reframed knows her actions were inappropriate; yet she also feels buoyed by the praise and encouraged by a new sense of *hope*.

This is what happened for fourteen-year-old Simon, a dynamo with an electric personality, an uncanny ability to irritate people, and an exceedingly dysfunctional home life. Although he harbors tremendous anger and is often rude, he can also be quite affable. Returning to his group home after school one day, he announced, "Guess what. The school secretary told me that I'm the first kid in twenty-five years who has gotten under her skin."

Camille, a staff member who overheard his comment, remarked, "That's fantastic! What an accomplishment. Just think of all the kids who sat in that office day after day, month after month, trying to push her buttons, and you're the only one who has succeeded. Boy, you have a *marvelous* ability to affect people!"

Simon was beaming.

"Now, Simon," Camille continued, "the problem is that this great talent of yours is hurting people's feelings and getting you in serious trouble. We've got to think up ways to let it work *for* you rather than *against* you."

A month later Camille, who by then had developed a solid relationship with Simon, felt called upon to reframe another of his rude remarks. She concluded by gently asking him if his excellent ability to deeply affect people might have something to do with his past.

After thinking for a moment, Simon replied, "Ma didn't give me much attention."

"Maybe this is your way of getting it—of *making sure* you are noticed," Camille suggested.

Simon's eyes glimmered with a flash of recognition.

Reframing can be used effectively in a variety of other situations as well. See figure 11–1 for ways to reframe some typical problem behaviors.

Figure 11–1

Reframing

Behavior	Strategic Interventions
Obnoxiousness	*You do an excellent job of keeping people at a distance. Who can blame you. What can we do to slowly move closer together?*
Restlessness	*You kids seem to have tremendous energy today. Let's complete this assignment and then go outside where you can run and play.*
Rudeness	*You get your point across very well, and people react strongly to it. Can we think of ways for you to do this without getting them so mad at you?*
Stealing	*You're very good at taking care of yourself. When you feel you need something, you figure out how to get it. Can we come up with ways for you to get what you need without stealing?*
Swearing	*You're very good at letting people know exactly how you're feeling. Let's figure out a way for you to do this without upsetting them.*
Tattling	*It's great that you care so much about people doing the right thing. But let's look at how you can care and still get along with the other kids.*

The Hydraulic Squeeze

Whereas reframing acknowledges a problematic coping behavior, the Hydraulic Squeeze *moves it to a setting in which it can do no harm*. This intervention—formulated by child psychologist Bernard Levine, PhD—"squeezes" a difficult behavior into a smaller, more clearly defined arena where it can turn benign and remain alive for investigation. Such an option is far preferable to either letting the behavior rage out of control or attempting to extinguish it, which may only give rise to more troublesome conduct. Misbehavior, after all, is a message, and messages need to be answered, not ignored or destroyed.

Reframing a child's acting-out behavior lets her know that she is valued and that people want to help her—a message that can be as significant as the intervention itself. Applying the Hydraulic Squeeze then helps her learn to channel her troubling emotions, showing her that her behavior has meaning, may even be indicative of a special ability, and simply needs to be demonstrated in a more productive manner.

The Hydraulic Squeeze has many creative applications, two of which are depicted below, along with a classic *mis*application of this technique. Additional uses of the Hydraulic Squeeze are listed in figure 11–2, on page 166.

Venting Anger

Marcos, age twelve, and Randall, thirteen, had experienced sexual abuse as young children and were fond of swearing, which often got them into trouble. Their swearing was a message to the world that they were angry kids with serious underlying issues. After two years of therapy, however, neither youngster had opened up.

When Vince first met with them for duo therapy, he established ground rules. The one they found most interesting was, "You can swear if you need to, as long as you do it while we're alone together. If you do it in the presence of others, you will receive a time-out and you may lose your swearing privileges."

No sooner was this pronouncement made than Marcos declared, "That's a fuckin' good rule. I like it."

Randall quickly followed up with, "Shit, I can say *shit* and not get shit for it!"

The three met regularly throughout the school year. During an early session in the school gymnasium, the boys went through the entire alphabet, coming up with a swear word for each letter. Vince, in turn, complimented their creativity (*reframing*). Before long, the boys were swearing less outside of therapy, suggesting that Vince's strategic intervention had succeeded. He had indeed *hydraulically squeezed* their need to discharge angry emotions into a one-hour-a-week time block.

Interestingly, with Vince's subtle assistance, the boys began to connect their swearing, particularly their sexualized swears, with the abuse they had encountered. Keeping the undesirable behavior alive not only inspired them to talk about their trauma but initiated the psychotherapeutic work needed to heal the scars it had left.

Making Fart Noises

Seven-year-old Freddy, like many troubled kids his age, liked to make fart noises in public and soon became known for his meticulously timed disruptive flatulence. His therapist, Bernie, informed him that he could make all the fart noises he wanted when they were together, but should otherwise try to hold them in. "When you make those noises in front of others, it gets you in trouble," Bernie gently added. "That bothers me, because I'm your friend." Weeks after applying this Hydraulic Squeeze, Bernie reframed Freddy's noise-making as wildly musical and encouraged him to tape-record all his noises, labeling each one with a name, such as the "Fabulous Flutter."

In time, Freddy's farting noises ceased altogether, and with Bernie's expert coaching, he was able to see that farting had a lot to do with "pooping"—another of Freddy's fascinations—and that poops were *messy*. While exploring the "messiness" of his past and working through much of his underlying conflict, Freddy discovered that his fascination with farting had been his way of letting people know that his life had been "very messy" as a result of serious power and control issues.

Figure 11–2

The Hydraulic Squeeze

Behavior	Strategic Interventions
Arguing	Organize a series of debates, letting the child pick the topic for each one and, more often than not, win the dispute.
Excessive talking	Provide regular opportunities for extra talking. Spend one-on-one time with the child; let her read the daily schedule aloud; have her read a book to you or a group of children.
Physical aggression	Divert the aggressive energy into sports or other physical activities, such as martial arts classes.
Sexualized behavior	Normalize the child's sexual feelings and model ways to manage them. When a child masturbates in public, for example, teach him about masturbation and hydraulically squeeze the behavior into private places, such as the bed or the bathroom.
Stealing	Suggest a board game that involves espionage or trickery. Or close your eyes, invite the child to take something from the room, then try to guess what is missing.
Venting anger: yelling, screaming, swearing	Let the child know that venting is acceptable only behind closed doors, where the loudness will not affect others.

Physical Aggression: A Classic Misapplication of the "Squeeze"
Eleven-year-old Gorman, who lived at a residential center, had poor impulse control and often acted out aggressively. One day he threw a lamp and, while on the verge of a tantrum, had to be removed from the unit until he regained control. I escorted him into my office and had him sit down. His body was tense, his face was beet red, sweat was pouring from his brow, and his eyes had a glazed, wild look. "I need to punch something! I can't sit here," he screamed.

"I know you're upset, but you don't need to punch anything," I told him calmly, despite the fierce pounding of my heart.

"I *need* to punch something," he repeated.

I explained that I was not going to let him act aggressively and that if he tried, I would have to hold him, which I did not want to do. It was touch-and-go for a few long minutes before he calmed down.

In future encounters with Gorman, I reminded him of the enormous self-control he showed that day, and suggested that he divert some of his aggressive energy into sports or other physical activities, such as karate. He joined a community basketball league and gradually saw that he could control his anger without becoming physical.

Regrettably, many aggressive children are encouraged to take out their anger on punching bags or pillows, which is *not* a good use of the Hydraulic Squeeze. Counseling a troubled youngster to strike out at an object, or providing a bag or pillow for venting purposes, may only reinforce his perception that he *cannot control himself without being physical.* Once reinforced, this belief is likely to promote future acts of physical aggression because in moments of anger, the youth is not apt to have a punching bag or pillow at his disposal.

The Three-Penny Exchange

The Three-Penny Exchange is an invitation to communicate that can profoundly affect children who hold in a great deal of mental anguish and let it out from time to time through misbehavior. Holding patterns of this sort are usually rooted in the belief that opening up will usher in more pain, disclose family secrets, or be perceived as a sign of weakness. Temporarily dissolving these holding patterns calls for a gentle and humorous intervention that turns the power over to the child and conveys the message "I really care about you"—the cornerstone of the Three-Penny Exchange.

This was the technique that eventually assisted Juanita, an extremely guarded eleven year old who was transferred to our residential center from a less intensive treatment setting. Throughout her first year with us, she resisted all appeals to talk about her problems, including her feelings toward her mother, an unstable parent who had been in and out of Juanita's life since the day she was born. Then one Sunday during Juanita's second year with us, I received a call from her unit supervisor, informing me that Juanita was stomping around the unit and refusing a time-out. Aware that she had a visit scheduled with her mother the next day, I went to Juanita's unit and asked her to return with me to my office.

While sitting in my office, we discussed the events that had just transpired. After about five minutes, I decided to try a new approach to help her express her underlying concerns. I took three pennies from my top desk drawer and said: "Look, Juanita, I get paid to help kids with their problems. If I don't do a good job, I don't get paid as much. I want you to take these three pennies and decide how much I'll earn today, if anything. Now, I happen to think that some of your agitation may have something to do with your visit tomorrow and that talking about the visit might feel a lot better. Of course, I could be wrong about this . . . Here's the deal: *If I'm one-hundred percent correct, you must pay me three pennies. If I'm mostly correct, you pay me two pennies. And if I'm only a little bit right, you owe me one penny.*"

I walked Juanita back to her unit to complete a time-out she had received for swearing. Two hours later, while doing paperwork in my office, I heard rustling outside the door and saw a small yellow Post-it note come sliding underneath. Taped to the note was a penny, and written across the top were the words, "You got one." Beneath the penny were two more words: "Mom's b-day." It was signed, "From, Juanita."

Her mother's upcoming birthday was evidently triggering unpleasant memories and, along with them, a myriad of conflicting emotions. With Juanita's permission, I explained this situation to her therapist, Beth. I also described Juanita's response to the Three-Penny Exchange, which Beth proceeded to use quite successfully in future therapy sessions with her.

The Millimeter Acknowledgment

The Millimeter Acknowledgment is a soft-touch approach that gently opens a small hole in the defensive shield of a child who is reluctant to disclose information for fear of increasing her vulnerability. It entails placing your index finger about one millimeter (less than one-twentieth of an inch) from your thumb and asking, "Do you think it's *slightly* possible that you might . . . ?" all the while hoping the child will take one millimeter of responsibility for her actions or feelings.

The Millimeter Acknowledgment, in realistically preparing you to expect defensiveness, will help dissolve some of the frustration you may feel while conversing with a youngster who refuses to own up to her actions. This attitude alone is apt to ease her into accepting more responsibility for her behavior and inching her way toward more open, direct communication. Examples of this intervention appear in the "little less correct" approach used with Teddy in chapter 2; in Jarrod's story, described below; and in figure 11–3, on page 170.

Eight-year-old Jarrod, a troubled public school student and the product of a chaotic home life, had negligible self-esteem, a short emotional fuse, an unwillingness to take responsibility for his aggressive acts, and a reluctance to talk about serious subjects. One afternoon Bruce, the school counselor, heard screams coming from a distant hallway and went to investigate the commotion. He came upon Jarrod standing in the hallway with the principal and a woman dressed in a blue uniform, both hovering over him. He was yelling, "I *didn't* hit the monitor! I *never* hit the monitor!"

"But, Jarrod, I *am* the monitor, and you definitely hit me," said the woman in blue.

Bruce quietly asked the principal if he could speak with Jarrod privately, and she agreed. Taking the boy aside, he asked, "Jarrod, what happened?"

"I got into a fight with Andy. He called my mother an asshole."

"Did the monitor try to break up the fight?"

"Yeah."

Bruce bent down to talk to him at eye level. "Now, Jarrod, do you think it's *slightly* possible," he suggested, making the sign of the Millimeter Acknowledgment, "that you could have quite accidentally hit the monitor as she tried to stop the two of you from fighting?"

"Yeah," he replied.

"Okay, thanks for letting me know this. I'm sure it wasn't easy for you."

He motioned for Jarrod to accompany him as he returned to the two women. "Jarrod admits to accidentally hitting you," Bruce told the monitor. "He's *very* sorry about it."

"I accept your apology," the monitor said to Jarrod. "But tomorrow I want you to stay closer to me during the lunch hour."

"Okay," Jarrod replied.

As the foursome broke up, Bruce again praised Jarrod for admitting to his mistake. Jarrod beamed with pride and relief, then turned and accompanied Bruce to his office to process the fight with Andy.

Figure 11–3

The Millimeter Acknowledgment

Situation	Strategic Interventions
A teacher talking with a student who has misbehaved	*Do you think it's* remotely possible *that some of your problems today might have a tiny bit to do with how hard the work is?* A *lot of kids are struggling with this material.*
A foster parent speaking with a child who may have stolen money	*Do you think it's* slightly possible *that you may have made a mistake by taking money, and that* maybe now you want to *return it?*
A youth worker approaching a child who is nervous about an upcoming visit with a parent	*Do you think there's this much of a chance that your behavior has something to do with the visit?*
A counselor addressing a new camper about her reluctance to go to an opening day ceremony	*Could you be a* tiny bit *nervous about attending the ceremony? All kids are nervous at the beginning of camp.*

Magical Metaphors

The use of metaphors can work wonders, especially magical metaphors—figures of speech that substitute inanimate objects for human conditions. Why? Because they tend to depersonalize difficult situations, diffusing tensions and instilling hope in children immersed in despair.

Impassioned lectures about how a child should behave or where she will end up if she misbehaves are far less likely to improve her conduct, much less sink into her awareness. Nor are stories about children overcoming hardship apt to make the difference we hope for; if improving a troubled child's behavior were that simple, we would make great strides in a matter of hours by showing the film of Laura Ingalls Wilder's *Little House on the Prairie*—a feat that to my knowledge has not been accomplished.

Magical metaphors, unlike confrontive lectures and happily-ever-after stories, impart images-in-process that offer long-term support and guidance. Metaphors similar to the three that follow can weave wondrous spells when used in conversation with an individual child or a group.

The Derailed Train

Problematic behavior becomes immediately objectified when portrayed as a train that has been derailed, with its wheels still spinning, oil leaking, steam billowing out its smokestack, and a need to get back on the track. This is an ideal metaphor to introduce to a restless class, foster children struggling with conflict, a family in stress, or a rambunctious group of youngsters in residential care.

Before working with a group of eight junior high school students who had significant behavior problems, I met individually with each one and explained that from my perspective, the youngster was a train that had fallen off the track. "Wheels are turning, steam is spewing out, but the train is going nowhere," I said. "The purpose of the group is to get all eight trains back on track." The kids seemed amused by the image.

They worked hard during our time together, courageously confronting many of their demons. Then during our last meeting, one of the students, named Sarah, surprised me with a curious question. "What kind of train am I?" she asked quizzically.

"Sarah," I replied, rapidly collecting my thoughts, "you're a very caring train with a strong engine. You're moving at a good speed even though you always stop to pick up people who need a ride."

"What about me?" Doug called out. "What kind of train am I?"

"Doug, you're an upbeat, funky train. You've got wild colors coating your engine and loud rap music playing in the passenger cars. You're a train alive with spirit, weaving and chugging your way to a good place."

One by one, each of the students wanted to hear what type of train they were; and one by one, I painted them word-pictures. They were indeed all back on track.

The Melting Snowball

Nervousness addressed as anxiety is hard to dispel; pictured as a snowball, however, it can gradually shrink. The graphic metaphor of a melting snowball helps counter anxiety about an upcoming change or event.

Seven-year-old Chuckie—who had been abandoned by his mother and had trouble trusting adults—was scheduled to leave his residential center for a foster home within a few days when Tom, his unit supervisor, received a call that he had run from his classroom. Finding him sitting outside on the stairwell, Tom slowly approached and asked what was wrong. Chuckie came right out and said he was scared to leave.

Tom supported his feelings and then proposed, "Chuckie, I want you to pretend that your nervousness about leaving is a big snowball sitting in the middle of your chest . . . How big is it?"

Extending his arms out to the side, Chuckie replied, "It's this big!"

"Well, Chuckie, every day you live with your new family that snowball is going to melt a little. In a few years it will probably be this big," said Tom, using his hand to form a circle about the size of a dime. "Chuckie, that snowball will always be there; it will never go away. But with luck and hard work, it should get small enough not to bother you too much."

A year later Chuckie's foster family brought him back to the center for a visit. When he saw Tom, he blurted out, "It's this big!" His hand was in a circle about the size of a dime.

The Fork in the Road
The image of arriving at a fork in the road is an invaluable metaphor to use with teenagers who make decisions that get them into trouble. It will challenge them to look ahead, think carefully, and choose the right path.

Sixteen-year-old Shawn, incarcerated at a juvenile detention center, had a long history of petty crimes. One afternoon he started an intense fight with another resident and had to be physically escorted to his room by Greg, the staff member on duty. After venting for a while, Shawn broke down in tears and spoke hopelessly about his life.

Greg listened compassionately and then said: "Shawn, you've had a tough life. No one can blame you for being so angry. But now you're at a fork in the road and you've got to decide which way you're going. The road to the left is easier. Kids who go left keep on acting out their anger and often end up in places like this. Prisons are full of people who've had tough childhoods. Take the *right* road and you'll see it's a harder journey—it's about controlling your impulses to lash out—but it leads to a wonderful place. Shawn, you've got to decide where you're heading. Which road will it be?"

Whether you are using reframing or a magical metaphor, exercise your patience and creativity. Each one of these interventions, when nurtured by time and intent, has the potential to inspire an extremely successful interaction. To generate the most promising outcomes, however, it is best to learn them all. The broader your range of strategic verbal skills, the better prepared you will be to turn difficult situations into learning experiences.

CHAPTER 12

LIMIT SETTING

Most teachers, foster parents, and child- and youth-care workers find that when it comes to dealing with maladaptive coping styles, talking is not enough. Many acting-out behaviors, they discover, reflect a need not only for the sense of promise sparked by thoughtful words but also for the security furnished by limit setting. Indeed, because troubled children often lack internal controls, they truly want the adults in their world to exert external controls that can keep them on the right path; without such limits, life as they know it becomes scary and confusing.

Limit setting reshapes problematic behavior by defining boundaries beyond which actions are meaningfully addressed. For youngsters who lack internal controls, fair limits provide an atmosphere of safety and caring, which enhances adult-child relationships as well as social functioning.

Limit setting progresses in five distinct stages: supportive interventions, logical consequences, physical management, processing, and reintegration. Together, these stages form a continuum of responses that can be applied to a group as well as an individual, and to any misbehavior, regardless of its severity or the context in which it occurs. The basic sequence of events occurring along this continuum is as follows:

→ When a troubled child begins to act out, warnings and other *supportive interventions* are used to encourage him to control his behavior. The objective is to support his capacity to make good decisions on his own.

→ If the problematic behavior continues—whether or not it triggers a serious incident—a time-out, loss of privileges, or other *logical consequences* are usually required. Once a logical consequence is given, there should be no turning back, for trust is now under scrutiny. Giving in to any protest against a logical consequence tends to increase the likelihood of more problems.

→ If the child has trouble accepting a logical consequence and if his safety or anyone else's appears compromised, *physical management* in the form of escort or restraint may be necessary.

→ After logical consequences have been given and physical management, if needed, has been administered, it is time for *processing* the incident with the child. This discussion should include a review of the event itself, the circumstances that led up to it, and healthier coping strategies to help the youngster avoid similar problems in the future.

→ The final task is to assist in the child's *reintegration* into his environment. This is accomplished by outlining how he will return to his life space prepared to meet adult expectations, fulfill his personal responsibilities, and move on.

Each stage of this limit-setting continuum (see figure 12–10) is described below. For best results, remain focused on the stage you are in at any particular time and keep your sights set on the goal—namely, helping the child feel safe enough to shift to a more adaptive pattern of behavior.

Supportive Interventions

When troubled children begin to demonstrate unacceptable behavior, their greatest need is for a supportive response that will empower them to take control of their actions. Supportive interventions help children become aware of their actions; learn the limits of acceptability; control their actions; de-escalate unacceptable behavior; learn to choose more productive forms of self-expression; and experience adults as caring people who are willing to assist them.

Following is a selection of time-tested supportive techniques. Through trial and error you will quickly discover which ones are likely to work best with which kids. You may also find that depending on the situation, some are more suitable than others. To become adept in the use of supportive interventions, practice them *all*.

Core Rules

Rules, which are often formulated jointly by children and adults, inform youngsters about important expectations and give youngsters the power to abide by them. Expectations that are *not* explicitly stated as rules tend to pose problems. For example, a child held accountable for swearing in a group home yet unaware that swearing is unacceptable to the staff, is apt to feel *un*supported and unfairly treated. "I didn't know I couldn't swear!" he may bellow, convinced that he has been set up for failure—a belief that is likely to retard his progress.

To handle the myriad of challenging behaviors in their midst, adults working with troubled children often overcompensate by covering their walls with one rule after another, creating an atmosphere that can compromise relationship building. Interior designs of this sort intimate that the adults in charge are far more rule conscious than kid conscious. Worse yet, try as we might, we simply cannot formulate rules for all contingencies, because forms of behavior that conflict with our unexpressed expectations are bound to arise from time to time.

How, then, are we to maintain order and sanity? By establishing *core rules* of safety and conduct while at the same time quelling our persistent desire to maintain control by realizing that working with troubled kids requires us to cultivate a higher than usual tolerance for emotional discomfort. The outcome of our efforts is kids who focus on living rather than complying.

When I first started working in residential care, I was overwhelmed by all the rules there were to learn. Then a staff member told me that the ultimate goal for child-oriented settings was to have *no* rules. When kids feel safe and nurtured in their relationships with caregivers, he explained, there is little need for formal regulations; any time expectations are not met, adults use their discretion and the kids trust them to respond fairly. "We'll never get to such a place in this facility," he said, "but we should still keep trying!"

This staff member knew—as do many of us—that in settings where children have difficulty trusting adults, preestablished core rules help create a safe and predictable environment, which in turn helps to dissipate insecurity-based anxiety. It is also true that in such settings rules created *in the moment* have the capacity to offer support and de-escalate tensions.

Examples:

"You're angry because I asked you not to say the word *sucks* in a negative way. Perhaps I should have been clearer about what unacceptable language is. Let's talk a bit and come to an agreement about this."

"You kids seem upset about who gets to the use computer and for how long. Can we come up with some rules for computer use?"

Verbal Cues, Reminders, and Warnings

When behavior begins to veer into undesirable territory, such supportive interventions as verbal cues, reminders, and warnings can help children get back on course. For greatest impact, these should be delivered in a calm, supportive tone of voice.

Examples:

"Elton, it's not such a good idea to run in the mall."

"Class, it's getting a little too loud in here. Let's see if we can use quieter voices. Thank you."

"Howie, remember what we talked about—you were going to try harder to share with the other kids."

"Kerri, we spoke about wearing too much makeup to school. It seems like you're going a little overboard. What do you think?"

"Remember, we need to clean up the room before going to the park."

"What do we always do before leaving the classroom? Yes, we line up and wait until everyone is quiet."

A Redirected Focus

Diverting the attention of children who are beginning to lose control of their behavior gives them a new focal point and an opportunity to rein in their actions. Depending on the situation, you may try posing a challenge, changing the subject, or asking for opinions on a pertinent topic.

Examples:

Two children are arguing in the backseat of a car. The driver calmly asks, "Hey, kids, how many Jeep Cherokees can you count in the next twenty minutes? I'll bet you can't count more than seventeen."

A class is growing increasingly restless. The teacher intervenes with, "What kind of food would you like me to bring in for our Friday afternoon party?"

Dinnertime at a group home has become chaotic. The adult in charge draws the kids' attention to the latest sports results and plans for the next field trip.

A Voluntary Move

When two or more children begin quarreling, a temporary separation—the "divide and conquer" approach—is likely to reduce the tension. *Suggesting* such a separation is supportive, for it leaves the kids in charge of the decision. Although the ideal strategy is to help children in conflict work out their problems, when time does not allow for mediation, a voluntary move is often a best possible response.

Examples:

"Bob and Primo, you seem to be having a tough time together. Maybe you should think about choosing separate activities for a while."

"Sheelu, would you like to change seats until dinner is over? You and Mark both seem to need more space."

"Juan, you and David have been having a lot of trouble sharing a room lately. Do you think it would help if you switched rooms for a few weeks?"

Humor

Humor used as a supportive intervention can significantly reduce the tensions prompting troublesome behavior by changing scowls to smiles. (For an in-depth discussion of humor, see chapter 8.)

Examples:

Two first graders are throwing crayons across the table at each other. Their teacher winds up a small toy ostrich and sends it strutting from one end of the table to the other.

"Jack, I would love it if you would put your clothes away. I would be sooo happy I might even cry tears of joy. Why, it could get so wet in here we'll need a boat and paddle to get out the door!"

Nonverbal Cues

Nonverbal cues can save the day. These attention grabbers often stop children in their tracks, wordlessly reminding them to take control of their troublesome behavior. Nonverbal cues, as described in chapter 9, include physical proximity; posters you can point to when the need arises; a "stop, think, and act" signal; creative facial expressions; ringing a bell or chime; rhythmic clapping; dimming the lights; and invented hand signals.

Examples:

A group of third graders is becoming boisterous. Their teacher circulates among them, sometimes positioning herself near an especially rowdy student.

A sixth grader starts eating pistachio nuts in class. The teacher slips a warning card onto his desk.

Fourteen-year-old Laura starts cursing under her breath. Her foster mother taps her forehead to remind Laura to "stop, think, and act."

The residents of a group home begin whispering as George, the adult in charge, spells out activities for the weekend. George stops talking.

Basic Verbal Interventions

All twelve verbal interventions presented in chapter 10 work quite well as supportive techniques. Reasoning responses, connecting statements, and empowering messages are especially effective during this stage of limit setting.

Examples:

Supportive comment—"I don't blame you for being upset. I'd feel the same way if I were you. Let's see if we can work together to help you make better choices."

Repeated statement—"So you're saying I've been unfair. Let's take a look at this."

Feelings update—"We've been dealing with many behavior problems today. Are a lot of you angry?"

Animated praise—"Casey, you seem to be having the same problem you had yesterday. Do you remember what you did to turn your day around? It was a super move."

Apologizing—"This hasn't been a very enjoyable class. I did say we would work outside today, but the ground's just too wet right now. I'm sorry I misled you."

Humor—[*Said with feigned anger to a nine-year-old child*] "You know, you're acting just like a nine year old!"

Reasoning response—"Hey, Gerry, I can't let you talk like that. What if we let every kid say those things? It wouldn't be a great place to hang out, would it?"

Connecting statement—"Jed, I don't want to give you extra homework. It's not me against you; we're on the same side. But if you don't start buckling down, you may never learn this material, and it will really help you down the road."

Empowering message—"Bruno, do you think you could come up with a better way to ask for that?"

Surface clarification—"Let me make sure I know exactly why you're angry, Carl. What did Rick do to get you so worked up?"

Explorative response—"It's getting pretty silly in here. Is something bothering you guys?"

Plan making—"Shauna, I don't want to have to separate you and Taylor. Can we come up with a plan to get through math class without any more disruptions?"

Vicarious Reinforcement of Another Child
Addressing a youngster's problem behavior may call unwanted attention to him, increasing his anxiety; however, complimenting another child for exhibiting more desirable behavior is apt to inspire him to control his actions in order to garner the same praise. This principle holds true for groups as well as individuals.

Examples:

Sarah is taking her time putting her books away. Julie is more on task. Their teacher comments, "Julie, thank you for stacking your books so quickly. You'll be one of the first to line up."

Several group home residents are making impulsive demands on a staff member. Their child-care counselor calls out, "Pete, I appreciate the way you asked so politely to see your point chart. I'll get it for you."

In the camp dining hall Paul is bouncing in his chair and giggling; Kyle, meanwhile, is sitting quietly beside him. Their counselor says, "Kyle, you are doing very well. You're showing me that you're ready to head outside. Great job."

Peer Support
Children can often be called upon to help a struggling peer. This intervention must be used with caution, however, because if the child fails to respond, the others may take their frustrations out on him.

Examples:

"Would those of you who have finished the assignment like to help the kids who are still working on it?"

"Hey, guys, Johnny is really angry about the cancellation of his brother's visit. He could use your help tonight. Maybe you could invite him to join you at the movies."

"We need to figure out how to get all these jobs accomplished. Can anyone think of a way to help Matt move the desks? Who else needs help?"

A Class, Group, or Family Meeting

Whenever tensions mount in a class, group, or family setting, an *immediate* well-run meeting can often de-escalate the situation and get the kids back on track. The more that participants share their feelings under the leadership of the adults in charge, the more they work through their conflicts, as opposed to acting them out.

In addition, *regularly scheduled* meetings held on a daily or weekly basis can be extremely supportive, spawning a feeling of familiarity in which barriers and defenses begin to loosen and fall. Regularly scheduled meetings can also give kids a greater sense of control over their environment.

Examples:

A teacher says to a class that is approaching chaos, "Please put your books away and join me on the rug for a class meeting. We need to talk about how the day is going."

A residential counselor explains to an agitated group of adolescents, "You guys seem to be on edge today. Let's step into the living room and have a short group meeting. We've got to work this out."

A mother announces to her three foster children, who for the past week have been picking on one another upon their return from school, "We will be having a meeting every day after school from now on until we start getting along better. We need to talk more and argue less."

If supportive interventions are not fruitful, when is it time to stop utilizing them? Sooner than you may think, because the overuse of these interventions can elevate anxiety levels, prompting kids to test whether or not you can keep them safe. When these techniques do not quickly inspire self-control, the atmosphere is apt to grow tense and trouble may begin brewing—signs that tighter limit setting is probably required. A good general guideline is, *if a couple of supportive interventions do not produce results, quickly shift gears and follow up with a logical consequence.*

A memorable example of what can happen when the shift to logical consequences is delayed appears in the movie *Kramer versus Kramer.* Here, a divorced father is sitting in the kitchen with his young son when the boy heads for the refrigerator, takes out a gallon of ice cream, and proceeds to eat it. The father tells him to put the ice cream back, but the boy ignores him and continues to eat it, slowly and tauntingly devouring one spoonful after another. The frustrated father, meanwhile, spouts out warning after exasperated warning. Finally, he becomes so angry that he forcibly yanks the ice cream away from his son!

Responding would have been better than reacting. After issuing two supportive warnings, the father could have transitioned into the next stage of limit setting by saying, "Okay, son, I've asked you to stop eating the ice cream. I don't want you to ruin your appetite, so please put the ice cream away, or——," filling in the blank with a logical consequence. Afterward, the two could process the incident, at which point the father might hear the message behind his son's behavior: he is upset about his parents' divorce. The shift to logical consequences would have both averted the father's anger and set the scene for more meaningful interactions.

Logical Consequences

The continued misbehavior of kids who do not respond to supportive approaches must be taken seriously, since it usually expresses a need for greater external control. In fact, the more out of control kids appear, the more *appropriately* controlling we must be to help restore their sense of safety and well-being.

Logical consequences provide the needed control by holding children accountable for their actions through various forms of discipline. Unlike supportive interventions, which empower youngsters to alter their problematic behavior on their own, logical consequences attempt to transform it *from the outside* while giving them an opportunity to reflect on their actions.

Such a shift, to be perceived as fair, must link a consequence to the unacceptable behavior in a *logical* manner, indicating that there is a reason for the response.

CHILD: Why did you take my radio away for the weekend?

ADULT: Because, as I told you, the volume was up so high that some of us couldn't sleep. I gave you two warnings and it wasn't turned down.

Although this child might be angry about losing his radio, he will invariably see the logic in the outcome. As a result, he is more likely to feel fairly treated and to keep the radio turned down in the future.

A consequence that is *not* linked to the unacceptable behavior will most likely be experienced as punitive, triggering mistrust and anger. Whereas logical consequences entail reasonable limits that prompt behavioral change, punishment inflicts emotional or physical pain, is rarely perceived as fair, and is apt to provoke retaliation.

Issuing effective logical consequences requires foresight and determination. First, you must be prepared to *follow through* with any consequence you set. Why? Because the children need to know that you can consistently and predictably take care of them, that "no" means no, and that protesting a limit will only exacerbate the situation. They must also learn to respect authority and rules of conduct.

It can be tough to stand firm when a child tries to persuade you to ease up on a limit you have set. Your first inclination may be to avoid confrontation, as in option #1 in the examples below. Option #2, however, is in both cases more likely to prompt a behavioral shift.

ADULT: Jack, I've warned you repeatedly about skipping steps. I'd like you to walk up those stairs again.

CHILD: No, Mr. Golden, I promise I won't skip steps anymore.

ADULT: (option #1) Okay, but next time——.

(option #2) Jack, please come back and walk up the stairs again. Thank you.

ADULT: Ed, will you please take a short time-out. I've asked you twice not to use that kind of language.

CHILD: I didn't say anything. It wasn't me.

ADULT: (option #1) Well, it sounded like you. Please watch what you are saying.

(option #2) The longer it takes you to get to the time-out chair, the longer you'll have to sit in it. Let's get started. Thanks.

In addition to following through, you must be prepared to *counteract resistance* in the form of "But I didn't do anything. I have a right to be mad. I shouldn't have to do this time-out!" Although kids should be permitted to protest anything they perceive as a misuse of authority, they must learn to do so at the right time and in the right manner. Toward this end, during a peaceful moment you could relate a personal anecdote, such as the following:

Imagine that I'm driving at fifty-five miles an hour down the highway when a policeman pulls me over and gives me a speeding ticket. Of course, I'm pretty mad, because I wasn't speeding. Yet I know that if I swear at the officer he could arrest me for misconduct; even though I have not broken the law, I have no right to act disrespectfully. So I tell the officer how fast I was going and then courteously accept the ticket, mentally planning to fight it later in court.

You see, adults, like kids, are at times unfairly accused of a violation. Still, there's a right and a wrong way to deal with authority. We all need to make good choices in tough situations.

To help stand your ground after setting a difficult limit, remind yourself of the Golden Rule of Behavioral Returns: *Pay now or pay more later.* In other words, instead of worrying about how the child will respond in the moment, think about how he might behave the next day, and the day after that, and the following month. Know that if you set firm and consistent limits he, together with any other kids who witness your actions, will learn to trust you, and you will all be better off down the road.

A third prerequisite to administering effective consequences is to *think progressively.* Ask yourself, "How often has this particular behavior occurred in the past?" The rule of thumb for progressive discipline is, *the more often a misbehavior has occurred, the stronger the consequence should be.*

Although kids are apt to fret and fume over stiffer consequences, the smoke will clear more quickly if they know in advance that consequences are administered progressively. This information can be conveyed in the following ways:

> "John, you made a mistake when you pushed Andy down. We've had a good talk and I know you're sorry. We've agreed that your consequence will be a one-day suspension from school. I don't like having to suspend you, but what if we allowed all the kids to push others down, even if they had good reasons to be angry? It wouldn't be safe around here. John, this is the first time you've done something like this. If you should become aggressive again, the suspension will have to be for a longer period of time."

> "Jill, I've had to give you three five-minute time-outs in the last hour because you're bothering people. I've tried to talk with you to see if something is on your mind, but you don't seem to feel like opening up. If in the next half hour you get another time-out for the same reason, you will need to sit for ten minutes, which will give you more time to think things over."

The fourth, and final, consideration before embarking on this phase of limit setting is to *avoid giving overly severe consequences.* Although it is important to increase the severity of a consequence in response to recurring problem behavior, it is equally important to cap this progression at a predetermined increment. Without setting an upper limit on a consequence, you are likely to head into a disciplinary impasse much like that of George, the child-care worker in chapter 9 who inched his way from a five- to a forty-minute time-out in response to Luke's swearing.

Had George capped the consequence at ten minutes and waited for Luke to settle down and begin his time-out, things would surely have evolved differently: Luke, feeling less provoked, would have had little reason to continue swearing. The simple truth is that the difficult behaviors of challenging kids will not "go away" in response to ever tougher disciplinary measures. They may well transform over the long term, however, in response to progressive consequences within reasonable parameters and a deepening sense of trust.

Issuing overly severe consequences for actions that are likely to recur is apt to not only infuriate the child but also restrict your disciplinary options. How, after all, do you respond to a seriously misbehaving youth who is already grounded for a week—by extending the grounding? What consequence do you give to one who has six detentions to serve—another detention?

Your resolve to put a limit on limit setting should, like your decision to use progressive discipline, be shared with the children. By informing them that consequences are administered progressively and peak at a certain point, you will be giving them two empowering pieces of information: one, that repeated offenses will often result in stiffer consequences, and two, that they can make mistakes and receive fair treatment.

The techniques themselves are detailed below, in an order of increasing severity. As you work with them, keep in mind that more serious behaviors usually warrant more rigorous responses. Remember, too, that in certain instances it is a good idea to use more than one logical consequence at a time. A child who slaps a peer, for example, could be given a time-out, grounded for a few days, and asked to write an apology.

Redoing
When a child has performed a task in a less than acceptable manner, it is often a good idea to ask for a redo. Asking the child to do it

over again demonstrates your belief that he *can* do it and that it is important. Depending on the situation, it may be best to explain that he will not be allowed to do anything else until he has redone the task correctly. If he refuses, or if the problem behavior recurs, a stronger consequence—such as a time-out or a restriction—may be needed.

Figure 12–1

Redoing Consequences

Problem Behavior	Response
Acting silly while lining up for a transition	Ask the kids to line up again and stand quietly.
Speaking inappropriately to an adult or a peer	Ask the child to express himself in acceptable terms.
Completing a chore unsatisfactorily	Ask the child to return and do it again until it is properly completed.
Running through a hallway	Ask the child to return and walk instead.
Putting little effort into completing an assignment	Ask the student to redo it.
Cutting into line	Ask the child to enter again and go to the back of the line.
Dashing across the center of the street	Ask the child to come back and walk in the crosswalk.
Dressing improperly for an occasion	Ask the youngster to return to his room and dress appropriately. If he needs help, provide assistance.

Reparative Actions

When misbehavior physically or emotionally injures people or property, remember that the child has most likely wounded himself as well. The misdeed, after all, has probably fueled his negative self-concept, leading him to think, "This is who I am—a kid who acts bad." Reparative actions are most advantageous when they not only help mend a compromised relationship but also alleviate some of the pain the child feels inside. The purpose of this consequence is twofold: to help the child understand the impact of his behavior and to help him learn that when he causes injury, the right thing to do is repair the damage and take responsibility for his actions.

Figure 12–2
Reparative Action Consequences

Problem Behavior	Response
Bullying one's peers	Have the child apologize to his peers and spend a few days helping disadvantaged children.
Continually throwing food during lunchtime	For a few weeks, require the child to stay fifteen minutes after lunch to help clean up the cafeteria.
Mistreating an animal	Require the child to volunteer at a local animal shelter, or to write a report about animal abuse or endangered species.
Writing swear words on a wall	Have the child remove the writing and repaint the wall. Also require him to develop a plan to reduce the amount of graffiti in the community.
Breaking a valuable item	Have the kid do odd jobs to repay the cost of the item.

Restriction of Privileges

Children who behave responsibly earn privileges such as walking to stores by themselves, watching television, using the phone, playing unsupervised in the park, riding their bikes, using the family car, and staying out late on weekends. Abuse of these privileges leads logically to restriction of the rights associated with them. In keeping with progressive discipline, the restriction period can be increased each time the violation is repeated, provided that an upper limit is set in advance.

Restriction Traps. Enticing though they may at first appear, limitations placed on certain privileges can be detrimental to a child's development and should therefore be avoided. One is *restricting time with friends*. Although it may seem logical to say, "If you can't behave by yourself, how can I expect you to behave with a friend?" such a consequence is counterproductive, for the power of friendship propels troubled kids to improve their behavior. Take away opportunities for peer relating and we unwittingly promote what they serve to eradicate—misbehavior. In fact, because troubled youngsters often

Figure 12–3

Restriction Consequences

Problem Behavior	Response
Using a computer improperly	For a specified time period, do not allow the child to use the computer, or allow him to use it only in your presence.
Talking too long on the phone	Do not allow the youngster to use the phone for a specified time period, or restrict the frequency and duration of calls.
Riding a bike without wearing a helmet	Prohibit the child from riding the bike for a specified time period.
Stealing from a store	Do not allow the child to go to stores unsupervised for a specified period of time. (Also have him apologize to the store owner and make restitution.)
Misbehaving while at a public facility such as a roller-skating rink, movie theater, or swimming pool	Do not allow the child to visit the facility for a specified time period.
Refusing to do homework or household chores	Withhold the child's free-time privileges, such as watching television or playing outdoors, until the homework or chores are finished.

have difficulty forming and sustaining friendships, and as a result severely compromise their self-esteem, as described in chapter 3, it is incumbent upon us to *facilitate* friendships.

If you are a teacher, for instance, consider allowing disruptive students to sit together on a provisional basis and offering them a second-chance option if things do not go well at first. "Okay," you might say, "as long as you behave well, I'll let you boys sit together, because I know you are friends. If you get silly or have trouble, I'll need to separate you, but I will give you another chance to sit together next week." You may have to put up with some acting out in the short term, but the payoff for the kids will be well worth it.

A second trap to beware of is *restricting food intake*. Many states that license residential and foster care programs prohibit the withholding of food from children. And for good reason: such an act erodes their trust in adults and leads to physical pain as well as intense, long-lasting rage. No matter how poorly a child acts, he should never be deprived of food. If he misbehaves during a meal, simply explain that he will be served as soon as he calms down, and that he need not worry about receiving the same amount of food as everyone else. If he is late for a meal, you can always give him something else to eat, or ask him to make something on his own and clean up after himself. If he is repeatedly late for dinner, he could temporarily lose the privilege of going out on his own since he has not demonstrated an ability to manage his time well.

As was described in chapter 3, many children who live in foster homes or residential settings hoard food under their mattresses, in closets, in roof panels—in any nook or cranny that can accommodate a bag of Twinkies. Most of these youngsters have had food withheld from them and are fearful that it will happen again.

A third trap to circumvent is *restricting recreational time*. Troubled children desperately need recreational time for releasing pent-up emotions, moving their bodies, and playing freely. Often, this is the only time of day they feel good about themselves. Child psychologist Dr. Bruno Bettelheim equated taking recreational time away from an emotionally disturbed child with taking cough syrup away from someone with a sore throat.[1]

If you are a teacher, be sure to think twice about restricting a child from recess in response to misbehavior. For one thing, there is nothing logical about this consequence unless the child has been violent enough to receive a severe initial consequence or unless the problem behavior has occurred during recess, in which case a preferred option would be increased supervision, as described on page 195. For another, a child who is told he may not attend recess is apt to continue misbehaving, since he has nothing to look forward to.

If you are a foster parent, try not to restrict your child from participating in sports or other forms of organized recreation, because these pursuits enhance self-confidence and provide a sense of normalcy to kids who feel "different." Interestingly, some troubled children with low self-esteem misbehave *in order* to lose these privileges, since they are afraid of being embarrassed on the field. "No homework, no sports," although a logical response, is often a self-defeating decree best replaced by "No homework, no TV till it's done—and if the problem persists, we may need to devote more weekend time to your schooling."

Removal of Troublesome Objects

When an object plays a role in problematic behavior, it is within the realm of logic to put it away for a specified period of time. Eleven-year-old Justin relinquished his basketball with full understanding of his misdeed when his foster mother said: "Justin, I've asked you nicely not to bounce the basketball in the house, but you seem to be having a hard time following instructions today. Will you please hand me the ball—I'll return it tomorrow. Thank you."

To apply progressive discipline, repeat this consequence, extending the period of relinquishment each time. Keep your options open by initially withholding the object for a *short* period of time, and make sure the maximum withholding period does not become unreasonable. Remember that removing objects from children requires you to exert power over them—a dynamic that can unduly provoke those who are hypersensitive to misuses of power.

Figure 12–4

Removal Consequences

Problem Behavior	Response
Riding a bike after being asked not to	Put the bike away for a specified time period.
Listening to a Walkman instead of doing homework	Remove the Walkman until all homework is completed.
Continuing to wear clothing that has been deemed inappropriate for the occasion	Put the clothing away for a predetermined period of time.
Tapping a ruler against a desk after being asked to put it away	Remove the ruler for a specified time period

Removal Traps. The strategy of taking away objects is often misused. One trap to beware of is *arbitrarily taking away personal possessions*. A child who is rude loses her favorite doll for a day. A kid who fools around at bedtime loses his comic books for a week. The adult's intent in such instances is to evoke within the child a sense of discomfort for having caused others a measure of grief. This approach to limit setting, however, is neither logical nor educational; it is instead a gross misuse of power, and as such, is likely to arouse anger and exacerbate misbehavior. The only possession that should be taken away from a child is one integrally associated with the problem at hand.

A second trap to avoid is *taking away allowance*. Making allowance contingent upon good behavior is an arbitrary and subjective practice experienced by many troubled children as unfair and unpredictable. An unconditional weekly allowance is critically important, for it gives children an ongoing chance to exercise delayed gratification, money management, and other mature behaviors.

When a child breaks or loses an item, rather than withholding his entire allowance to pay the costs of fixing or replacing it (a reparative consequence), it is more instructional to have him pay the necessary costs through a brokered arrangement. One foster mother I know negotiated a deal: "Geoff, you broke the window. You receive an allowance of five dollars a week. Do you think that paying three dollars a week for a month, combined with some extra work around the house, would be a good way to handle this?"

Proximity Manipulation

A child who misbehaves is often sending the message "I'm not controlling myself very well. Keep me close." It is therefore logical to require such a child to stay within close proximity of you. You might explain: "Don, you've had a hard time getting along with people today. I've tried to help you out. But now I'd like you to please stay by me for the rest of the day. Thanks." The more problematic the behavior, the closer the proximity. Through good behavior, the child can then earn back your trust and his autonomy.

Any time a child's problematic behavior raises serious concerns, it may be wise to assign him to one of the designated levels of supervision described on the next page. When he shows an ability to maintain behavioral standards, allow him to move to a less restrictive level. As with any intervention, it is best to involve him in the decision making.

Following are three designated levels of supervision often used in treatment settings for troubled kids. They appear in an order of increasing intensity.

Close supervision: The child must let you know where he is at all times.

One-to-one supervision: The child must remain in close proximity of you at all times.

In-sight supervision: The child must remain within your range of vision at all times. This level is most appropriate for children who are abusing themselves or demonstrating other unsafe behaviors.

While issuing these consequences progressively, it is important to regularly assess the child's behavior and inform him of ways to move to a less restrictive level of supervision. Autonomy, to be reliably welcomed, must be regained *gradually* through actions that restore trust. Sadly, some very troubled kids, such as those with histories of sexual perpetration against others, require intense levels of supervision round the clock for months, if not years.

Figure 12–5
Proximity Manipulation Consequences

Problem Behavior	Response
Teasing a sibling in the living room while you're in the kitchen cooking dinner	Ask the child to join you in the kitchen until dinner is prepared.
Throwing objects in the school cafeteria	Ask the student to sit near one of the lunch monitors.
Fooling around while walking to the school bathroom	Tell the child he will be escorted to the bathroom for a specified number of days.
Misbehaving while walking in line	Have the child walk with you at the back of the line.
Acting disruptively during recess, study hall, or free time	Confine the child to a space that can be easily monitored.
Acting rowdy at a recreational facility	Have the children stay nearby, and monitor them closely on subsequent trips until trust is restored.

An Early Bedtime

Just as doing well at bedtime may earn the privilege of staying up later than usual, fooling around at bedtime could result in retiring earlier the next night. In such instances a child who misbehaves should be given a supportive warning: "Jake, if I have to ask you one more time to stop knocking on the wall, you'll have to go to bed a half hour earlier tomorrow night. It's important for you to get your sleep."

    The Bedtime Trap. An early bedtime is often a logical response to problems occurring at bedtime. An early bedtime for problems occurring in the afternoon, however, is not. If you tell an angry twelve year old at 4:30 P.M. that because of his misbehavior he will have to go to bed early, what incentive will he have to do well *until* bedtime? If he continues to misbehave, what can you do *next?* Contaminating bedtime by using it as a catch-all consequence for negative behavior compromises fairness, which is likely to upset the child further, escalate the behavior, and leave you with little recourse.

    Sending children to bed early generally makes good sense when they misbehave within thirty minutes of bedtime; when misbehavior occurs prior to this point, they should receive a different logical consequence, such as a time-out. In chapter 13 we will examine other methods for helping children settle down at bedtime.

A Directed Chat

When trouble is brewing, a meaningful one-on-one conversation held some distance from the festering turbulence can provide the increased

Figure 12–6
Directed Chat Consequences

Problem Behavior	Response
Fooling around in class	*Billy, could you please talk with me outside the classroom for a minute.*
Misbehaving during dinner	*Garth, could I please talk to you out in the hallway. Thanks.*
Acting rudely to one's foster parent	*Larry, let's go into the living room and have a chat about what's been happening here. Thanks.*
Collaborating to disrupt others	*Could the three of you please join me in the other room. Thanks.*

attention a child needs to get back on track. This change of location serves a twofold purpose: it helps the youngster gain emotional distance from the disturbance and, by removing him from an audience of peers who may be contributing to the problem, save face.

Time-Out

A time-out gives a child who is misbehaving a chance to cool off and reflect on his actions. It can also de-escalate the behavior of a youngster whose behavior is disrupting a group.

A time-out for a child who is misbehaving and has not responded to supportive interventions entails asking him to go to a designated location—a chair, desk, couch, seat in a hallway, stairway step, or bedroom—and to sit quietly and comfortably for an open-ended or specified period of time. Upon completion of the time-out, adult and child process the incident and help him reintegrate into the original milieu.

Why Use Time-Out? Time-out has several advantages over many of the other logical consequences highlighted in this chapter. Three of the most significant benefits are described below.

- *Time-out is an immediate consequence.*
  Learning theory dictates that the sooner a consequence is given for low-level misbehaviors—such as rudeness, obstinacy, minor aggressiveness, and silliness—the more likely it is to reduce future misconduct; and conversely, that the longer a consequence is delayed, the less effective it tends to be. Time-out, a quick and firm response, reduces problematic behaviors by letting children know that their actions are not acceptable. Allowing misbehavior to continue, on the other hand, can send a flawed message such as "What you're doing isn't that serious" or "You probably can't help yourself," neither of which is apt to catalyze change.

  Interestingly, a large number of schools and child-care settings address low-level problem behaviors through the use of *delayed* consequences, such as restrictions, groundings, detentions, and suspensions. These types of responses are relatively nonconfrontational, easy to administer, and of proven value in untroubled populations. However, they are often ineffective against the aggressive and disrespectful behaviors of troubled kids, especially in settings where group stability is at risk. Here time-out is often needed to immediately promote a sense of safety and well-being, and to convey that the adult world holds higher expectations.

Another reason for the success of this immediate consequence is that short time-outs can be repeated if a troubled child continues to misbehave. By contrast, a delayed consequence may only escalate the problem behavior, because the child may feel he has nothing more to lose. "Why should I behave? I've already lost my recess time," he may declare, or "I never do well enough to stay up late. I'm always in trouble." Time-out, unlike a delayed consequence, enables children to deal with an incident, put it behind them, and start over again with a clean slate.

- *Time-out provides a reasonable "out" in a "three strikes and you're out" alert*
  The popular "three strikes and you're out" approach to warning children about inappropriate behavior can backfire when the third strike brings on an excessive consequence. In many elementary schools, for example, the first time a student misbehaves, his teacher places a check ("strike one") beside his name on the chalkboard and tells him that if he gets two more checks he will have to miss recess.

  Although this technique often succeeds with students who have adequate coping styles, it is fraught with pitfalls when applied to troubled children. Why? Because placing checks on a chalkboard is often ineffectual in curbing aggressive and disrespectful behavior; sets a low standard for social interactions; can stigmatize a child whose name appears repeatedly on the board; and by failing to hold students immediately accountable for their behavior, can negatively affect a group's sense of safety and security.

  Consider the example of Jack, a troubled elementary school student who is disrespectful at 9:00 A.M. and again at 10:30 A.M.

On both occasions his teacher places a check on the board next to his name and warns him that with the third check, he will have to stay after school. At 11:30, twenty minutes before lunch, Jack blurts out another disrespectful remark. His teacher is reluctant to issue the consequence, however, because Jack has had a relatively good morning and has responded well to the supportive interventions. Although his remark was inappropriate and should be addressed, she is suddenly concerned that the consequence may be too extreme and, if issued, likely to provoke an outburst. The teacher is caught in a quandary: she must either ignore the rude remark or warn Jack again to stop misbehaving without checkmarking him—options that will compromise her stature as a limit setter.

Many teachers, foster parents, and professionals who utilize a "three strikes and you're out" system with troubled kids find themselves in a similar dilemma if the consequence is too severe. They are reluctant to follow through with the promised consequence because the third-strike behavior, in and of itself, does not warrant such an extreme outcome. "One more nasty word and you'll go to bed!" a foster parent asserts. Yet ten minutes later, when the child utters his third inappropriate comment, the foster parent chooses not to take action because the behavior does not seem objectionable enough to justify her sending the child to bed. "Any more fooling around and you'll all stay for detention," a junior high school teacher announces to the kids in his resource room. Yet two minutes later, when a student begins whistling, the teacher is reluctant to follow through because such behavior does not seem to warrant a mass detention.

When it comes to challenging behavior, the "three strikes and you're out" disciplinary method involving a potentially extreme "out" poses a Catch-22. Follow through and you may be acting too harshly; fail to follow through and you could be viewed as a weak limit setter who is unable to keep youngsters safe. The best way to avoid this paradox is to make sure the third-strike consequence is *reasonable,* and that is where time-out comes in. Such a consequence is not only much easier to administer but far more likely to lead to happier and more highly functioning children.

- *Time-out creates an atmosphere of safety and caring.*
  Low-level misbehaviors exhibited by kids at risk often escalate in the absence of meaningful limits. Why? Because such youngsters yearn to know where the lines will be drawn and will continue to test the environment until they find an answer. Time-out serves to draw that line in a fair and predictable manner which, in turn, calms the children and establishes an environment of safety and caring.

  In group situations, where safety must be preserved at all costs, time-out is an extremely effective intervention. The message it relays is: "This is a safe place with high standards. We do not condone inappropriate behavior, regardless of the reason for it. We want to know why it is occurring, but our job is to help you express your feelings in a nonhurtful manner."

The use of time-out, in addition to its many advantages, gives rise to questions, such as "What if you give a kid a time-out and he blows up?" and "What if you give a kid a time-out and he refuses to take it?" The truth is that the controlling nature of this intervention creates a potential for confrontation that occasionally leads to a need for physical management. Physical management, which is described on pages 221–231, is indeed a serious and complex stage of limit setting, but avoiding confrontation is often *more* hazardous, for it can foster a more chaotic, out-of-control environment. Ultimately, troubled kids appear to experience more emotional growth and progress in environments where time-out is used regularly—and physical management is employed when necessary—than in environments where staff rely primarily on delayed consequences.

It may take a while to feel comfortable giving time-outs. Certainly, this intervention is more anxiety producing than a delayed consequence, or than repeatedly warning a child without ever "drawing the line." Rest assured, however, that with practice, you will become more and more at ease with this delicate yet powerful tool. And so will the children whose lives you touch, for they will come to know that a respectful adult is in charge and really does care about them.

Time-Out Considerations. Below are some of the most frequently asked questions about time-out, together with helpful answers.

• *What sorts of behaviors call for a time-out?*
  Behaviors such as rudeness, silliness, teasing, disrespect, and low-level aggressiveness that are not curbed by a couple of supportive prompts often warrant a time-out. In addition, failure to heed a request is often cause for a time-out, as is indicated in the following scenario:

  > "John, could you please stop making those noises. Thank you."

  > (John continues to snort.)

  > "John, could you please take a short time-out to think about listening and controlling yourself a little better. Thanks."

  A child who is too engrossed in an activity to register a request can be addressed again, even more supportively. However, when a pattern of ignoring begins to take shape, as it has with John, it is usually time to become more directive in order to prevent the behavior from undermining your authority and threatening the cohesion of the group.

• *When is a time-out not enough?*
  Serious misbehaviors such as threatening, stealing, committing violence, or destroying property often warrant both an *immediate time-out* and a *delayed consequence*. For example:

  > "Luther, I'd like you to chill out for a half hour (*time-out*); it's very upsetting when you threaten people. I'm also going to keep you in tonight (*delayed restriction of privileges*). Considering the way you're talking, I don't think you've

demonstrated that you're in good enough shape to do well in public tonight."

Severe acts of aggression often require a more extreme consequence, such as an *extended separation*. An extended separation, discussed on pages 212-217, is essentially a time-out that lasts longer than an hour.

- *How long should a time-out last?*
Effective time-outs tend to range from a few seconds to an hour, depending on the circumstances. Time-outs that are issued for a predetermined amount of time, as in "Judy, could you please take a five-minute time-out to think about what you said—thanks" are *universal*. Others are *open-ended,* or left to the discretion of the child or adult, as in "Judy, could you please take a time-out in the chair. Come back when you think you are ready to be more respectful. Thanks."

Open-ended time-outs give children more control over problematic situations. Their drawbacks, however, are worth noting. Because open-ended time-outs are rooted in subjectivity and are less consistent than universal time-outs, they are often harder to administer to children who are mistrustful of adults and to kids in group settings. Serious power struggles can ensue when a child and adult disagree about how settled the youngster is, or whether he sat out long enough before returning. In group settings that are governed by predictability and structure, kids often monitor how equitable their consequences appear, and react harshly to a perceived partiality.

In relaxed settings, in one-on-one situations, and with highly functioning kids, open-ended time-outs are often more empowering. In settings governed by a need for consistency, predictability, and fairness, universal time-outs may be more effective. The best way to know what will work in a given situation is through experimentation: try open-ended time-outs first, and prepare to switch to universal time-outs if necessary.

Some child-care experts recommend giving children who misbehave one minute of time-out for each year they have been on the earth—a sad price to pay for growing older, and an unwieldy guideline to follow while working with a mixed age group. From a more practical standpoint, it is a good idea when issuing open-ended time-outs to base the duration of the consequence on the severity of the offense and on when you and the child believe he is ready to return. When using universal time-outs for low-level misbehaviors, plan on an initial consequence of one to five minutes for children under the age of ten, and two to fifteen minutes for older kids.

In group settings, where universal time-outs are often the consequence of choice, it is sometimes helpful to establish *minimum* sit-out times for swearing, threatening, stealing, or minor acts of aggression. Consequences for such behaviors can range from ten minutes to one hour, depending on the severity of the offense, age of the youngster, and context of the incident. (Responses to more violent acts are discussed under Extended Separation, on pages 212–214.) Other than designating a set amount of time for swearing—for example, swearing = a ten-minute time-out—it is advisable to treat such behaviors on a per-incident basis. Establishing a minimum consequence informs kids that the more severe their actions are the more severe the consequence will be.

Consequences, like rules, need to fluctuate in relation to the climate of a group. For instance, to establish an atmosphere of safety in an adolescent group home that has recently experienced several violent episodes, the time-out for threatening may need to be temporarily increased from thirty minutes to one hour. Residents will benefit immediately by seeing that the adults are "upping the ante" in order to protect them. (*Note:* In such instances, it is often wise to couple the increase with proactive interventions, such as counseling aimed at uncovering the source of turbulence, as well as added incentives to boost morale and motivation.)

- *Where should a time-out be served?*
A time-out should take place in a location far from heavy traffic and excessive stimulation yet accessible to supervision. The ideal

choice would be a site integral to the environment—such as a couch, desk, comfortable chair, or step—rather than one used exclusively for time-outs, which can cause undue humiliation.

Choosing a time-out area often calls for creativity and flexibility. If a classroom has insufficient space for a time-out area, time-outs could be served in another classroom or in the hallway. Although it is difficult to supervise a student in the hallway, it may be the best possible option, in which case the teacher would need to check on him at frequent intervals.

In a home setting, the time-out site could be a stairway step, hallway bench, or bedroom. Although some professionals contend that a child using his bedroom for time-out can project negative associations onto his place of refuge, it too may prove to be the best possible option, especially in a home that is overly stimulating or problematic.

- *How should a time-out be served?*
  To settle down and shift gears, a child taking a time-out needs to be relatively quiet and comfortable. Engaging the youngster in conversation during this interlude, forcing him to stand, or requiring him to face a wall is apt to be counterproductive. If he, like many troubled kids, has trust and separation issues, and is facing a corner, unable to see what is happening behind him, he is likely to feel both humiliated and anxious. Watching the action, on the other hand, may keep him more positively engaged. If he is in a group setting and begins to provoke his peers, it may be best to have him move to a less stimulating area or turn his chair so that he is not looking directly at his peers.

  Children serving a time-out of five minutes or more could be given the option of working on class assignments, reading, or filling out a processing form. Listening to music or playing a game, however, is taboo, as time-out is an occasion for reflection, not entertainment.

  Above all, children should be told that time-out is to help them "chill out" and think about better decisions to make in the future. When this supportive message was delivered to one fourth grade class at the beginning of the school year, a student replied, "Wow! Last year, time-out meant we were bad."

Administering Time-Out Progressively. In a group setting or in a situation involving multiple caretakers for an individual child, a preestablished time-out progression similar to the one outlined in figure 12–7 serves three important functions. First, such a progression lets it be known that misbehavior is handled in a *predictable* and *fair* manner. Second, it enables adult caretakers to respond in a consistent way. And third, it provides a framework for dealing with resistance, thereby reducing the likelihood of confounding the situation with an exasperated "If you don't sit in the time-out area, you'll be grounded for a week!"

Figure 12–7

A Typical Time-Out Progression

Problem behavior➤
Two supportive interventions

      Continued problem behavior➤
      First logical consequence: a five-minute time-out

      Refusal➤
      Two warnings

            Continued problem behavior➤
            Second logical consequence: a ten-minute time-out

            Continued refusal➤
            A contextual decision about how to proceed

The Case of John. Here is how the time-out progression outlined above might unfold for John, a fifth grader who has just flung a piece of paper across the room.

First supportive intervention:

"John, could you please pick up that paper you just threw. Thanks."

"No way. I didn't throw it."

Second supportive intervention:

"I'm sorry, John, but I just saw you throw it. If you don't pick it up, you will need to take a five-minute time-out. Let's not make this a big deal."

"I didn't throw it and I'm not taking a time-out."

First logical consequence:

"John, could you please take a five-minute time-out. Thanks."

"I'm not going to. I didn't do anything!"

First warning:

"John, if you don't head for the time-out chair in a few seconds, you'll have to take ten minutes."

(John refuses to move.)

Second warning:

"I'm counting to three. If you haven't moved by then, you'll need to take ten minutes. One, two . . . three." (Counting to three is a good technique to use, provided that the child has had a few seconds to vent his emotions before the counting begins.)

"I'm not going."

Second logical consequence:

"John, you now have ten minutes to do. Could you please go to the time-out area."

"No way!"

"If you don't start your time in a few seconds, you will need to ——"

John's teacher would now have to decide on a reasonable course of action depending on the context of the situation. Major contextual factors include the effect a child's refusal and behavior are having on the group; the child's age, issues, and capabilities; the human and physical resources available; adult expectations; and the nature of the setting. John's teacher, to be truly effective, would already have in place an established selection of contextual decisions that covers all contingencies.

Contextual Options. Troubled children and youth need to know *well beforehand* what will happen if they refuse to do a time-out, and why. Listed below are several responses that can hold resistant children accountable for their actions at this stage of the time-out progression.

- If the child refusing a time-out is not being disruptive, the response might be, *"Frank, please let me know when you're ready to begin your time-out. Thanks."* Another possibility could be: *"Marion, you have ten minutes in which to sit and think. You won't be able to go anywhere (to recess, out to play, to the movies) or do anything (use the computer, play with a friend, talk on the phone) until you've finished the time-out and we've had a chance to talk. Why don't you get it started—don't ruin what's been a good day."*

  When a nondisruptive refusal to take a time-out is creating group tension or unrest, a consequence that the child can control—such as, *"Do the time-out and you are free to join the others"*—is often an effective response.

- If the youngster refusing a time-out *is* being disruptive, he could be told, *"Chris, we've asked you nicely to leave the room with us. If you can't make the decision to come with us, we'll have to help you move."*

  An appropriate consequence for a child who needs to be physically escorted from the room as a result of refusing a time-out often depends on the setting. In a residential center, where children tend to harbor extreme anger and mistrust of adults, such a child may need to cool down and perhaps be restricted to his living quarters for a predetermined period of time. An appropriate response to a thirteen year old might be: *"Harris, two hours ago we had to help you move to the quiet room. We don't think it makes sense for you to go anywhere tonight. We want to make sure you're feeling more in control and making good deci-sions."* (When to physically intervene with a resistant child and how to respond to physical interventions are examined in greater detail in the following chapter.)

In a public school setting, a disruptive child who is refusing to accept responsibility for his actions could be told: *"Larry, you know what happens next: you will need to go to the office (or another designated location). If you can walk with me to the office without any problems, you'll only have to sit there for a mini-mum of thirty minutes. If you misbehave on the way to the office (by kicking a wall or giving "the finger" to a classmate), you will be there for at least two hours. If you continue to refuse to move, then we'll need to ask the principal to help you—in which case your parents will be called and you could be suspended for a day."* The consequences, in other words, need to become progressively more intense as a child's refusal and concomitant behaviors escalate. The message this approach sends is: "You are not an out-of-control kid who can't make good decisions. Even when you get mad, you have the capacity to handle your anger in an appropriate manner." This is a message of normalcy and hope—one that is important to deliver to troubled students trying hard to succeed in public school.

Modifying Time-Out Progressions. Time-out progressions can be modified in countless ways to meet the needs of a particular child or group. Imagine, for example, that your twelve-year-old foster daughter Emily speaks disrespectfully to you and you are inclined to try a more empowering open-ended time-out rather than a universal one. In such an instance an established limit-setting progression might be something like this: *"Emily, will you please go chill out on the couch. I'm uncom-fortable with your language. Thanks."* If she returns before settling down, you could ask her to go back and spend a longer period of time reflecting on her use of language, explaining: *"Emily, you were only on the couch for ten seconds. Because your words really hurt my feelings, I believe you should spend a little more time thinking about what you said. Thanks."* If she again returns before settling down, you could ask her to sit for a specified period of time, such as five minutes.

Another modification is to reduce the duration of time-outs for younger children. A good progression for youngsters twelve and under is: *two supportive interventions → a one- or two-minute time-out → two warnings → a five-minute time-out → a contextual decision about how to proceed.*

A third modification is achieved by collapsing the traditional two-tiered configuration into a single-step progression. A one-step approach is most helpful when time and resources are not conducive to repeated interactions with an unruly child. A busy teacher with little lag time in the course of her day, for instance, may prefer to work with this variation: *two supportive interventions → a five-minute time-out in the classroom → two warnings → a ten-minute time-out in the hallway or a different classroom → a thirty-minute time-out in the office, or in a resource or reflection room.*

When time and resources are *not* limited, a two-tiered on-site progression is recommended, since it is more likely to keep troubled kids engaged in their setting. Six months after instituting a two-tiered format for progressive time-outs, a third grade teacher reported that the overall behavior of her class had improved considerably and that the group appeared more cohesive. Her students, too, spoke favorably about the procedure, stating, "We can make mistakes and still stay in class—unless we get too wild."

Time-Out Tips. Whether you are interacting with a strong-willed five year old or a teenager new to a group home, it is a good idea to keep the following points in mind.

1. Always say "please" and "thank you" when giving a time-out. Also control the volume and tone of your voice, as well as your body language. Remember that a child will be most sensitive to the messages *beneath* your words.

2. Use respectful terminology. Children between the ages of two and ten are apt to respond well to the term "time-out." Older kids may prefer another term—a preference that, if honored, is likely to improve their response to this intervention. When working with an older youngster, ask him what he would like

time-out to be called. The more empowering you can be, the better. Here are some possibilities:

"Bo, I asked you not to swear. Could you please chill out on the bench for a while. Thanks."

"Barry, could you please go to your room and cool off for fifteen minutes. Thanks."

"Amy, you could probably benefit from some think time[2] to help you gain more control. Could you please go to the reflection area. Thanks."

Of course, if a child under the age of ten would prefer one of these terms, respect his wishes and enter it into your disciplinary lexicon.

3. Keep all supportive interventions and other warnings *time limited* rather than *cumulative*. If a student who has been acting rowdy responds positively to your initial prompts, be sure to return to the start of the limit-setting continuum should he become rowdy again later. In other words, if eight-year-old Timothy has responded well to one or two warnings to stop making silly remarks, do not give him a time-out when twenty-five minutes later he makes another silly comment; instead, start over again with supportive interventions.

4. Once you have given a time-out, *follow through* with it. Failure to do so is likely to provoke continued testing on all fronts. Why? Because the "troubled-kid Internet," a phenomenon that long predated the computer Internet, broadcasts such information. Any time an adult loses resolve, every troubled kid within a one-hundred-mile radius knows about it before 2.7 seconds have passed!

5. When using a universal time-out, figure in every minute spent sitting quietly. In other words, do not restart a time-out if a child begins misbehaving partway through it. Instead, let

him know how much of his time-out he has completed and how much is left. Or simply let him know that the time spent misbehaving does not count toward fulfillment of the consequence, as in "Martin, mumbling like that doesn't count toward the completion of your time-out."

6. When a child is taking a time-out, try not to give him a timer or place him beside a clock, for he may be tempted to shift his focus from reflecting to timekeeping. What matters is not so much how long children sit as how contemplative they are and what they learn from the experience. Set amounts of time are used simply to establish a sense of consistency and fairness. If a mistrusting child insists on seeing the time, however, it is fine to acquiesce.

7. When a time-out is over, be sure to process the incident with the child, if only briefly. After a short time-out given for a minor misbehavior, it is often sufficient to look in the child's direction and say, "Okay, Mary, you can get up. Let's try to be a little less silly. Thanks." In more critical instances—for a child who has reacted emotionally to the intervention or who has been given a time-out for a serious or recurrent misbehavior—it is wise to process the incident in greater depth before he returns to what he was doing. (See Processing on pages 231–240.)

8. Expect to give time-outs over and over again for the same misbehavior. Looking for immediate results or viewing time-out as a cure-all is a set-up for disappointment. Time-out does not cure anything; rather, it is a management tool that, when used correctly, can keep disorderly situations under control and, *over a period of time,* help children examine their coping styles and discover better alternatives.

Extended Separation

Extended separation is essentially a long time-out lasting anywhere from one to twenty-four or more hours. This very serious form of discipline is practiced most often in residential and detention centers, where safety concerns must be immediately and firmly addressed. It is usually issued to older kids who have committed acts of violence or other dangerous offenses.

Although a properly conducted extended separation can be an appropriate deterrent to violent behavior, use of this intervention requires certain safeguards. First, no youngster should be asked to sit in time-out for more than an hour unless he is *intensively supervised; allowed to sit comfortably; permitted to regularly stretch his legs; offered regular meals and snacks; allowed to read, write, and complete class assignments;* and *given opportunities to process the incident with an adult.* Second, the director of the agency should authorize the duration of the consequence. Why are these conditions of paramount importance? Because acts of violence tend to evoke extremely intense feelings, occasionally causing staff members to become too emotionally involved to render an appropriate consequence.

In addition to ensuring that extended separations meet these conditions, the agency should thoroughly document the separation, forwarding a copy of all records to pertinent collaterals, such as lawyers, parents, state officials, and legal guardians. An extended separation that cannot be conducted in the fair and humane manner described above has no place in an agency's repertoire of responses.

The Extended Separation Procedure. The purpose of an extended separation is to encourage a troubled kid to look at his violent actions and to think empathically about their ramifications. Your job is therefore to have the youth settle down in a comfortable, well-supervised location and begin to process the incident with you. You may want to have him fill out a form asking why the behavior occurred, what better choices were available, and how these options can be used in the future. In addition, you could give him an education assignment on a relevant topic. A youngster who has punched a peer, for instance, could be asked to read or write a story portraying the negative consequences of fighting, and to compose an apology.

When the extended separation is over, be sure to process the incident with the youngster. Processing in this instance entails giving him an opportunity to explore his feelings and choices, as well as spelling out further consequences, such as loss of privileges, an intensified supervision level, and increased counseling to step up therapeutic interventions and antiviolence work. Most kids who have committed an offense of this magnitude benefit by losing personal privileges and by remaining in close proximity of adults until they gradually earn back trust. Many times, some form of restitution is also helpful.

Numerous factors influence the duration of an extended separation, including the age of the youngster, severity of the action, frequency of the misbehavior, safety of the group, and circumstances leading to the incident. As with other consequences, the duration should increase progressively each time the youth repeats the problem behavior and should be circumscribed by an upper limit. The responses listed in figure 12–8 include a variety of separation times, each of which is based on these considerations.

Figure 12–8
Extended Separation Consequences

Violent Behavior	Response
A thirteen-year-old group home resident throwing a glass at a staff member	Ask the resident to take a three-hour extended separation.
The same youngster throwing a fork at a staff member the following week	Ask the resident to take a five-hour extended separation.
A fifteen-year-old resident of a youth detention center punching a counselor in the chest	Ask the youth to serve a six-hour extended separation.
A ten year old at a residential center breaking a window in anger	Ask the child to sit for a two-hour extended separation.
A twelve year old aggressively pushing his foster parent	Ask the child to take a two-hour extended separation.
A seventeen-year-old resident of a youth detention center ripping a sink from its molding	Ask the youth to serve a four-hour extended separation.
A sixteen year old viciously assaulting a staff member at a residential center	Give the youngster a twenty-four-hour extended separation. (Police involvement is a viable option.)

Voices of Controversy. Extended separation is a highly controversial method of discipline. Some professionals believe that having a child sit for more than one hour reinforces his negative self-image, interferes with his emotional well-being, and is counterproductive and punitive. Consequently, many licensing officials restrict the extended separations issued by residential providers to no more than an hour or two.

Opponents of extended separation tend to rely on one or more of the following approaches in lieu of a lengthy time-out:

- **Discharging.** Discharging a youngster in response to a violent incident sends a strong message that his behavior will not be tolerated, but it also undermines the hard work that has gone into establishing a therapeutic relationship with him. Moreover, it is not always possible to immediately discharge a resident. To maintain a violence-prone youth until a new program can be found, many facilities will separate him from the group for an extended period of time (drawing heavily on available resources) or will include him in group activities (sending the erroneous message that violent behavior is not all that serious).

  A third flaw in this alternative to extended separation is that since troubled kids are sent to treatment centers or specialized programs *because* they are at risk for violence, discharging them for violent actions fails to serve a remedial purpose. As a rule, the most helpful group-care settings maintain violence-prone kids through a combination of appropriate incentives, strong consequences, and ongoing therapeutic work.

- **Filing charges.** Filing charges against a child for violent or destructive behavior lets him see how serious such actions are. Court involvement can also add leverage in dealing with the youngster. In spite of these advantages, however, treatment providers who file charges against a youngster risk damaging the therapeutic relationship they have worked hard to develop; losing the youth to a juvenile detention center or another court-appointed setting; and having to contend with his more volatile emotions until such placement has occurred.

The regrettable truth is that some emotionally disturbed kids *are* going to commit acts of violence. The job of treatment providers is therefore to prevent it to the best of their ability. If they are too quick to sever ties with the kids in their care, they may forfeit the opportunity to truly help.

- **Giving a one-hour time-out followed by one-to-one supervision.** Some residential programs respond to serious acts of violence with a one-hour time-out followed by one-to-one supervision for a lengthy period of time during which the child is allowed to participate in everyday group activities. Such a policy can unwittingly reward misbehavior by suggesting to the other kids, "Act violently and you will receive the one-on-one attention you desire." Another pitfall is that the personalized attention given to the misbehaving child may compromise the care that others receive. In essence, when one youngster draws excessive attention to himself and resources are drained, the group as a whole can suffer.

  A further flaw in responding to a violent incident with a one-hour time-out is that this practice fails to account for how group members will feel when the individual so quickly returns to the group. Imagine that you are a fourteen year old living in a group home. While watching television, another resident loses control and punches you in the jaw. What will it be like when one hour later that resident is watching television with you? You might wonder, "Is this what happens when violence occurs—you sit for an hour and then return with a personal escort?" Or you might feel like screaming with rage, or perhaps throwing the remote control unit at him. The point is that regardless of how tough life has been for a youngster, violence that is not seriously addressed begets more violence.

Although all these alternatives to an extended separation are in many ways valid, their flaws often outweigh their merits. Many residential and detention centers in which kids are separated for brief interludes after serious behavioral episodes report a higher than usual incidence of violent and dangerous behavior. Why? Because in underplaying

the seriousness of problem behavior, we adults inadvertently reinforce it. Simply put, *in times of peril the needs of the collective must
supersede the needs of the individual.*

The needs of the collective require extended separations to help curb
violent behavior. Such separations are most effective, however, when viewed
as part of a comprehensive approach to violence prevention. Other
components of this holistic approach include talking respectfully to kids;
giving them ongoing opportunities to build self-esteem; setting fair and
appropriate limits; extending plenty of personalized attention; using
humor liberally; providing peer mediation or individual, duo, group, or
family therapy when indicated; offering techniques in social skills and
anger management; offering food unconditionally; modeling and teaching good values; providing consistent structure; and most of all, giving
love and hope. Violence prevention, in other words, requires a sustained
total-environment approach.

Grounding

This consequence, which is often applied after a time-out or extended separation, is usually a good response to acts of aggression or
violence, stealing, staying out without permission, suspension from
school, running away, destroying property, inappropriate sexual
activity, drug abuse, or other health or safety violations. Typically,
a child who is grounded is required to remain at home or in his living unit for a set period of time, although he is permitted to attend
school and keep all essential appointments and team commitments.
The message behind the grounding is: "Because you have not handled your freedom very well, you will have to lose it for a while. We
need to keep an eye on you until you earn back some trust."

The duration of a grounding should be commensurate with
the seriousness of the precipitating behavior, whether or not it is
recurrent, the child's age, and your ability to supervise him while
he is grounded. Effective groundings usually range from one to
several days, with longer durations reserved for repeated offenses
or major safety or rule violations. In keeping with progressive limit
setting, each time the unwanted behavior recurs, the consequence is
strengthened up to a designated limit.

Because grounding a child, particularly a young one, restricts the adult as well, it is best to use this consequence only after a long talk with your observing ego. One good way to guard against retaliatory reactions is to decide on the duration of a grounding *after all involved parties have taken time to collect their thoughts,* even if this means the next day. Upon greeting her fifteen-year-old foster son when he returned home with no alibi long past curfew, one mother said: "Alex, you are going to be grounded for staying out until three A.M. You had us all worried sick! Tomorrow, we'll decide how long you'll have to stay home—I'm too tired and upset right now."

Emotional distance is needed in order to issue a fair and reasonable consequence. And remember, many troubled kids who are grounded increase their instigating behaviors because they are bored, antsy, and angry, so don't exhaust your options by giving too stiff a consequence at the outset!

Figure 12–9

Grounding Consequences

Problem Behavior	Response
Fighting at school for the first time	Ground the child for a period of two to five days, depending on his age and the severity of the incident.
Experimenting with drugs	Ground the child for a least one week, as drug use represents a major health and safety violation. In addition, install some means of drug education.
Stealing	Ground the child for two to fourteen days, depending on his age and the seriousness of the act. Also have the child return the stolen item and apologize for the theft.
Destroying property	Ground the child for two to fourteen days, depending on his age and the seriousness of the vandalism. Insist that he work to pay for the damage.
Running away	Ground the child for two to fourteen days, depending on his age, the extent of the excursion, and the number of previous incidents.
Committing an act of violence	After having the child serve an extended separation or general time-out, ground him anywhere from half a day to a couple of weeks, depending on his age and the severity of the incident.

Figure 12–9 illustrates how grounding can be used as a consequence. The length of time included in each response is simply an approximation; allow your responses to be guided by the factors listed on page 217.

Suspension

Suspension is typically used in school settings for students of all ages. It may last from a few hours to several days, depending on the nature of the offense. In the best of situations, the decision to initiate this consequence comes from the principal or assistant principal, and the process is well documented.

In-House Suspension. An in-house suspension is issued for excessive tardiness, disruptive classroom behavior, acts of aggression, vandalism, and other dangerous or antisocial behaviors. A student given an in-house suspension is required to spend a predetermined amount of time in a nonstimulating location. As with an extended separation, the student should be allowed to sit in a comfortable chair, have appropriate snacks and lunch, and stretch his legs on a regular basis.

Because many kids who receive an in-house suspension need extra attention and guidance, it is a good idea to structure suspension time with this reality in mind. While a youngster is serving an in-house suspension, you may want to oversee the completion of his homework and also give him an assignment related to the targeted behavior, such as reading educational pamphlets or writing an essay on the negative outcomes of the misbehavior. You could also ask him to fill out processing forms about healthier actions and devise plans for doing better in the future.

In some instances it is helpful to issue a reparative consequence, such as writing an apology or contributing to the school community by cleaning a designated area or by reading to younger students. Educational and therapeutic components that are added to an in-house suspension are likely to trigger a positive difference in the student's life and reduce the incidence of problematic behaviors.

Out-of-School Suspension. An out-of-school suspension is issued for bringing drugs or dangerous weapons to school, or otherwise infringing on the welfare of the student body. Safety is always the main concern. A child given this consequence is required to remain off school grounds for a specified period of time.

The decision to suspend a student is often motivated by a lack of resources. For schools without sufficient personnel to conduct meaningful in-house suspensions, sending a child home for a number of days constitutes a best possible response. The preferred approach, however, is to deal with troublesome behavior through in-house consequences. One reason is that troubled kids who are returned to their homes rarely receive the support and guidance they so desperately need. Another reason is that many troubled students experience suspension as a rejection reminiscent of an earlier abandonment, which only reinforces their negative self-image.

Schools that are committed to helping *all* their students will try to creatively replenish their pools of resources enough to assist those who are struggling emotionally. After all, they are aware of the message most likely to spark behavioral change: "We care about you and don't want to send you away just because you've made a serious mistake. We want to deal with the issue *here* and help you make better decisions in the future."

Expulsion

To ensure the safety of a school community, it is occasionally necessary to expel a student who has committed a major violation such as selling drugs, bringing a gun to school, or performing repeated acts of violence. As with suspensions, the decision to expel a student, if it is legally possible to do so, should come from the principal or assistant principal and should be well documented. Many enlightened school officials are aware that students who are expelled for such infractions are in desperate need of help, and rather than abandoning them to the streets will arrange for them to participate in specialized programs.

Physical Management

Physical management—the next stage on the limit-setting continuum—entails taking control of an irrational child's actions through physical means. This consequence is used only when safety is jeopardized and all other interventions have failed to curb the threatening behavior. Whereas most youngsters will eventually respond to logical consequences, emotionally challenged kids at times require the skilled use of physical management. The caregiver's job in such instances is to *hold the troubled child in the least restrictive yet most secure manner possible until he is able to control his actions.*

This form of intervention sparks major debates about liability factors, psychological dynamics, safety, and resource availability. Nevertheless, the fact remains that you cannot "legislate" away a troubled child's pent-up rage, disturbance, and confusion; you cannot alter his behavior by telling him that tantrums are forbidden. If it were only that easy! You can establish consequences for serious misbehavior and incentive systems to improve social functioning; you can use a solid limit-setting framework and proactive child-care practices; but to assume that an emotionally wounded kid will never require physical assistance to gain control of his behavior is shortsighted and likely to do him a great disservice.

The reality is that troubled kids often lack the internal controls that guide sound decision-making, especially when they become agitated. At such times, if their actions pose a threat to personal or group safety, they are apt to respond well to being held by adults trained in physical intervention techniques. For some youngsters, being held in these ways satisfies an early developmental need for nurturance, connection, and physical contact—a need that in less dire circumstances would be fulfilled through hugs, pats on the back, and handshakes.

Agitation tends to run high when an emotionally wounded child first enters a structured setting such as a new home, school, or child-care facility. Angry, scared, and concerned about his safety, the youngster may physically lash out to test the "holding" capacity of the unfamiliar environment, wondering, "Can these people keep me safe? Will I blow out of this place too?" Adults who pass such a test usually discover that the need to use physical management with that particular child soon diminishes, and in some instances disappears.

The important point to remember is that some troubled kids urgently *need* to be held, and that our job as caregivers and teachers is to respond to this need by meeting them exactly where they are developmentally, not where we think they should be. To meet them where they are, we must acquire resources, seek training in physical management, and mentally prepare ourselves to maintain tough kids in environments in which they might not otherwise succeed. Kids who physically lash out are calling for help; and scores of troubled kids turn their lives around in the presence of adults who offer sustained support and commitment and who are willing to hold them, both emotionally and physically.

Physical Management Techniques

The two most widely used physical management techniques are physical escort and physical restraint. To be performed safely, *both methods require training and practice.* (Programs offering training in safe holds and maneuvers are listed in the appendix, on page 269.) In addition, the reasons for initiating the intervention should be stated; the episode must be processed when it is over; and the management approach needs to be thoroughly documented.

Physical Escort. This technique involves physically moving a disruptive or defiant child to a less stimulating environment. A relocation of this sort takes place only after the child has been asked to make the move on his own and has taken no action. The decision to physically escort a child calls for considerable forethought, because placing your hands on a troubled youngster can intensify his aggression.

Physical Restraint. Physical restraint is more intrusive, and entails one or more adults holding a child to prevent him from hurting himself or others, or from damaging property. Some youngsters need to be physically restrained after reacting violently to attempts to escort them to another location, whereas others require physical restraint upon losing control under other circumstances.

To Intervene or Not to Intervene?

That is the prevailing question, for physical intervention is not always a realistic option. Before deciding to move a defiant child, be sure to explore these three concerns:

- *How might the child respond to being physically escorted?*
  Is he hypersensitive to touch? Will the intervention escalate his behavior? If so, what are the possible ramifications? (Will the child need to be restrained? Will other children become upset upon seeing this intervention? Will the child be humiliated or embarrassed in front of his peers?)

- *How is the child's refusal to leave the room affecting the group?*
  If the child's defiance is exacerbating tensions, it may be best to take action by either escorting him out of the room or excusing the other children before doing so. Refusing to take action may not only fail to mitigate the brewing tension but also adversely affect future adult-child relations, because your unwillingness to follow through with limit setting is likely to be seen as an inability to keep kids safe. Unable to maintain order, you may be viewed as an adult who cannot be trusted.

- *Is it safe to intervene?*
  Under no circumstances should you attempt to physically escort a youngster if you are incapable of restraining him or if you have not been trained in physical management techniques. A one-hundred-fifty-pound youth counselor, for instance, would be foolish to try to restrain a two-hundred-thirty-pound out-of-control adolescent. By the same token, placing a violence-prone youngster, particularly an adolescent, in a setting that cannot furnish physical management is an invitation to disaster. Physical management is safe *only if enough skilled adults are on hand to intervene.*

Contingency Plans

Physical interventions can sometimes be averted by implementing one or more contingency plans. Those that follow were designed to be used with adolescents, although they are equally effective when used with younger children.

- Tell the defiant youth what the consequences will be if he walks on his own to the time-out area versus what they will be if he is physically escorted. You might say, for example: "Robert, you know how we do things. If you can walk with me, you'll only have to sit in my office for fifteen minutes; if we need to help you, you'll be there for the rest of the day." This course of action frequently empowers youngsters to make good decisions for themselves.

- Base the duration of the consequences on how well the youngster responds to your directions. You might explain: "Dan, you are going to be suspended for smashing that window and throwing the desk. We will talk about how long the suspension will last when you come to my office. The sooner you can calm down and take care of business, the shorter your suspension will be."

- Move the rest of the group to a different location, and call in another adult to work with the youngster—preferably one who has a meaningful relationship with him and an ability to influence his decision making.

- Summon a person in authority, such as the principal or program director. An individual with more emotional distance from the situation, or more leverage in the youngster's eyes, can often change the current.

- Call the youth's parents. The parent-child relationship can furnish the incentive needed to help youngsters regain control.

- Ask the group to assist the youngster. In specialized therapeutic settings in which groups serve as catalysts for emotional growth, other kids are often able to encourage a defiant youth to help himself by doing what is right. Yet although peers can be an invaluable source of support, they should *never be asked to physically intervene with another child.* (*Note:* Enlist the aid of a group only after considerable deliberation, because this plan can backfire if the children turn against a youngster who does not heed their advice.)

- Keep your distance and call the police. Sometimes the threat of police intervention is enough to stem the tide of violence. Even when it is not and the dangerous behavior continues, police involvement can be the safest solution.

Physical Management versus Isolation Tactics
Any time physical management becomes a necessary option, you need to physically escort the defiant child to a time-out area or a supervised quiet room. In volatile situations, such as groups composed solely of troubled kids, the swift use of this intervention can prevent one kid's provocative behaviors from inciting the entire group. Moreover, it sends a promising message: "We can take care of you here. We can set limits and follow through with them. We will keep you and the group safe."

Physically escorting a child to a quiet room or isolation booth with a door that is held shut from the outside has an altogether different impact. Out-of-control kids who are isolated in such rooms tend to act out all the more—sometimes running against the closed door, or punching or kicking it while screaming. The message behind this all-too-common intervention is: "It's us against you, kid. We don't want to deal with you."

Creating a painful me-against-you separation for kids with a poor self-image and major attachment issues is a psychologically, if not physically, damaging practice. And yet it is the practice of choice in many child-care settings faced with a dearth of human resources. When an insufficient number of people are on hand to apply proper physical management, there often appears to be no choice but to put an agitated kid in a room and hold or lock the door—a practice that in many states is now illegal. If you are working in a setting that allows such a practice and your primary mandate is to maintain safety in the best manner possible, please do not rest content with forced isolation as a best possible response. Instead, advocate for additional staff and training so that youngsters who call out for help and attention can be held rather than sequestered.

Follow-up Consequences
In the interest of creating an enduring sense of safety, it is a good idea to follow up a physical intervention with one or more logical consequences. Toward this end, after holding an out-of-control child, you should process the incident together, have the child complete his time-out responsibilities, and then issue a further consequence agreed upon in the processing session, such as proximity manipulation, a restriction, a grounding, or an in-house suspension. The message to convey is: "Since you just went through a difficult experience and did not show good self-control, I need to monitor your actions very closely to be sure you are back on track and able to make better decisions. You don't seem ready to go outside (down the block, to the park, to the mall), where it would be more difficult to help you if problems arise."

The nature and duration of any such consequence should depend on the severity of the incident, how well the child reintegrates into his milieu, his temperament, and his age, as illustrated in the following examples.

"Tom, you've just had a pretty rough time. I'd like you to hang out with me for a while. Once I see that you're settled down and back on track, we'll talk about your going outside."

"Julie, you've just had a rough morning. We'll need to ground you to the downstairs area for two hours. If by then you appear to be doing well, we can talk about a trip to the park."

A seven year old who has required frequent restraining at a residential facility could be grounded to his living unit for thirty minutes to three hours, depending on when he demonstrates an ability to handle more stimulating activities. If after three hours he is still not in shape to go out, the grounding can be extended—or better yet, he can receive one-to-one supervision outdoors. (Troubled kids undergoing difficult phases need plenty of fresh air and exercise.)

A twelve year old who needed to be held by her foster mother could be grounded to the house for a day or two, depending on the severity of the incident, her capacity to reintegrate, and her temperament.

A large fifteen year old who has required frequent physical management at a residential facility could be grounded to his living unit for twenty-four hours to several days, depending on the severity of the incident.

Adolescents require extremely strong follow-up consequences. For them, behavioral expectations must be raised because adults, regardless of their experience and skill, are occasionally hurt while attempting to physically manage large kids, and sometimes the kids themselves are hurt. To prevent the likelihood of future injury, adolescents must come to see that behavior necessitating physical management will bring heavy consequences, such as an extended separation, significant grounding, or an extensive loss of privileges.

Raising the ante for teenagers at risk is best accomplished by telling a troubled child on the cusp of adolescence: "Yes, you have problems, but you need to understand how dangerous it is to act in a manner that places you and others at physical risk. If you lose control and need physical assistance, you will be given strong consequences that will limit the activities, freedoms, and privileges you enjoy. Safety is vital." The heartening news is that many troubled teenagers who are helped to understand that violent behavior has serious ramifications are at decreased risk of causing harm to themselves and others later in life.

Although most youngsters requiring physical management benefit from logical consequences, some do not. Here are three exceptions to the rule:

Exception #1: A raised ante in dangerous settings. Any time the security of a group has been compromised, it may be necessary to stray from established practices in order to restore order and safety. In some situations this may mean issuing strict consequences, such as an extended separation, to *anyone* who requires physical management, regardless of age, temperament, or contextual considerations.

Such a measure proved successful in the early stages of reforming a youth center where safety issues had spiked dramatically. A number of staff members had been injured while attempting to physically manage residents, many of whom were deliberately refusing time-outs to provoke these confrontations. Because most of the kids had tragic histories and pronounced emotional problems, the situation was verging on perilous. To preserve safety, we instituted a new rule: any resident requiring physical management would receive a two-hour extended separation. Within days, the number of restraints had dropped dramatically.

The reasons these youngsters wanted to be restrained were clear: they were feeling threatened by a chaotic and unfair environment, and their personal needs for attention were being overlooked. In the months that followed, staff members strove to improve the overall quality of care and to give each resident more attention—goals they could not have achieved until safety was restored. In time, the two-hour extended separation was replaced by more logical consequences.

Exception #2: Modified plans for seriously disturbed kids. Some seriously troubled children who require extreme amounts of physical management benefit from special behavioral plans that do not overly restrict their activities, freedoms, and privileges. In the absence of specialized plans, many such kids become so buried under oppressive consequences that they are unable to dig themselves out, resulting in increased misbehavior and retarded emotional growth. Programs that create individualized behavioral plans guard against such downward spirals by allowing kids to get out and enjoy life, develop meaningful relationships, and build self-esteem, while still taking responsibility for serious infractions.

Exception #3: Increased supervision (but not restrictions or extended separations) for psychiatrically impaired kids. Youngsters confined to a psychiatric institution have already received the message that serious acting out brings serious consequences. The outcome of their emotional pathology and extreme symptomatology (such as self-abuse, suicidal ideation, or violence) was placement in a restrictive, albeit therapeutic, environment. In such settings, which are designed to be controlling, children who act out and require physical management have few freedoms and privileges left to lose. Consequences for their loss of control have, in effect, been administered; the reins have been pulled in.

For youngsters in this situation, a behavioral episode leading to physical management generally warrants an increased level of supervision over an extended period of time. A long extended separation, however, is usually inappropriate, since such kids in crisis who have lost self-control tend to require ongoing attention. Only after they have acted responsibly enough to move to a less intensive setting is it appropriate to hold them more accountable for their actions.

The Adult Mind-Set
The emotional aspects of physical intervention are as significant as the technical aspects. The reason is that as adults working on the front lines with troubled kids, we are often subjected to provocative and threatening behavior that can trigger within us a retaliatory reaction. Such a reaction, if unchecked, may add fuel to an already raging fire.

Kids at risk, most of whom have been at the receiving end of torrents of verbal abuse, can be remarkably adept at provoking adults. No area is sacred. They will make fun of your height, weight, physical features, even disabilities; they will swear profusely, use sexually explicit language, and deliver intimidating remarks. Confronted by a barrage of demeaning comments, you may be swayed into physically managing the offender, if only to restore your sense of power and control.

Such a scenario usually builds up slowly. At first, you may be inwardly irritated, silently wishing the kid would just knock it off. A few minutes later, you may feel gripped by a sense of impotence and anger, *especially if you are inexperienced in such matters.* Before long, you are likely to be consumed by a desire to show the kid who's boss. This urge, combined with an impulse to allay your emotional discomfort through revenge, can cause you to verbally provoke the youngster into needing physical management to gratify your own need for control.

It is a continuing challenge to learn to tolerate swearing, insults, and taunts without unleashing retaliatory remarks. Furthermore, fear of injury is psychologically and physiologically arousing, causing a rational adult to sometimes act in an irrational manner. But the fact remains that helping troubled kids is often synonymous with taking in their pain and becoming a receptacle for their feelings, which they often need to vent in order to heal. While serving as a container for these feelings, you are apt to experience a variety of emotions ranging from anger, rage, hatred, and vengeance to vulnerability, powerlessness, and fear. Your job, however, is to feel the emotions without acting on them. In other words, it's okay to feel extreme anger toward a kid, yet it is *never* okay to verbally abuse him, hit him, or provoke him into a restraint.

How can you muster adequate self-control in such situations? By remaining acutely aware of the emotions surfacing within you; activating your knowledge of self-management techniques, as described in chapter 2; and calling forth a strong observing ego, as illustrated in the following dialogue.

KID: You're a fag. Why don't you drop dead?

ADULT'S OBSERVING EGO: This kid is really provoking you. You hate it when he calls you a fag. But that's your issue, not his. Come to grips—don't overreact. Stay cool and look disinterested.

ADULT [*calmly*]: Steve, let me know when you're ready to talk.

KID: Fuck you, asshole. I'm not gonna talk. Why don't you come over and I'll give you my fist.

ADULT'S OBSERVING EGO: You're getting angrier. Relax—he doesn't really mean what he's saying. He's had a tough day and a tough life. Think about something else. Remember, you're a filler, not a talker, so stay cool. Distance yourself from him and his words. He can't keep this up much longer; he'll eventually run out of steam. Wait him out, pal.

KID: You're a snot-nosed wimp.

ADULT'S OBSERVING EGO: Okay, he's got a point there. That's it . . . let the humor flow. Use the "force," Luke.

KID: What do I need to do to get out of this room and back to the kids?

ADULT'S OBSERVING EGO: Bingo!

ADULT: We need to talk about what happened outside, and create a
    plan for getting you back on track.

In working through the feelings evoked by an agitated child on
the verge of losing control, this adult was able to avert a physical
confrontation. Certainly, with training, support, supervision, and
experience, *many* youth welfare workers learn to withstand verbal
attacks and maintain self-control.

   Times arise, however, when as a result of either an adult's loss
of control or a troubled child's overriding need to be held, physical
management becomes unavoidable. To use it in a remedial way, we
must transcend our anger and fear, and *place the youngster's needs
before our own.* Doing it right with a troubled kid is an awesome
and challenging task, yet the rewards can be magnificent.

Processing

Any time a child misbehaves, whether or not physical management
has occurred, the incident should be processed. Low-level misbehaviors such as rudeness or excessive silliness are usually followed
by immediate consequences and then a brief period of processing,
whereas serious misconduct such as running away or committing acts
of violence or destruction are succeeded by a processing session in
which the episode is fully explored and the child helps to determine
his consequences.

   This fourth stage of the limit-setting continuum makes use of
many of the skills described in earlier chapters. To begin a processing
session, you will want to conduct a pretalk routine. Working through
the behavioral incident with a child, you will be calling upon verbal
and nonverbal strategies, the affect scale, differentiations between content and message, and the effective use of body language. To review
these techniques, refer to chapters 9, 10, and 11.

Preliminary Considerations

A behavioral incident can be processed in any number of ways,
depending on the context of the situation. To decide on the most
effective approach, be sure to reflect on the following key factors.

The Nature of Your Relationship with the Child. If you enjoy a meaningful relationship with the child, you may be able to use humor and explorative responses to uncover the source of his agitation. If you are less familiar to the child, it may be better to rely on connecting statements, apologizing, and a feelings update—verbal interventions that display vulnerability, build trust, and prevent the likelihood of a power struggle.

The Severity of the Offense. Following a brief time-out for a minor misbehavior, a child may need only minimal processing. A simple statement may suffice, such as "Jim, are you ready to rejoin the group? Let's save the silly jokes for recess. Thanks." More serious actions are likely to require a longer and more comprehensive processing session. For example, a student who has punched a classmate, needed subsequent restraint, and been sitting in the quiet room for half an hour will probably demand a more profound level of engagement. Any time a child's behavior has warranted physical management, be sure to ask if he is physically okay and if he has any concerns related to the restraint before zeroing in on the initial misbehavior and follow-up consequences.

Time Availability. The ideal time to process a behavioral incident is right after it has occurred, while the events and motivations are easy to recall. Such immediate processing, however, is often a rare luxury in a busy foster home, shorthanded classroom, activity-driven summer program, or understaffed residential facility. If you are operating under similar time constraints, making a plan to talk at a later time and apologizing for the delay will let the child know that he is important to you. As one seventh grade teacher explained to a student who had just completed a ten-minute time-out, "Roland, I'm sorry I can't talk right now. Tomorrow we'll have a long talk after class."

Initial Assessment: Is the kid ready to talk?

Once you have explored the contextual considerations, it is time to talk with the child about his behavior and assist him in transitioning smoothly into his life space, *provided that he is ready to engage in a conversation.* If he appears calm, you could begin the intervention right away. If he is still upset and unwilling to talk, it may be best to let him remain in the neutral setting until he is prepared to communicate. In such instances, you could respectfully tell him that you will try again a little later, then keep coming back until he is more communicative. "Hank," you might say, "I'll be back in a few minutes to check on how you're doing. When you're ready, we'll talk about what happened and figure out a better course of action for the future."

Sometimes a child will appear calm but will refuse to talk or take responsibility for his actions. Such a child is best approached in a low-key manner and engaged through supportive comments and repeated statements. If he remains unwilling to talk, you could release him from his completed time-out and step up his supervision until he is ready to process, explaining, "I'm sorry you won't talk with me, because this makes it harder to know how you're feeling and to discuss what happened. Because of your silence, I'm going to keep you close to me for the next few hours. When you are ready to open up a bit, we'll have a productive talk—then you'll be freer to move around."

The same approach can be used with a youngster who, upon completion of a time-out, still denies his culpability. In this situation you could explain, "I hear what you're saying. You're really good at protecting yourself, but I'm not so sure about the facts you've described. I think what happened might be somewhat different. As a result, I want you to stay close to me for the next few hours. If at any time you want to talk again, we can try to work through this incident, and then maybe you can go outside to play."

Proximity manipulation is a logical consequence for kids who are resistant to processing. Whereas those who engage readily in processing help determine the consequences for their breach of conduct, those who refuse subject themselves to yet another round of imposed consequences. Always, the child chooses the path he will take.

Goals of a Processing Session
Most kids make good use of processing. Why? Because this intervention, when properly conducted, invites them to safely explore the past, the future, and the possibility of personal transformation.

Properly conducted sessions, although free of any fixed format, share the following five goals.

Goal #1: Clarifying the Incident—What occurred and why?

Exploring what happened and why it transpired is often a good way to start a processing conversation. Toward this end, you could ask, "What happened?" or "What was that all about?"—in essence, encouraging the child to tell you his version of the episode and the factors that caused his breach of conduct. Your job at this point is to listen carefully and avoid judging the child or his actions.

By contrast, some adults will start off by asking, "Why are you taking a time-out?" or "What did you do wrong?" Such openers can prompt a still agitated child to think he is being treated unfairly all over again, since the implication is that he alone is responsible for the problem. A youngster who has taken a brief time-out for a minor incident is apt to be less upset by such a direct approach, although he, too, would probably prefer the open-endedness of "What happened?"

Examples:

Questions to ask a child who has completed a brief time-out—

"Eric, why did that happen?"

"Steve, were you being a little silly?"

Questions to ask a child who has committed a serious offense and now seems calm—

"Lynn, what was that all about? What happened?"

"Abbie, are you ready to tell me what caused you to act that way?"

Questions to ask a disgruntled child who has completed a time-out after two or three attempts to do so and thinks you were wrong to have given him a consequence—

"Hey, Brian, you still seem upset. What ticked you off?"

"Jean, what caused all this to happen? You still seem really angry."

Questions to ask a child who broke a window, was physically restrained, and has been settled for a while—

"Carmen, I'm sorry we had to hold you. Are you feeling okay? Is something bothering you?"

"Roland, that was a difficult few moments. Are you okay with what happened? Do you understand why we needed to hold you?"

The purpose of the opening line is to *engage the child in conversation.* Subsequent responses need to keep the child engaged until the story has been told, as in the following dialogue.

ADULT: Madge, what caused all this to happen? You still seem really angry.

MADGE: You never let me do anything, but you always let Natalie do whatever she wants!

ADULT: It seems that you're really mad at me (*supportive comment*). You think I've been playing favorites (*surface clarification*). It's awful for a kid to feel that way (*supportive comment*).

Goal #2: Reviewing Alternative Actions—Were there better choices?
Discussing alternatives to the offending behavior helps children make better decisions in the future. As the session moves into this arena, processing becomes a learning experience in *self-management.* Exercises in self-management are available through many schools, particularly those that offer courses in conflict resolution, peer mediation, or "bully proofing." Incorporating these techniques—such as role playing, which can help youngsters rehearse new ways of

behaving—into the reviewing segment of a processing session can help children break out of inappropriate modes of expressing anger or getting their needs met. Although some seriously troubled children often have difficulty internalizing self-management strategies since they have no perceived sense of "self" to manage, most others exposed to these skills eventually do make better decisions on their own.

Example:

FOSTER MOTHER: Okay, I understand. You were mad at me because I promised we'd go out tonight and then called it off when I suddenly remembered your brother needed a ride to hockey practice. Is that right?

KATIE: Yeah, I really wanted to go to the mall.

FOSTER MOTHER: I apologize for breaking my promise. So, you knocked over the books because you were mad?

KATIE: Yeah, I was so mad at you.

FOSTER MOTHER: Was there a better way to let me know how upset you were? What other choices could you have made?

KATIE [*smiling*]: I could have thrown paint in your face.

FOSTER MOTHER: Let's talk about my makeup later. What matters now is that you were mad and you knocked over the books. What else could you have done to let me know I disappointed you?

KATIE: I could have told you I was angry.

FOSTER MOTHER: That would have been a *great* choice.

KATIE: Yeah, but I still wouldn't have been able to go to the mall.

FOSTER MOTHER: Not tonight. What else could you have said?

KATIE: I could have gotten you to promise you'd take me soon.

FOSTER MOTHER: That would have been smart. Let me ask you something else. What if you get mad at me and don't feel like talking—what choices do you have then?

KATIE: I could run to my room and scream into my pillow.

FOSTER MOTHER: That would be a much better decision! You could also try counting. When I get mad and feel like exploding, I sometimes close my eyes and count.

KATIE: So when can we go to the mall?

FOSTER MOTHER: We'll talk about that in a minute, but first I'm wondering, do you get into trouble in other places when you lose your cool?

KATIE: Yes, I do.

FOSTER MOTHER: So what's another good thing to think about when you get mad and want to lash out?

KATIE: Think about the trouble I might get into?

FOSTER MOTHER: Yup. Hey, sometimes I get so frustrated with my boss I want to yell at him. But then I think, "That might feel great but I'd lose my job, which would be worse." So I just fantasize about shouting at him. Fantasies don't get you fired.

KATIE: Are you going to fire me?

FOSTER MOTHER: No, but I'm not going to take you out for a few days because of what you did. Do you think that's fair?

KATIE: I guess so.

FOSTER MOTHER: If you had made a better choice, we might have gone to the mall tomorrow. And while we're talking . . . I've got a few questions about your new boyfriend—

KATIE: One . . . two . . . three . . .

FOSTER MOTHER: Oh good, our talk has helped.

Goal #3: Determining Appropriate Consequences—What will the payback be?

Follow-up consequences can prove problematic if a child is not consulted in advance, for he may feel alienated and hostile. He is far more likely to complete a consequence if he has had a say in what it will be. Inviting a youngster's input sends an empowering message: "You made a serious mistake, but I still value you and want you to be part of this process. I trust you to make a good decision and be accountable for your mistakes." As you go on to discuss consequences, remember to evoke a sense of fairness through the use of reasoning responses and connecting statements.

Examples:

> "Bruce, you made a big mistake by skipping school today. What if every stepparent allowed her child to skip school (*reasoning response*)? I don't enjoy giving you a consequence, but I must do so because I care about you (*connecting state-ment*). So what do you think we should do about this?"

> "Cheryl, it wasn't a good idea to throw that milk carton. Kids who throw things can hurt people (*reasoning response*). What do you think a proper consequence should be?"

Whenever you ask a youngster to help determine a consequence, be sure to have some range of limits already in mind. When fourteen-year-old Laura was caught shoplifting, her stepfather was prepared to require a two- to four-week grounding and a face-to-face apology to the store owner:

STEPFATHER: So, Laura, how do you think we should deal with this? It's pretty serious to shoplift.

LAURA [*after a long pause*]: I think I should have to return to the store and apologize . . . I should also be grounded for two weeks.

Because Laura's reply was within the parameters her stepfather had considered fair, he praised her, saying, "That sounds like a reasonable consequence. I'm proud of you for coming up with it." If Laura had instead replied, "I think I should have to return to the store and apologize; I should also be grounded for a few days," her stepfather would have reasoned with her to arrive at a more serious consequence. When determining appropriate consequences, the guideline is: *Empower, but do not unreasonably give in.*

Goal #4: Exploring Underlying Issues—What precipitated the behavior?

Once a child is calm enough to contemplate consequences for a troublesome episode, he is often ready to gently explore underlying conflicts or issues. During this exploration, the child may discover that in acting out his emotional pain and anxiety he has displaced his anger from its true target onto someone else. The disruptive behavior can then be seen for what it is—namely, a cry for help—at which point you can respond by setting aside time to assist him in coming to grips with the more deeply rooted disturbance.

Example:

GUIDANCE COUNSELOR: This has been a pretty good talk, and I'm proud of the way you have handled yourself. I'm curious, though—you seemed extra upset today. Could something else be bothering you?

BILL: My foster parents were arguing last night.

GUIDANCE COUNSELOR: Oh, that's a hard thing to hear (*supportive comment*).

BILL: They were really yelling.

GUIDANCE COUNSELOR: Can we talk about that?

Goal #5: Making a Plan for the Future—What are the short- and long-term expectations?

Making a plan entails creating a strategy for coping with ongoing situations and upcoming events. Ideally, such a plan will inspire the child with a sense that things can indeed improve.

Example:

TEACHER: Okay, Kiel, thanks for sharing all that with me. So what's the plan? What do you need to do to get back on track (*short-term expectation*)?

KIEL: I need to go to my seat and rewrite the vocabulary words. After that, I can have my snack.

TEACHER: And what's our plan to prevent the same problem from occurring again (*long-term expectation*)?

KIEL: To not rush while I'm writing—to try to be more patient.

TEACHER: I'm going to start a temporary sticker chart to show when you've taken your time and correctly completed your writing assignments. I'm also going to send you home with a new writing notebook you can use for practice. I think we have a pretty good plan, don't you?

KIEL: Yeah.

Reintegration

Reintegration, the final stage of the limit-setting continuum, guarantees that the child is ready to return to the life space. It also prepares the child for the reentry via a brief preview of pertinent logistics: where to go, what to do, who to report to, and most importantly, how to function more appropriately. After securing a guarantee of the child's readiness and conducting the preview, you may want to reaffirm any plans or commitments he made during the processing stage.

Example:

ADULT: Okay, Akil, are you ready to return and get along with people in a better way?

AKIL: Yup.

ADULT: That's great. And what did we agree you need to do?

AKIL: I need to go back to the kitchen and finish my chore. Afterward, Mr. Kennedy and I will work on my class assignments.

ADULT: All right, head on back. That was a good talk we had. And remember, next time you get mad, what are you going to try to do?

AKIL: Take a few deep breaths, count to five, and think about what will happen if I screw up.

ADULT: See you tomorrow.

Figure 12–10

The Limit-Setting Continuum

Supportive Interventions

Core Rules
Verbal Cues, Reminders, and Warnings
A Redirected Focus
A Voluntary Move
Humor
Nonverbal Cues
Basic Verbal Interventions
Vicarious Reinforcement of Another Child
Peer Support
A Class, Group, or Family Meeting

Logical Consequences

Redoing
Reparative Actions
Restriction of Privileges
Removal of Troublesome Objects
Proximity Manipulation
An Early Bedtime
A Directed Chat
Time-Out
Extended Separation
Grounding
Suspension
Expulsion

Physical Management

Physical Escort
Physical Restraint

Processing

Reintegration

CHAPTER 13

BEHAVIOR MODIFICATION

Everyone enjoys an occasional reward in recognition of a job well done, and troubled children are no exception. In fact, for many such children, rewards for improved behavior can go a long way toward helping them further modify their conduct and sustain their progress.

The practice of providing rewards for desirable behavior as well as consequences for inappropriate actions is known as *behavior modification*. The underlying premise of this method is that rewarded actions are likely to recur whereas actions that have called for logical consequences will tend to diminish. The use of logical consequences was addressed in detail in chapter 12. Now it is time to consider how firm and predictable limit setting *coupled with the promise of predictable rewards* can often motivate troubled children to improve their conduct. Numerous incentives are possible, such as rewarding a struggling student with extra attention for improved behavior; compensating a child who demonstrates good bedtime behavior during the week with later bedtimes on weekends; and promising an anxious young child a variety of colorful stickers for behaving well in a store.

Many troubled children respond well to a behavior modification plan. Kids at risk who struggle with power and control issues frequently thrive on the consistency, predictability, and structure such a plan provides. Because it dispenses on cue either prizes or penalties, it infuses their seemingly uncertain surroundings with something they can truly control. For a child who feels "all over the place," it gives shape and form to the environment.

A behavior modification plan is also a boon to troubled youngsters who do not trust adults and therefore have great difficulty delaying gratification—kids who demand, "I want my needs met *now!* I don't trust that you will fulfill them later." Every time we appropriately reward such a child, we send the message "I can deliver on my promises. I can be trusted . . . and maybe other adults can as well."

In addition, the creation of a behavior modification plan can provide a forum for adult-child interactions. In resource-limited settings where adults cannot give kids an adequate amount of one-on-one attention, behavior modification can to some degree help meet this need.

Thumbs-Down Perspectives

Many child development experts argue that caregivers and teachers sometimes employ behavior modification in lieu of more meaningful interactions, or use rewards to "buy" good behavior. Bribing a child in this way, they warn us, usually brings about short-term compliance at a great cost—namely, long-term tensions in the adult-child relationship.

Both critiques are certainly valid, because what troubled children really need from caregivers and teachers is ample doses of *love* and fair and predictable *limits*. Shortchanging either the love (through excessive rewards without enough meaningful contact) or the limit setting (through misuses of power) can lead to more intense behavioral problems in the future. Youngsters who receive insufficient love and attention often end up misbehaving, sending the message "Help me. I want more meaningful care!" Or they may think, "I'm not worth being around," a notion that can fuel frustration or anger, forms of self-punishment, and continued misbehavior.

In general, adults who circumvent their child-care responsibilities by using behavior modification in lieu of attentive outreach risk weakening the adult-child bonds that drive healthy functioning. The children, upon repeatedly experiencing the superficiality of these relationships, may unconsciously choose to please neither their caretakers nor themselves, and hence make no efforts to alter their behavior.

Another reason for the long-term dissonance resulting from a liberal use of behavior modification is that the gains achieved through the dispensing of rewards are not always internalized or sustained. Why? Because heavy reliance on behavior modification can retard the development of internal controls, which in troubled populations is already delayed. Heavy reliance on behavior modification can also stifle creativity. Ultimately, children act appropriately because it *feels right* to do so, not because they will earn tangible rewards. A primary goal in child-care work is therefore to encourage youngsters through our caring interactions to strengthen their internal controls by practicing better self-management—in other words, by making good decisions on their own.

Despite these sound critiques of behavior modification, in *carefully chosen situations* many troubled children will improve their behavior markedly and sustain the gains when a well-crafted behavior modification plan is in place. The key is not to overuse this practice unless contextual factors warrant its overemphasis.

The extensive use of behavior modification is justified in at least two situations. The first is when in a home, school, or treatment setting ongoing behavior problems cause so much instability that adult-child relations are strained or safety is compromised. In such circumstances, *short-term* behavior modification can immediately fortify the environment, invigorate adult-child rapport, and promote better functioning. As the child's behavior, self-esteem, and interpersonal dynamics improve, the rewards are then decreased and eventually extinguished. In these situations, the use of rewards becomes a *means to an end,* a way to get a struggling youngster or group back on track.

The second situation calling for a wholesale use of behavior modification is in a home, special education class, or other group setting composed of difficult youngsters. In such settings *long-term* behavior modification can provide the consistency and structure needed to meet educational, therapeutic, and relationship goals.

Short-Term Behavior Modification

If day after day a troubled child is disruptive, she may be feeling too unsafe and insecure to attach to significant adults in her environment. Schools are filled with such students, and although a solid education can be their ticket to a productive life, they are at great risk of losing this passport to success. Many have serious learning and emotional disabilities, are grades behind, and face the possibility of inadequately learning the three Rs. For those who struggle with poor self-esteem and have highly developed defense mechanisms to avoid further emotional pain, acting out or truancy is sometimes preferable to studying for a test, completing an assignment, or tackling classwork likely to result in yet another failure or cause them to look "stupid" in front of their peers and significant adults.

What is a teacher to do in such instances? Rather than write off a student as "unmanageable," it is far more advantageous to step in with a short-term behavior modification plan. A disruptive student who relies on rewards to learn her multiplication tables will *not* "unlearn" her tables when the incentives are removed. Nor will an agitated, insecure student who learns to read by way of rewards stop reading when the plan is terminated. To the contrary, in both instances the student's learning curve may increase, because her self-esteem will no doubt have shot up and her social relationships will have become more meaningful.

The same holds true for group home residents. I am often asked to assist in situations in which a youngster appears to have lost control and staff members seem worn out and at their wits' end. Most times, an immediate, well-conceived short-term behavior modification plan coupled with firm and predictable limit setting restores stability fairly quickly, paving the way to enhanced adult-child rapport and overall functioning.

Such a plan helped stabilize the living environment for Lynell who, seething with anger and despair, entered our residential facility at the age of twelve. Sexually abused early in life and abandoned by her mother, Lynell trusted no one, and her rage was never far from the surface. For weeks she periodically kicked and swore at staff members and, rarely willing to accept limits without a major tantrum, needed frequent physical management. Then we drew up a short-term behavior modification plan with her: for any hour in which she did an excellent job of meeting her responsibilities and was free and clear of time-outs, she would receive two stickers to be placed on a "Lynell's Meeting My Responsibilities Chart"; for any hour in which she did a good job and was issued one or more time-outs that were completed without difficulty, she would earn one sticker. At the end of each week, she could add up her stickers and trade them in for "fun time" with an adult. Twenty-five stickers would earn her fifty minutes with a staff member of her choice. Due to our limited resources, I was often the adult most available to her.

Lynell responded well to this incentive system. She loved coming to my office and playing games with me, or working at my computer. The more we cultivated our relationship, the more trusting she became. Then about a week after we introduced the chart, Lynell's behavior began to improve. Within four months we were able to wean her from the chart and introduce into her treatment experience other forms of added attention, including a therapeutic horseback-riding program.

Lynell, like Ashley and Brandy—the foster sisters the Cartrights eventually adopted, as described in chapter 5—simply needed more attention and a more stabilized environment in order to move ahead. For her, as well as for thousands of other troubled kids, short-term behavior modification served as a springboard to less contrived human interactions.

Creating and Implementing a Short-Term Plan

A short-term behavior plan is an incentive system developed in collaboration with a child or group, and designed to be utilized for a specified time period. Such a plan, which spells out the granting of rewards, is most effective when used in conjunction with limit setting.

While designing and carrying out a short-term plan for a child at risk, be sure to keep the following points in mind.

✔ **Reward improvement.**
Because challenging behavior often results from years of difficult interactions, change is most often a slow, step-by-step process.

Expectations that are too high at the outset are apt to dissuade the child from investing in the system. Rewards for *gradual* improvement, however, will offer her opportunities to quickly enjoy success, promising an immediacy that is likely to inspire continued improvement. A good guideline to use in constructing a short-term plan is to offer rewards that a child or group has an 80 percent chance of achieving immediately.

✔ **Use best possible rewards.**
When deciding on the rewards themselves, you could ask the child what she would like to earn, all the while preparing a number of options to present. In many instances the most desirable and corrective reward is *individual time with an adult* who can nurture the child and help her gain better control of troublesome behavior. For example, a second grade student who earns thirty stickers in a week for making better choices could trade them in for thirty minutes of one-on-one sports, game, or art time with the teacher's aide or the guidance counselor; perhaps she could invite a friend to join them, creating an added bonus if she has trouble making friends. An angry, defiant, or withdrawn child can benefit enormously by earning even more one-on-one time with an adult; such extended interactions might boost her self-esteem and self-confidence, help reveal her underlying issues, and accelerate any number of other gains.

The second best option is usually *a nonmaterial reward* such as a special activity trip, additional free or recreational time, a later bedtime, extra computer time, more time to play video games, choosing the music to be played for a period of time, or assisting another child for a while. A group or class might enjoy a no-homework day, additional recess time, a field trip, or a video (with popcorn).

In lieu of nonmaterial incentives, you might offer *a material reward* such as school supplies (a pencil, eraser, colored marker), food (a granola bar, apple, trail mix, chips, candy, soda, or juice), a comic or crossword-puzzle book, a small action figure, money, a cassette or rented video, a gift certificate, library card, book, or sports cards. Whenever possible, try to keep material rewards not only enticing but also healthy and wholesome.

Interestingly, what often motivates *young* children to improve their behavior is not so much the reward as the *medium of exchange*. For youngsters up to age seven, choosing a "gold" coin or iridescent sticker twice a day for good behavior allows them to accumulate tokens of their success. The more visually interesting these tokens are, the more likely they are to inspire behavioral change.

In a fourth grade class I once visited, students earned fake dollar bills with their picture in the place of George Washington's; the teacher photographed each child's face, taped it to the center of a dollar bill, then photocopied it. Hence Billy, by doing well, earned "Billy dollars," which he could trade in for a designated reward. One week the exchange rate was ten Billy dollars for ten minutes of extra computer time; the following week Billy was permitted to use his dollars to select from a menu of rewards. A foster parent I know superimposes her own face onto dollar bills, allowing her two foster children to earn "Dotty dollars."

✔ **Slowly raise the expectations in response to improved behavior.** Gradually raising the expectations will help the child learn to control her behavior for longer periods of time. For example, a defiant child who receives points toward a reward for completing time-outs could, upon earning the maximum number of points, begin a new round in which points are awarded for incurring fewer time-outs in addition to completing them without difficulty. In such instances the idea is to progressively boost the expectations until the child is at last weaned from the incentive plan and better able to accept limits.

Similarly, a teenager who frequently "cuts" school could be rewarded for showing up more often. As her attendance increases, so should the expectations. All the while, incidents of truancy or other problematic behaviors should be met with appropriate consequences.

✔ **Keep the plan simple and easy to administer.**
Take into account the time available for record keeping and the resources on hand for granting the rewards. For example, if you have a busy schedule and are in charge of a large group of children, you may come to resent a plan that requires you to record a youngster's behavior every hour, and in fact may not have time to do it properly. A scaled-down plan that is administered well accomplishes more than a comprehensive one that is either carried out inconsistently or too complicated to remember.

✔ **Follow through!**
The more committed you are to carrying out your part in the plan, the more tempted the child will be to invest in it and to trust you. Forget once to fill in a child's points—or to pass out stickers with enthusiasm—and she may lose interest altogether. Occasionally, a youngster may test your willingness to follow through by misbehaving just before receiving her reward. In such instances it is best to set an appropriate limit and *then* follow up with the reward. If, for example, a child has earned a special activity trip to a local arcade but started a fight with her brother ten minutes before departure time, you could say, "You will receive your reward—you've earned it. But I'm not comfortable taking you to the arcade while you're acting this way. We'll set up a new time for the trip tomorrow."

✔ **Set aside time to discuss why the child did or did not earn a designated incentive.**
A built-in processing time can help reinforce the learning experience. To effectively communicate your message, make use of the verbal interventions highlighted in chapter 10. Incentive processing has three goals: to encourage a child to take responsibility for her positive as well as negative actions, to explore alternative behaviors, and to uncover the origins of her misconduct.

✔ **Discuss and award incentives at the same time each day or week.**
The consistent awarding of incentives provides structure and

security. For maximum effectiveness, arrange for the processing and awarding to take place as soon after your assessment as possible. For example, a foster child who earns points for afternoon behavior will benefit most from a reflection meeting held at 5:00 P.M. The longer the wait between behavioral assessment and the discussion and provision of rewards, the less meaningful the plan will be.

✔ **Provide frequent assessments and rewards if the child's behavior is extremely problematic.**
Ideally, a child who is constantly misbehaving should receive her medium of exchange and earned incentives on a frequent basis— every hour, if possible. As her conduct improves, the interval could extend to every two hours, then twice a day, and gradually once a day. Eventually, she may no longer need the feedback and motivational assistance you have been providing.

Of course, if human and physical resources are too limited for hourly feedback, strive for a best possible frequency. It is usually better to regularly assess and reward a troubled child once a day than to inconsistently carry out a more intensive plan.

✔ **Be flexible!**
Prepare to change the medium of exchange and rewards as needed to keep the plan going. Modifying the incentive system you design is apt to reinvigorate the child's interest in it. Creativity is a must!

✔ **Build in a time limit.**
While introducing an incentive system, it is often helpful to identify an evaluation point, explaining, for example, "We'll try this for the next five weeks, and then we will discuss how helpful it has been." It generally makes sense to terminate the initial trial phase at a natural breaking point, such as the end of the month or just before the next school vacation. Establishing an evaluation point helps kids and adults focus concerted energy on the work at hand.

✔ **Create an easy-to-read behavior chart.**

Young children usually respond well to colorful charts filled
with interesting stickers or artwork. Older ones tend to prefer
rather bland documents marked with points, checks, or other
ordinary-looking graphics.

There are a myriad of ways to construct a behavior chart.
One popular approach is to draw a grid with boxes large enough
to accommodate stickers, stars, tokens, chips, imitation gold
coins, points, checks, or whatever the medium of exchange will
be. It is often a good idea to end with a column for total incentives earned and to spell out beneath the grid the target goal and
terms of the plan.

One teacher used a chart of this sort to help her student Neil
remember to raise his hand in class instead of calling out. She
labeled it "Neil's Raising My Hand Chart" (see figure 13–1). A
similar chart can be constructed to assist a child in mastering
academic tasks, completing chores, being respectful to peers and
adults, or achieving numerous other behavioral changes.

For a child who is somewhat pessimistic about changing
her ways or acquiring new skills, consider drafting a "Road to
Reading (Writing, Spelling, Arithmetic) Chart." Such a chart
proved to be a perfect catalyst for Jenn, a bright student with
a high IQ who entered her third grade inclusion class unable
to read. She would often lament, "They've tried phonics and
everything, but nothing works." She was frequently disruptive in
class, in part because she felt cursed by her inability to read.

One day Jenn's teacher taped together three sheets of green
construction paper, cut out several one-by-two-inch "cobblestones" from pale gray construction paper, drew a "road" about
eight inches wide down the three sheets of paper, and labeled it
"Jenn's Road to Reading Chart" (see figure 13–2). "Learning
to read," she told Jenn, "is like building a road—you do it one
cobblestone at a time." She went on to say that every time she
made a concerted effort to read she would receive a cobblestone
to glue onto the road, and that each time she completed four
rows of cobblestones, she would receive a reward for her accomplishment.

Figure 13–1

Neil's Raising My Hand Chart

	Math	Reading	Science	English	Total
Monday					
Tuesday					
Wednesday					
Thursday					
Friday					

Target goal: Raise hand instead of calling out

Incentives: 3 stars—Did a super job of raising his hand
2 stars—Did a good job of raising his hand
1 star—Did a fair job of raising his hand

Frequency: Trade in all stars at the end of the week

Reward: Each star can be traded in for 1 minute of fun time with an adult.

Figure 13–2

Jenn's Road to Reading Chart

Target goal: Improve reading skills

Incentives: 1 cobblestone—made a good effort at reading
6 cobblestones make a row

Reward: 4 completed rows entitles Jenn to a submarine sandwich for lunch.

READING WITH MISS CAMBY ☆	READING GROUP ☆	☆ SPELLING PRE-TEST	☆❋ READING BUDDIES	READING GROUP ☆	YEAH! LIBRARY TIME
ALPHABET WORK ☆	READING BUDDIES ☆	READING WITH MISS CAMBY ☆	YAHOO! SPELLING TEST	READING WITH MRS HARSEN ☆	☆ LIBRARY TIME

Within five months, Jenn was reading and feeling very proud of herself. Two months later, she and her teacher decided that the road was complete and she no longer needed the chart. By then her behavior had improved remarkably, as well.

Thirteen-year-old Kevin, who was having a hard time controlling his behavior, used a similar chart. His counselor labeled it "Kevin's Road to Doing Better Chart" and gave him "cobblestones" for achieving self-control. After completing four rows of cobblestones, he earned a pizza. By the time he finished his road, he had made major behavioral strides.

✔ **Reward behaviors on a contingency basis.**
If you are targeting a behavior that is problematic for the child or her environment, it is a good idea to construct a behavior chart and inform her that she will receive incentives upon meeting the goal *as long as she commits no other serious offenses during the recording period.* For example, if her targeted goal is to talk nicely to people, tell her she will receive all earned incentives provided that she has not committed a serious misbehavior during that time period.

Granting an incentive *un*conditionally may only reinforce her violent behaviors and negatively influence her self-concept, conveying the message "Kid, you're so out of control that I must reward you even though you hurt someone." A more constructive message to relay is, "Sandra, I'm very proud of you for talking more politely this morning, but because you punched Sally, you didn't earn any points. Safety comes first."

It is often helpful to target the *most* problematic behavior. For example, if a child in a group setting is refusing to take a time-out and group stability appears compromised, the behavior to target is the youngster's refusal to accept limits. In such instances, consider using a grid resembling "Sandra's Meeting My Responsibilities Chart," illustrated in figure 13–3, or a similarly constructed "Making Good Choices Chart." By all means, avoid the temptation to create a "Doing Time-Out Better Chart" for a defiant kid, since the real objective is to eliminate the *need* for time-out.

Figure 13–3

Sandra's Meeting My Responsibilities Chart

	Math 8–9	Reading 9–10	Science 10–11	English 11–12	Total
Monday					
Tuesday					
Wednesday					
Thursday					
Friday					

Target goal: Work hard in academics and be respectful to peers and adults

Incentives: 3 points—Showed outstanding effort in completing classwork was respectful to kids and adults; and did not receive a time-out

2 points—Showed good effort in both areas, and received three or fewer time-outs but handled them well

1 point—Showed fair effort in both areas, and received more than three time-outs, handled one or more with difficulty, but was not asked to go to the office

Frequency: Trade in all points at the end of the day

Reward: A minimum of 5 points can be traded in for the chance to select from a menu of rewards including extra computer time, snacks, and painted beads

✔ **Exercise honesty and discretion in settings where other children are not on a behavior modification plan.**

If you are in a classroom or group home, once the child's plan is up and running, a troubled child who is *not* on an incentive program may ask, "Why don't *I* get stickers and extra privileges?" Or higher functioning children may complain about *their* inability to earn rewards for good behavior. In either instance your job is to explain that every youngster is treated differently and has unique needs and abilities. In addition, strive to praise and acknowledge the successes of *all* the children; keep behavior charts in a separate room or in a notebook; and award incentives in a private manner. If necessary, you could always award the child with a bonus point for not bragging about her incentives or rewards—a best possible intervention.

A Plan versus a Contract

Whereas a behavior plan is often recommended for nonaggressive offenses, a contract is routinely advised for more alarming behaviors, particularly those committed by adolescents. In such instances kids who have acted violently toward themselves or others are asked to help design and then sign a contract ensuring that the dangerous behavior will not recur. The document usually lists rules to abide by and states the consequences that will follow any violation of the terms set forth.

For eighteen-year-old Sam, whose contract appears in figure 13–4, the penalty for breaking any of the stipulations he agreed to is expulsion from his foster home.

Figure 13–4

Sam's Contract

I, Sam, agree to:
    (1) Refrain from hurting myself and others
    (2) Take my medication without difficulty
    (3) Attend group and individual therapy once a week
    (4) Go to school every day

I understand that if I fail to meet any one of these conditions I will jeopardize my placement in this home.

Signed:_____

Program official:_____

Parent(s):_____

Date:_____

While it is understandable to want a violence-prone child to refrain from engaging in dangerous behaviors, the one-more-and-you're-out implication of a contract can, like the three-strikes-and-you're-out approach described on pages 199–200, place you in a precarious position: one more infraction and you must either follow through with an extreme consequence or be perceived as untrustworthy. Following through on a discharge notice such as Sam's is likely to eliminate your opportunity to help the youth, which may only exacerbate his condition. Not following through is apt to magnify his insecurity and cause him to lash out in a cry for help.

To guard against double-binds of this sort, consider installing a *plan* in lieu of a contract. In response to alarming behavior, you could then explain, "Let's create a behavior plan to address these serious concerns." Plans are often verbal agreements that serve to connect kids with adults; contracts are signed documents that appear to place kids and adults on opposite sides of a transaction. What's more, plans can be modified whereas contracts, as a rule, cannot be.

Long-Term Behavior Modification

The extensive and permanent use of behavior modification in settings composed exclusively of troubled youngsters can ensure the predictability and safety needed to help kids grow emotionally, learn, and respond to other therapeutic interventions. In some inclusion or special education classrooms, teachers use point systems that allow students to earn stickers, points, or checks throughout the day and then trade them in for various rewards or privileges at the end of the day or week. Similar systems are in effect in some foster homes and residential facilities. These long-term systems rely on many of the same principles as short-term plans.

Strategic Applications

The ongoing use of behavior modification is especially effective at routinely problematic times of day, such as bedtime, mealtimes, the preschool period, and chore time. Such strategic applications help diffuse stress by providing additional structure and stability.

To help close the day for a troubled child who is often anxious about going to bed, you could use a bedtime star chart similar to the one illustrated in figure 13–5. Here a star has been entered for each day Carl, Fred, and Hank have gone to bed with no difficulty; each star adds twenty minutes to bedtime on Friday night, and if that goes smoothly, on Saturday night as well. Carl, for example, has earned a 9:30 P.M. Friday bedtime. If he gets a star on Friday night, he will have the same bedtime on Saturday night; if not, he will go to bed at his normal weekday bedtime of 8:30 P.M. Fred, who is the same age as Carl, also has a weekday bedtime of 8:30 P.M., whereas Hank's usual bedtime is later because he is older.

Figure 13–5

Bedtime Star Chart

Name/ Bedtime	Friday	Saturday	Sunday	Monday	Tuesday	Wednesday	Thursday	Friday	Saturday
Carl 8:30	★	★	—	★	—	★	★	10:10	
Fred 8:30	—	★	★	★	—	—	★	9:50	
Hank 9:00	★	★	★	—	★	★	★	11:00	

There are many variations on this theme. Some therapeutic facilities use a bedtime incentive system that rewards anyone who earns seven stars in a row by adding an extra half hour to her usual bedtime. The extended bedtime remains in effect until the child fails to earn a bedtime star, at which point her bedtime reverts to the original hour. Other programs balance the dispensing of rewards with logical consequences on a day-to-day basis. In these settings kids who misbehave at bedtime receive an earlier bedtime the following night, and those who demonstrate good bedtime behavior are generally rewarded with an occasional "late night."

The bedtime star chart or one of its variations can also be constructed to help children control their behavior at other times, such as during meals, while getting ready for school, and while performing chores. In such instances, each star they earn could entitle them to a certain block of time for a privilege related to the targeted behavior.

Level Systems

Many group homes, residential and detention centers, and special education classrooms employ level systems, a more intricate form of long-term behavior modification. Whereas some programs rely on extremely complex level systems, others keep their protocols rather simple. In all instances the underlying principle is the same: kids earn points for good behavior and for following through on assigned tasks; points are tallied on a regular basis, either daily or weekly; and the more points a kid accumulates, the more likely she is to climb to the next level, where she can earn even better privileges.

The model described below is a composite drawn from various systems currently in use. It illustrates how a level system can operate in a residential setting composed of adolescents.

RAP: A Demonstration Model. The fictitious Right-Way Adolescent Program (RAP) uses a trilevel point system in which level one offers the most privileges. Each morning, afternoon, and evening, residents earn points for good behavior; each night, the points are added up and recorded on a "point slip." A resident's total number of points at the end of a week determines the level she will be on the following week.

During each time period, RAP allows kids to earn between one and three points, amounting to a maximum of nine or a minimum of three points a day. To earn three points in any time segment, a youngster must behave respectfully; do all assigned chores and tasks, including homework; and be helpful to others. To qualify for level one privileges, she must earn fifty-five points by the end of the week. Forty-five to fifty-four points places her on level two, and fewer points on level three (see figure 13–6).

RAP also has a temporary level for kids who seriously misbehave. A youth who runs away or commits an act of aggression or self-abuse is placed on "reentry" for a predetermined period of time before being reinstated into the level system. Residents on reentry are kept close to staff members at all times and their privileges are restricted.

Another important component of RAP is the dialogue that occurs

Figure 13–6

The RAP Level System

Level One Privileges (55 or more points)

- A 10:00 P.M. bedtime on weeknights; midnight on Friday and Saturday nights
- Two extra phone calls
- One extra hour of Nintendo time
- An extra late-night snack on Friday and Saturday
- An $8.00 allowance

Level Two Privileges (45 –54 points)

- A 9:30 P.M. bedtime on weeknights; 11:00 P.M. on Friday and Saturday nights
- One extra phone call
- An extra half hour of Nintendo time
- A $6.00 allowance

Level Three Privileges (fewer than 45 points)

- A 9:00 P.M. bedtime on weeknights; 10:00 P.M. on Friday and Saturday nights
- A $5.00 allowance

before points are recorded on the point slip. Through dialoguing, staff members provide the residents with ongoing feedback about their behavior, as illustrated in the following conversation.

STAFF MEMBER: Okay, Paul, what do you think you earned for the afternoon?

PAUL: I'd say a three.

STAFF MEMBER: A three means you had no problems. Didn't you have a few problems after lunch?

PAUL: Yeah, but Dan was picking on me. He was calling me a skinhead!

STAFF MEMBER: And that ticked you off?

PAUL: You bet it did.

STAFF MEMBER: So how did you handle the teasing?

PAUL: I told him to fuck off.

STAFF MEMBER: Was there a better way to handle your anger?

PAUL: Yeah, I guess so. I could have told him to knock it off, or I could have just walked away.

STAFF MEMBER: Either of those would have been a better choice.

PAUL: But that incident was the only problem I had.

STAFF MEMBER: You're right—otherwise you seemed to be trying very hard. I really liked the way you helped Wayne with his chore.

PAUL: Okay, maybe it was a two.

STAFF MEMBER: That sounds more accurate. I appreciate that you're taking some responsibility here. I know that's not always easy for you.

Key Principles of Level Systems. Strive to keep the following guidelines in mind while implementing a level system.

✔ **Dialogue before awarding points.**
Always try to talk with a kid before recording her points. If time does not allow for a conversation at this juncture, talk with her as soon afterward as possible. The more you empower a youth to process her positive accomplishments *and* her misconduct, the more likely she is to improve her behavior.

✔ **When necessary, modify your expectations.**
Because kids at risk tend to have low self-esteem, you may need to periodically adjust the criteria for point attainment so that

an extremely troubled youngster is not continually on the lowest level. Why? Because remaining on the lowest level for weeks
on end is apt to reinforce the youth's already poor self-image.
In a setting that uses the RAP level system, for example, such a
youngster may begin to take on an identity as a "level three kind
of kid"—negative labeling at its worst because it is perpetuated
by a program selected for its therapeutic value.

To avoid magnifying a child's poor self-image, it may at times
be necessary to alter your expectations. Adjusting your expectations for one or more kids *without disrupting the integrity of the
group,* however, may prove extremely challenging. In moments
of ambivalence, remember that any program for youth is best
judged by how well it meets the needs of its most troubled cli-
entele.

✔ **Determine rewards carefully.**
While assigning rewards to each level, be sure all children will
have access to a *baseline of unconditional privileges* such as phone
usage, allowance, special activities, and visits with friends. Once
these "givens" are in place, they can be expanded upon, or a
variety of conditional privileges can be added. For example,
every youngster living in a residential setting should have a
guaranteed amount of phone usage, and whereas good behavior
could earn additional phone privileges, negative behavior should
not reduce the original entitlement.

Never should essential needs and rights be presented as privileges to be restricted. Reducing the number of phone calls that
can be placed or received may only heighten a lonely kid's despair.
Decreasing her allowance might hamper her ability to learn money
management and to buy items that will soothe her. Manipulating
her time with friends is apt to be equally counterproductive, since
friendships often promote improved behaviors.

A further word of caution: strive to keep bedtime consequences and rewards *logically connected to bedtime behaviors.*
In other words, announce an earlier bedtime only in response to
misbehavior occurring at bedtime, as was mentioned in chapter
12. Similarly, reserve an extended bedtime for improved bedtime

behavior. Extending bedtime as a reward for attaining higher point levels may reduce an extremely troubled kid's motivation to improve her bedtime behavior.

✔ **Communicate clearly.**
Beware of overly relying on "level lingo." Referring to levels and points rather than the behavior in question may depersonalize your relationship with a youth who desperately yearns for direct communication with a trusted adult. Troubled kids need to know about the positive and negative feelings their actions arouse, and they need to remain focused on their *behavior* rather than on their point slips.

To upgrade your powers of communication, steer clear of the following remarks:

"Please knock it off or you'll drop a level."

"If you don't get that done, you'll lose points."

"You've got to really shape up if you want that extra point."

More personal statements include:

"I can't take you with me if you're having trouble listening. Is something bothering you?"

"If you don't get that done, you'll have to stay behind to finish it."

"You've got to really shape up if you want to earn some of those privileges you've been shooting for. Your behavior is not sending me the message that you can handle more autonomy."

The Pros and Cons of Level Systems. Level systems, like so many other interventions, have their champions and their critics. Proponents of this form of long-term behavior modification profess that in distancing adults from children's undesirable behavior, it reduces the incidence of angry outbursts, power struggles, and questions about fairness. They also assert that it eases the adults' task by allowing the disbursement of privileges to be guided by a structured system rather than left to the caregivers' discretion, and in so doing it offers concreteness and consistency. "You didn't earn enough points to make an extra call," a caregiver might say. "It's not my decision." Opponents, on the other hand, question the benefits of generalized privileges; the sustainability of the resulting behavioral improvements; the effect of depersonalization on meaningful relationship development; and the psychological impact of artificially reducing behavior to points and levels.

Both sides of the level systems debate raise intriguing issues. Indeed, abandoning the use of a level system is often risky, signaling the need for a more discretionary approach that may disrupt adult-child relationships. Yet such personalized encounters lie at the foundation of a good treatment plan. The objective of out-of-home placements, after all, is to therapeutically replicate events that transpire in the youngsters' homes rather than artificially construct dynamics that will exist only in a corner of their world.

Ultimately, our task is not to make the job easier, but to prepare kids for success in less supportive environments—settings devoid of level systems and governed by adult decision-making, some of which is bound to be unpopular. When a program hires talented people, trains them well, and nurtures and supports them fully, it is often able to furnish consistency and predictability without intricate behavior modification systems. When these steps are not taken, or when resources are depleted, a program can indeed benefit from the installation of a level system. As with so many child-care practices, when the ideal path is riddled with too many curves and obstacles, the wisest course to take is the best possible route.

EPILOGUE

THIS BOOK CONTAINS DOZENS OF INTERVENTIONS CAPABLE OF BRINGING ABOUT change in a troubled child's behavior, many of which often yield impressive results. Sometimes the gains are sustained; too often, however, a child's behavior will eventually regress.

Why the reversal? A growing body of research indicates that behavioral regression is linked to waning support for the child, as well as for the primary adults in his world. Resources run dry; funding runs out; caregivers exhaust their reserves of patience, energy, and eventually, commitment.

Ask any teacher who is struggling with a difficult class what would help her the most and her answer will invariably be, "More support." Press her for details and she may add, "Such as an extra teacher or two." Give that worn-down teacher more assistance and she will almost certainly manifest greater patience, energy, and hope. This dynamic holds true not only for teachers but for parents, foster parents, and residential counselors as well. The end result: assist more caregivers and more kids will flourish.

It's too bad that kids at risk can't vote, because if they could, increased assistance would win hands-down. But today's sober reality is that many troubled kids and the adults who care for them are grossly undersupported. For example, each year thousands of kids in foster or residential care have the rug pulled out from beneath their feet at age eighteen, when they are "set free" from the social service system. After years of reaching out to these kids, many of whom have appalling histories of abuse and neglect, states have decided that at age eighteen they should be ready for independence. "See ya later, pal. You're on your own!" they are told as they are ushered out of intensely supportive environments and, too often, left to fend for themselves.

Human beings, however, are not meant to "go it alone." And while many of these young adults still require significant assistance to sustain their gains, precious few are able to find the people and services capable of helping them succeed. Instead, large numbers of "relinquished" kids, as well as thousands of other lonely and emotionally wounded adolescents, enter into questionable associations.

Our society tends to denigrate teenagers for knowingly entering into abusive relationships, cults, gangs, radical "religious" groups, or single parenthood, unaware that many troubled kids gravitate toward these domains to feel a sense of connectedness that is otherwise nonexistent in their lives. Certainly, all citizens must be held accountable for inappropriate actions, but at some point we need to collectively attack the issue of "wayward teens" at its source rather than react to its symptoms. In short, more boot camps and prisons is not the answer.

From this perch, the source of the problem is the deteriorating sense of support experienced by troubled kids and their families. Too many individuals are leading a life without enough meaningful connections. And the more isolated they become, *the more they tend to misbehave.* Little strains become big pressures when people do not have enough friends, relatives, colleagues, and others to turn to for assistance.

In recent decades, despite some enlightened progress, we have back-pedaled into a "me first" society concerned with personal comfort at the expense of human relatedness. Friendly mom-and-pop stores have given way to impersonal chain outlets. Computers keep people cocooned in their homes. Towns are being built without sidewalks. Revered sports teams are being pulled from cities and relocated so that owners can be more financially secure. Participation in bowling leagues and other group activities has dropped dramatically. Lists of children waiting to be matched with mentors grow longer every day . . . Amid this landscape of isolation and *the added stress it produces,* is it any wonder that more and more kids across all socioeconomic fronts are grappling with behavioral issues?

For children already at risk this predicament spells double jeopardy. Not only do they have a difficult history to contend with and a compromised ability to make friends, but they also have few adults they can count on and parents similarly devoid of strong support networks. Many of these kids stand on the outskirts of meaningful human relations—a grave reality that their behavior vividly reflects.

If correctional institutions and programs are not the answer, what *is?* The solution, pure and simple, is for every one of us to reach out even more to kids and families, to make compassion, sacrifice, and generosity a bigger part of who we are. And the way to begin is by looking in our own family mirrors for signs of estrangement.

A few years ago, when the picture of dwindling support first crystallized in my mind, I took a look in my family mirror and did not like what I saw. Neither side of my family was getting together, as we had in the past. Cousins had lost track of one another. Phone numbers were misplaced or forgotten. Everyone, it seemed, had become too busy, too preoccupied with personal matters to engage with family members. Consequently, our comfort zones had shrunk dramatically.

In response to the disintegration I saw, my wife and I decided to host a large Thanksgiving dinner for my mother's side of the family. It was a glorious event. We reestablished meaningful connections and met new members who over the years had joined the clan. We laughed, we argued, we caught up and made promises to stay in touch—vows we have since kept. While glancing repeatedly at my young nieces and nephews, I could see how important it was for them to know their family.

Did we change the world that day? Hardly. But we did make a statement—namely, that some things are worth the sacrifice of personal initiatives, and that at the top of the list is family.

As child advocates like you and me look beyond children's misbehavior to the big picture, we cannot help but see the devastating impact of alienation. Having seen it, we may then be moved to stretch our comfort zones a bit in order to build strong support networks in our families and communities, and for the people we help. The more outreach we offer, the more children we will see growing up loved and lovable.

In the world of support building, little miracles happen every day, and in response, kids' lives are changed, as the following anecdote suggests. Dan, a troubled kid who attended a special education high school, tried hard to push people away by misbehaving, which lessened his risk of "getting close" to them and being rejected. But he could never push away Mary, his teacher and friend. Mary got in Dan's head. He knew she believed in him and cared for him unconditionally.

After graduating, Dan began to call Mary every few weeks to keep in touch. Early one spring many years later, he phoned her with special news. "Mary," he said in an excited tone, "my landscaping company made eighteen thousand dollars last week putting in a sprinkler system!"

"Oh, Dan," Mary exclaimed, "that's fantastic! I always knew you'd be successful."

For a few seconds there was silence, then Dan said, "Yeah, that's why I keep calling you."

I can think of no better way to describe the power of support and of going the distance with troubled children and youth. Kids are only kids once. Let's make it special for them.

I wish you well, my friend.

APPENDIX

Physical Management Training Resources

Crisis Prevention Institute
3315-K 124th Street
Brookfield, WI 53005
800-558-8978
e-mail: cip@execpc.com

Therapeutic Crisis Intervention
c/o Cornell University
Family Life Development Center
33 Thornwood Drive, Suite 300
MVR Hall
Ithaca, NY 14853
607-254-5210
e-mail: eas20@cornell.edu

NOTES

Chapter 3

1. David W. Winnicott, "The Capacity to Be Alone," *International Journal of Psychoanalysis* 39 (1958): 416–420 and *The Maturational Processes and the Facilitating Environment* (New York: International Universities Press, 1965).

2. Margaret S. Mahler, *On Human Symbiosis and the Vicissitudes of Individuation* (New York: International Universities Press, 1968); Margaret S. Mahler, "Rapprochement Subphase of the Separation-Individuation Process," *Psychoanalytic Quarterly* 41 (1972): 487–506; and Margaret S. Mahler, Fred Pine, and Anni Bergman, *The Psychological Birth of the Human Infant* (New York: Basic Books, 1975).

3. Edith Jacobsen, *The Self and the Object World* (New York: International Universities Press, 1964).

4. Heinz Kohut, *The Analysis of the Self* (New York: International Universities Press, 1971) and *The Restoration of the Self* (New York: International Universities Press, 1977).

5. John Bowlby, *Attachment* (New York: Basic Books, 1969).

6. René A. Spitz, *The First Year of Life* (New York: International Universities Press, 1976).

7. Abraham H. Maslow, *Toward a Psychology of Being* (New York: Harper & Row, 1962).

8. Margaret S. Mahler, Fred Pine, and Anni Bergman, *The Psychological Birth of the Human Infant* (New York: Basic Books, 1975).

9. Joyce Edward, Nathene Ruskin, and Patsy Turrini, *Separation-Individuation: Theory and Application* (New York: Basic Books, 1981).

10. See Note 8.

11. See Note 9.

12. Erik Erikson, *Childhood and Society* (New York: W. W. Norton, 1950).

Chapter 7

1. Robert Crichton, *The Great Imposter* (New York: Random House, 1959).

Chapter 9

1. Thomas Gordon, *P.E.T.: Parent Effectiveness Training* (New York: Penguin, 1970). Information is also available through Parent Effec-tiveness Training, 531 Stevens Avenue, Solana Beach, CA 92075; 619-481-8121.

Chapter 12

1. Bruno Bettelheim, *Love Is Not Enough* (New York: Avon Books, 1950).

2. J. Ron Nelson, "Designing Schools to Meet the Needs of Students Who Exhibit Disruptive Behavior," *Journal of Emotional and Behavioral Disorders* 4, no. 3 (July 1996): 147–161.

RECOMMENDED READING

Bettelheim, B. *Love Is Not Enough*. New York: Free Press, 1950.

Bloomquist, M. L. *Skills Training for Children with Behavior Disorders*. New York: Guilford Press, 1996.

Brendtro, L. K., M. Brokenleg, and S. VanBockern. *Reclaiming Youth at Risk: Our Hope for the Future*. Bloomington, IN: National Education Service, 1990.

Brooks, R. *The Self-Esteem Teacher*. Circle Pines, MN: American Guidance Service, 1991.

Cotton, N. S. *Lessons from the Lion's Den*. San Francisco: Jossey-Bass, 1993.

Durant, M. *Residential Treatment*. New York: Norton, 1993.

Elkind, D. *Miseducation*. New York: Knopf, 1987.

Erikson, E. H. *Childhood and Society*. New York: Norton, 1950.

Fraiberg, S. M. *The Magic Years*. New York: Scribners, 1959.

Goldstein, A. P., R. P. Sprafkin, N. J. Gershaw, and P. Klein. *Skill-Streaming the Adolescent*. Champaign, IL: Research Press Company, 1980.

Hallowell, E. M., and J. J. Ratey. *Driven to Distraction: Recognizing and Coping with Attention Deficit Disorder*. New York: Touchstone, 1994.

Peck, M. S. *The Road Less Traveled.* New York: Touchstone, 1978.

Phillips, B. *Good Clean Jokes for Kids.* Eugene, OR: Harvest House, 1991.

Rathvon, N. *The Unmotivated Child.* New York: Fireside, 1996.

Redl, F., and D. Wineman. *Children Who Hate: Disorganization and Breakdown of Behavior Controls.* New York: Free Press, 1951.

Redl, F., and D. Wineman. *Controls from Within: Techniques for the Treatment of the Aggressive Child.* New York: Free Press, 1952.

Shapiro, E. S., and C. L. Cole. *Behavior Change in the Classroom.* New York: Guilford Press, 1994.

Train, A. *ADHD: How to Deal with Very Difficult Children.* London, UK: Souvenir Press, 1996.

Trieschman, A. E., J. K. Whittaker, and L. K. Brendtro. *The Other 23 Hours: Child Care Work in a Therapeutic Milieu.* Hawthorne, NY: Aldine de Gruyter, 1969.

Whittaker, J. K., and J. Garbarino. *Social Support Networks.* Hawthorne, NY: Aldine de Gruyter, 1983.

ABOUT THE AUTHOR

Charles D. Appelstein, MSW, provides training, consultation, and motivational presentations in residential, foster care, and public and private school settings nationwide. He is the former program director and treatment coordinator of the Nashua Children's Home, a southern New Hampshire-based residential facility for kids at risk and their families. His award-winning first book, *The Gus Chronicles: Reflections from an Abused Kid,* is used as a training aid in hundreds of child welfare programs and colleges throughout the United States and Canada. Charlie lives with his wife and daughter in southern New Hampshire.

To learn more about his new work, including his training videos, DVDs, and speaking engagements, visit www.charliea.com.

THE GUS CHRONICLES
Reflections from an Abused Kid

About: Sexual & Physical Abuse, Residential Treatment, Foster Care, Family Unification, and Much More

"By drawing us into his worldview, Gus gives the reader fresh perspectives on what it might be like to live in one of these places we adults call treatment centers. This book will take its place in the training literature . . . Textbooks just can't say it like *Gus* does."
—Dr. Larry Brendtro
Department of Special Education, Augustana College

"A thoroughly believable account of an abused and troubled youth. Gus's recollections of his first day in residential care were so chillingly similar to mine that I quickly forgot Gus was not real."
—Dr. John Seita
Kellogg Youth Initiative Partnerships

THE GUS CHRONICLES II
Reflections from a Kid
Who Has Been Abused

In his second literary outing, Gus is a year older and a wee bit wiser. Join him as he journeys through his final months in residential care.

"For those of us who work in residential care, it's a rare opportunity to read something that speaks in real and practical terms to the reality of our almost impossible jobs. This book is invaluable training for line workers, clinicians, administrators and policymakers who seek to understand the world of troubled youth from the inside out."
—Robert E. Lieberman, MA, LPC
President, American Association of Children's Residential Centers

"This powerful book evokes laughter and tears, and places the reader squarely in the shoes of at-risk kids who have been removed from their homes."
—David Pelzer
Author of *A Child Called It*

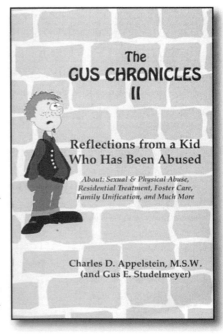

Our New Book!

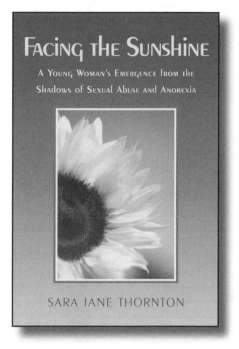

FACING THE SUNSHINE

A YOUNG WOMAN'S EMERGENCE FROM THE
Shadows of Sexual Abuse and Anorexia

SARA JANE THORNTON

Facing the Sunshine **is a true account of a journey to well-being following a childhood lost in the shadows of sexual abuse. At age sixteen, Sara Jane Thornton left home and spiraled into self-starvation, which nearly took her life. Hospitalized for two years after a suicide attempt at age twenty-one, she was subjected to seclusion, shock therapy, restraint with medication, and other adverse treatments. Aided finally by psychotherapy, self-empowering interactions, and her own innate resilience and determination, she defied expectations and was discharged. A failed attempt to live independently then convinced her to move in with her father, her abuser of many years, where she wrote this book and discovered the healing power of forgiveness. Merging her past with the present, she succeeded in shaping a radiant and meaningful future.**

"A must-read for any helping professional or loved one of a person momentarily swept up in the 'perfect storm' of childhood sexual abuse, intimacy problems, and eating disorders."
—Linda T. Sanford, LICSW
Author of *Strong at the Broken Places* and
Assistant Professor, Simmons College
of Social Work

"Readers of this book will develop a deeper understanding of the cognitive state of anorexics [and] the challenges professionals can expect to experience when working with patients with severe eating disorders. *Facing the Sunshine* is an invaluable resource for professionals."
—David Hirshberg, EdD
Executive Director, Germaine Lawrence School
Arlington, Massachusetts

"This story raises important questions about the treatment of the mentally ill and highlights grave deficiencies in the medical community, while leading us along a path of suffering, perseverance, and, finally, recovery."
—Melissa R. Gerson, LMSW
Psychotherapist and eating disorders specialist

CDs That Make a Difference

"Charlie Appelstein has taken his immense understanding of troubled kids and used it to reach kids through their favorite medium . . . music. If you want to reach and teach troubled teens, buy and use this CD. It will make a difference."
—Richard Lavoie
Author of *It's So Much Work to Be Your Friend* and creator of the F. A.T. City Program

"*One-Line Raps for Girls and Chaps* is an entertaining and powerful tool to help kids learn more effective ways of dealing with anger, communicating with respect, developing self-esteem, and relying on positive coping strategies. Charlie Appelstein and The No Bad Kid Band are to be applauded for this impressive CD."
—Robert Brooks, PhD
Coauthor of *Raising Resilient Children* and *The Power of Resilience*

"I have long been a fan of using the arts to promote the cause of healthy child development. *Parent Rapsody* is an excellent addition! I recommend it to anyone seeking a way to [help parents make] the lives of children better in this time when so many parents are confused and distracted."
—James Garbarino, PhD
Director, Loyola University of Chicago's Center for the Human Rights of Children

"Charlie Appelstein could teach the telephone book and make it interesting. I highly recommend *Parent Rapsody* to any parent or agency wanting to make a difference and strengthen relationships with young people."
—Mel Kennah, BA, MA, MBA
President, New Brunswick Association of Youth Residential Services Inc.
Executive Director, Moncton Youth Residences Inc.

Training Videos from ATR
NEW PERSPECTIVES ON ACHIEVING SUCCESS WITH TROUBLED CHILDREN AND YOUTH

Creating and Maintaining a Strength-Based Environment
Explores the important features of strength-based practice, an emerging form of care that affirms, emphasizes, and builds on an individual's attributes, inspiring changed behaviors

Managing Number One and Putting In the Bricks
Examines why adults tend to lose control of their emotions when dealing with difficult children, and provides practical strategies for maintaining composure and effectiveness

Key Concepts for Preventing Problem Behavior & Building Self-Esteem in Troubled Children and Youth
Identifies primary factors that contribute to challenging behavior and presents tools for enhancing self-esteem

Order Form

Appelstein Training Resources (ATR) provides strength-based materials to help parents and professionals better understand and respond to the needs of at-risk children and youth. The items listed below, other than *Facing the Sunshine,* were written or produced by ATR's president, Charles Appelstein, MSW.

Quantity   **Amount**

Books

_____ *No Such Thing as a Bad Kid* ($19.95)   _____
_____ *The Gus Chronicles* ($12.00)   _____
_____ *The Gus Chronicles II* ($12.00)   _____
_____ *Facing the Sunshine* ($19.95)   _____

CDs

_____ *One-Line Raps for Girls and Chaps* CD ($12.95)   _____
_____ *Parent Rapsody* CD ($15.95)   _____

Training Videos

_____ *Creating and Maintaining a Strength-Based Environment* ($69.95) _____
_____ *Managing Number One and Putting In the Bricks* ($149.95) _____
_____ *Key Concepts for Preventing Problem Behavior &*
        Building Self-Esteem in Troubled Children and Youth ($59.95) _____
_____ Complete set of videos ($250.00)   _____

Shipping and handling: for orders up to $25.00, please add $2.50;
for orders over $25.00, add 8%; for Canadian orders, add 15%;
minimum Canadian shipping charge is $4.00.   _____

Total amount enclosed   _____

Quantity discounts available

Method of Payment

❏ Check or money order enclosed (payable to Appelstein Training
   Resources, LLC in US currency only)
❏ MasterCard   ❏ Visa

Account #_____

                              Expiration Date_____

Ship to: Name _____

              Address _____

              City / state / zip _____

              Phone / e-mail _____

ATR

Hope Is Humanity's Fuel

Appelstein Training Resources, LLC
12 Martin Avenue, Salem, NH 03079
Phone/fax 603-898-5573
www.charliea.com • charlieap@comcast.net